For Kin or Country

XENOPHOBIA, NATIONALISM, AND WAR

Stephen M. Saideman and R. William Ayres

COLUMBIA UNIVERSITY PRESS   NEW YORK

COLUMBIA UNIVERSITY PRESS

Publishers Since 1893

NEW YORK   CHICHESTER, WEST SUSSEX

Library of Congress Cataloging-in-Publication Data

Saideman, Stephen M.

For kin or country : xenophobia, nationalism, and war / Stephen M. Saideman and R. William Ayres.

p. cm.

Includes bibliographical references and index.

ISBN 978-0-231-14478-0 (alk. paper) — ISBN 978-0-231-51449-1 (e-book)

1. Europe, Eastern—Ethnic relations—Political aspects.   2. Former Soviet republicas—Ethnic relations—Political aspects.   3. Nationalism—Europe, Eastern.   4. Nationalism—Former Soviet republics.   5. Xenophobia—Europe, Eastern.   6. Xenophobia—Former Soviet republics.   7. Europe, Eastern—Ethnic relations.   8. Former Soviet republics—Ethnic relations.   9. Post-communism—Europe, Eastern.   10. Post-communism—Former Soviet republics.   11. Europe, Eastern—Politics and government—1989–   12. Former Soviet republics—Politics and government.   I. Ayres, R. William.   II. Title

DJK51.S24   2008

320.540947—dc22

2008006050

FOR KIN OR COUNTRY

Dedicated to

the men and women of the Central and Eastern Europe Division of the Joint Staff's Directorate of Strategic Planning and Policy, 2001–2002

—SMS

Richard Herrmann, Don Sylvan, and Peg Hermann

—RWA

CONTENTS

THIS PROJECT DEVELOPED OVER THE COURSE OF more than a few years, so the debts are many. First, we are very grateful to the Council on Foreign Relations for the International Affairs Fellowship, and in particular to Elise Carlson Lewis, Aoki Lane, and Allison Valencia. The fellowship provided funding for the first trip to Hungary and part of the second. More important, the fellowship put one of the authors (Saideman) on the U.S. Joint Staff in the Directorate of Strategic Planning and Policy (J-5), working on issues relating to Bosnia, Kosovo, and other parts of the former Yugoslavia. This experience had a significant impact on this project by providing contacts in Hungary and by shaping how we think about policy, the foreign policymaking process, the Balkans, and irredentism. While we would like to thank all of the officers who served in the European division of J-5, several stand out. Pat Anonietti, Harold Buchholz, and Brad Mitchell provided much information, including the first contacts, and Brad even provided housing for the first trip to Budapest. The members of the Central and Eastern European Division not only welcomed the strange academic in their midst—including nicknaming him "The Irredentist"— but also engaged in a series of conversations about a variety of topics, including the enlargement process, the dynamics of irredentism, and the potentially destructive consequences of domestic politics. Jim Church, Jim Ransom, Ray Hodgkins, Chris Cook, Tom Eisiminger, Doug Legenfelder, Tony Cucolo, Debbi Gray, Jeff Jackson, Kelli Goss, Dre Norris, and Martin Pankove all were generous with their ideas.

Second, we are quite thankful for the funding provided by the Canada Research Chairs program, McGill's Research Development Fund, and the Research Group on International Security. They funded the second trip to Hungary and the Romania research. Over the course of the project, we were able to hire a series of very sharp, hardworking undergraduates and graduate students at McGill, including Amy Cox, Vania Draguieva, Gisele Irola, Michelle Meyer, David Lehman, Claudia Martinez Ochoa, Sarah-Myriam Martin-Brûlé, David Steinberg, Suranjan Weeraratne, Lori Young, and especially Ora Szekely, who did much of the heavy lifting at the end of the process. We owe each a big debt and letters of recommendation for the next decade or so. Helen Wilicka and Emilia Scognamiglio proved instrumental in facilitating the research via their navigation of McGill's bureaucracy on our behalf—no easy task, for which we are very grateful.

Third, we benefited from a variety of generous people as we planned and executed our interviews in Hungary and Romania. Zsuzsa Csergo provided several helpful contacts as well as reading several chapters and giving us insightful comments on several chapters. Members of the Hungarian embassy in Washington, D.C., particularly Andras Dekany, offered not only interesting insights but also very helpful contacts in Hungary. Members of the U.S. Embassy in Budapest, including Kyle Scott, Sandy Hart, and Kati Halasz, were also very helpful. Arpad Szurgyi provided very perceptive views and suggested several people to interview, all of whom proved to be quite informative. Eva Blenesi served as translator for one interview and provided some useful contacts for the Romania research. Raluca Popa proved to be indispensable, selecting the most appropriate potential interviews, setting them up, and arranging for additional translation. In addition, she helped to provide a base of operations at the Institute on Public Policy, made the interview experience in Romania incredibly easy and most informative, and read the Romania chapter and provided very useful comments. Ionuţ Lăcustă served as translator and provided insights on Romanian politics and society. Robert Gilchrist and other members of the U.S. Embassy in Bucharest were most helpful, too.

Fourth, a variety of colleagues read pieces of this work and/or commented during presentations. Various chapters and drafts were presented at U.S. Air

Force Academy Assembly in 2004, the International Studies Association meetings in 1999 and 2005, the Midwest Political Science Association meeting in 2004, the American Political Science Association meetings in 2001 and 2003, and the Central and East European International Studies Association/ International Studies Association meeting in 2003. We are grateful to the reviewers of our previous articles in *Nationalism and Ethnic Politics*, *Security Studies*, *Journal of Politics*, and *Foreign Policy Analysis* for comments that informed this project. Pat James and Stuart Kaufman read the entire manuscript, for which we are most thankful; they not only did some hard work, but also gave us much to think about. Richard Caplan, Elise Guiliano, Erin Jenne, Will Moore, David Romano, and Sherrill Stroschein provided helpful suggestions. Miles Kahler not only shaped the thought process that guided much of this work but also reviewed the first chapter, helping us to clarify our ideas. Conversations with Charles Gati, Dave Burrow, Larry Sondhaus, Charles King, Carol Leff, Patrice MacMahon, and Anna Grzymala-Busse provided much illumination. Juliet Johnson has been a terrific colleague, providing feedback on the Russia chapter and serving as a sounding board through much of the project. In sum, we have been lucky to meet and know so many smart people who are so generous with their time and expertise.

Fifth, we would like to thank Peter Dimock for shepherding this project with great patience and Kabir Dandona for facilitating the process and answering our questions. Gregory McNamee was very helpful in the editing process. Most important, Columbia's reviewers provided us with very helpful comments and suggestions.

We also owe a big debt to our coauthors on other projects, who carried heavier burdens and were patient as we worked on this project. Likewise, we owe our spouses and children, who were quite patient as we stared at our computer screens for years on end, even if it looked as if we were just surfing the Net.

We are grateful to all of these people, but to be clear, we are solely responsible for the information and arguments presented in the pages that follow and for any errors that remain.

LIST OF TABLES AND FIGURES

FOR KIN OR COUNTRY

Introduction

A nation is a society united by delusions about its ancestry and by common hatred of its neighbors.
—WILLIAM RALPH INGE

W HEN EMPIRES DECLINE AND FALL, WAR SEEMS inevitable. Boundaries shift, families are divided, political and economic systems fall into disarray. Such events give rise to leaders who promise to return that which has been lost—peoples and territories. Aggressive foreign policies may then follow, leading to devastating wars that are always costly, usually of only marginal success, and frequently self-destructive.

The end stages of the Austro-Hungarian and Ottoman Empires triggered a series of wars, including, ultimately, two world wars. Violence ushered the end of European colonization of Africa and Asia, and violence accelerated after the departure of the Western powers. The demise of the Soviet Union and the end of its domination of Eastern Europe were accompanied by war and atrocities not seen in Europe since the Second World War.

These aggressive efforts to change boundaries in order to reunite lost kin are a phenomenon known as irredentism.[1] Broadly defined, irredentism refers to territorial claims made by one state that are based on ethnic ties to an ethically related minority population that resides within another recognized state.[2] Nationalism—the desire to create a state to match one's nation (Gellner 1983)—can manifest itself in many ways.[3] Irredentism is perhaps one of the most virulent and damaging forms.[4] Irredentist wars produce tremendous costs for both aggressors and defenders, with considerable danger for the state attempting to regain "lost" territories and populations.

Why, then, do some countries engage in irredentism, when it can lead to their self-destruction? Why do others assert ethnic claims—perhaps in ways short of conquest—that risk the interests of the state in the international community? Is irredentism unavoidable?

If so, why have other states, given similar opportunities, refrained from the practice? Why do they remain "silent dogs" that do not engage in aggression? Some of the biggest surprises of the post–Cold War era are the wars that did not occur. While Armenia, Croatia, and Serbia engaged in expensive conflicts to enlarge their countries and incorporate kin living in neighboring territories, most of Eastern Europe and the former Soviet Union remained largely at peace. Hungary nursed its grievances over territories lost after the First World War, but did not engage in aggression against Romania, Slovakia, or Serbia after the end of the Cold War. Romania, undergoing a very troubled transition, refrained from annexing Moldova, despite the existence and popularity of its "Greater Romania Party." The end of the Soviet Union left twenty-five million Russians outside of Russia, and a political system ripe for nationalist rabble-rousers, but there has only been some talk of reunion with Belarus, far short of what could have been expected.[5]

Most studies of irredentism tend to consider only the most aggressive efforts (Gagnon 2004). To truly understand how irredentist wars develop, however, we have to consider the cases in which it could be expected, yet does not occur. Are there factors that cause one country to pursue a difficult and risky foreign policy of invasive war, and another state to stay way from such a self-destructive path, given similar opportunities?

The answers to these questions lie in the domestic politics within each country, specifically with the issue of what it takes for politicians to gain and stay in power. By looking at the impact of the domestic situation on foreign policy and studying cases that range across the spectrum—doing nothing, following assertive foreign policies on behalf of kin, and going to war—we can obtain a more coherent picture of the causes of war and the incentives for peace between states that share complex histories and ethnic groups.

In taking such an approach, we find a crucial irony played by nationalism in today's (and yesterday's) international politics: xenophobia—fear or hatred of all things foreign, and a central component of many extreme nationalisms—can serve as a brake on irredentism. Hate may actually produce peace, as troubling as that may sound. This is easiest to consider if one imagines ir-redentism as producing a massive wave of immigration. Any effort to enlarge a country's boundaries would result in the inclusion of two kinds of foreign-ers in the new state—ethnic kin who reside nearby and other groups of peo-ple who do not share ethnic ties with the populace of the aggressive state. While some citizens (though not all) would prefer their kin to be members of their country, most would seek to exclude the other foreigners. Understand-ing that this dynamic might be in play requires us to take seriously what it means to be a successful nationalist, that is, a politician that is able to attract support via nationalist appeals,[6] inasmuch as the answer is a bit more compli-cated than one might expect. By getting into the content of nationalisms—what does it mean to be a nationalist in one context versus another—we can understand why some nationalists seek territorial expansion while others would prefer to avoid it.

While the dynamics of xenophobia and nationalism are interesting in themselves and highly relevant for students of comparative politics and of Eastern Europe, they are primarily important here because of their impact on irredentism—on whether or not states will engage in potentially catastrophic wars with their neighbors.

Why Study Irredentism?

Understanding irredentism is important for two reasons. On a practical level, it can be incredibly destructive and dangerous to the welfare of states and peoples, and as a political phenomenon it has broader implications.

Irredentism has posed serious challenges to global security. Because it in-volves one state claiming the territory of another, and because states are very reluctant to part with their territory (Toft 2003),[7] irredentism causes war. A quick tour of the twentieth century illustrates the danger of irredentism to international security. Serb irredentists, who sought a Greater Serbia at the expense of the Austro-Hungarian Empire, triggered World War I, with many causes at a variety of levels. Most dramatically, irredentism helped to spark World War II, as Adolf Hitler sought to reunify the German peoples and territories lost in the aftermath of World War I. Other countries, includ-ing Hungary and Romania, developed fascist governments that were, in part, built on irredentist agendas, and then allied with Hitler in pursuit of lost territories.

In the postwar period, irredentism has remained a serious cause of instability and conflict. Somalia's recent history is a particularly good illustration of irredentism and its legacies. It tried during its democratic period in the early 1960s to gain Djibouti, along with parts of Ethiopia and Kenya.[8] During a subsequent authoritarian regime, in 1977, Somalia invaded Ethiopia, ultimately losing this war after the Soviet Union and Cuba intervened (Farer 1979; Patman 1990). The resentment over the costs of that war, including the flow of refugees from Ethiopia into Somalia, led to a series of rebellions, eventually pulling down the Siyad Barre regime and creating the mess that is Somalia today (Laitin 1999).

The "troubles" of Northern Ireland—a euphemism for a conflict that has killed more than three thousand people—are essentially an irredentist problem. The demand has generally been to unify the island—to bring Northern Ireland under Ireland's sovereignty. Thus, progress on a peaceful settlement requires not just the groups in Northern Ireland to accommodate with each other but also some kind of settlement between Ireland and Great Britain. Declining interest by Ireland in unification does seem to be related to the improved chances of settling this conflict.[9]

Cyprus was one of the most significant irredentist hotspots of the Cold War period, causing NATO members Greece and Turkey nearly to go to war with each other. Beginning in the 1950s, when Cyprus was still controlled by Britain, Greek Cypriots sought *enosis*—unification of Cyprus with Greece—while Turkish Cypriots, fearing discrimination at the hands of Greece, demanded *taksim*, separation (and, implicitly, their own unification with Turkey). This conflict delayed the granting of independence to Cyprus until 1960, and it forced the parties to set up a delicately balanced government that proved to be unworkable and collapsed in the 1960s. Increasingly violent intercommunal conflicts throughout the 1960s, coupled with a military coup in Greece in 1973, led to Turkey's invasion of the island in 1974, nearly touching off a general war between Greece and Turkey. As of 2007, the island remains partitioned, and a political solution to reunify Greek and Turkish Cypriots and protect them both from the irredentisms of their mother countries remains elusive, despite the accession of Cyprus (but not of Turkish Republic of Cyprus) to the European Union. The issue also remains a serious thorn in the side of Turkish-European relations and is a major complicating factor in Turkey's drive to join the European Union (EU).

Irredentism has produced much of the conflict of the post–Cold War period in Eastern Europe and the former Soviet Union.[10] The most noted irredentist effort was that of Serbia to annex parts of Croatia and Bosnia, producing approximately 50,000 and 200,000 deaths respectively (Ayres 1997). Croatia, despite the challenge it faced from Serbia, engaged in its own efforts to "reclaim" parts of Bosnia occupied by Croats, prolonging that conflict. Croatia and Serbia continue to pay the costs of irredentist campaigns that ended more than a decade ago. Their admission to European institutions will occur long after most countries in the region have become members. The domestic politics of Yugoslavia's successor states are damaged by the legacies of the war, including the assassination of Serbia's Prime Minister Djindjic (Ramet and Pavlakovic 2005), Bosnia's paralyzed political system induced by the Dayton Accords (Woodward 1999), Croatia's belated transition to democracy in the post-Tudjman era, and the grip of organized crime upon all three (Andreas 2005; Miljkovic and Hoare 2005).

Irredentism continues to threaten parts of the former Yugoslavia. While Albania may not be as enthusiastic about the possibility of a Greater Albania, the ties between the Kosovo Liberation Army (KLA) and Albanian forces in Macedonia (the National Liberation Army) suggest that a Greater Kosovo might be a goal of some factions (Judah 2001; Kola 2003). Conflict broke out in Macedonia in 2001, leading to yet another NATO intervention—Task Force Fox—to supervise the Ohrid Accords, which seem to have settled things, at least for the time being (International Crisis Group 2002). The KLA also remains a potent force, delaying a permanent resolution of the Kosovo issue. Although the Balkans have fallen out of the headlines, the region remains politically unstable because of these overlapping and competing irredentist claims.

Armenia stands out as the one recent case of successful irredentism: it won a war against Azerbaijan to gain the Armenian-populated territory of Nagorno-Karabakh. While Armenia has settled its conflict de facto by controlling the Karabakh region, ongoing tensions and a lack of international legitimacy to the lines of control have hampered development and investment in the area, in particular cutting off a potential route for Caspian Sea oil to reach international markets. Continued uncertainty between Armenia and Azerbaijan draws in neighbors (Turkey, Iran, and Russia), creating a source of regional instability, while the potentially lucrative oil and gas reserves in the Caspian Sea basin remain underutilized.[11] And, of course, the economic and human costs of prolonged conflict and tense stalemate have hampered efforts to develop both Armenia and Azerbaijan from their relatively poor post-Soviet condition.

Finally, Pakistani efforts to gain Kashmir have brought South Asia to the brink of nuclear war on more than one occasion since India and Pakistan developed nuclear capabilities, as well as significantly complicating global efforts to stem terrorism. Kashmir's status was contested when the subcontinent was partitioned. Since then, Pakistan has sought to unify India's portion of Kashmir with its own. While there are other dynamics that cause India and Pakistan to engage in rivalry (Paul 2005), the competing claims over Kashmir and Pakistan's support of groups seeking to join Kashmir with itself have been a central part of the conflict (Saideman 2005). Tension has continued there for decades, with tens of thousands of casualties, and the issue continues to tie up Indo-Pakistani relations on even basic humanitarian questions such as the 2005 earthquake.

Finally, irredentism plays a significant role in both Afghanistan and Iraq. One of the central points of tension between Afghanistan and Pakistan is over their border. President Hamid Karzai cannot commit to the current international boundaries, since he needs to appeal to the Pashtuns of Afghanistan, who would like a Greater Afghanistan to include the Pashtuns of Pakistan. This creates much animosity and fear in Pakistan, which helps to explain their frictions with the Afghani government (Smith 2007). Similarly, the Kurds of Iraq are part of a long-standing irredentist crisis, involving kin in neighboring Iran, Syria, and Turkey. Balancing the interests of Turkey and the Kurds has been a full-time job for the United States, greatly complicating the plans before the war and the occupation afterward.

This tour of the world's irredentist hot spots demonstrates that the too little studied topic of this book is important and relevant for understanding not only past conflicts but also potential confrontations in the future. Irredentist conflicts have been responsible for hundreds of thousands of deaths over the past forty years, and they remain at the heart of the instability in several key regions around the world. This review also shows that some countries have sunk an enormous amount of political capital in these efforts, sometimes with success, but often to complete and very costly failure. The question remains why countries will engage in such efforts despite the dangers.

Relevance for Broader Debates

Not only does irredentism threaten lives and undermine economic development, but it also presents us with an important question: When will politicians lead their countries into such self-destructive courses of action? Irredentism is rarely successful (Ambrosio 2001), and countries that engage in it are likely to pay high costs, even if they win. We pose this question: When will politicians pursue policies that may reunite ethnic kin abroad (irredentism) and when will they direct resources instead to try to improve the situation of those already inside their country? This trade-off exists because of irredentism's costs, which are unlikely to be borne equally. As we discuss at greater length in the next chapter, aggressive efforts will probably antagonize neighboring states and interested outsiders, leading to some isolation, which again imposes some pain upon the domestic population.

The question of irredentism is relevant for more than just scholars of ethnic conflict. First, irredentism poses a challenge to deterrence theorists (Jervis, Lebow, and Stein 1985; Huth 1988, 1999; Morgan 2003), as some states, regardless of the likelihood of success, have engaged in costly aggression to no avail. Somalia attacked its neighbors both when it was relatively strong and when it was relatively weak, which should trouble those who focus on relative power. If we find that politicians are willing to endanger their country on behalf of their kin (hence our title) under certain circumstances, then deterrence theory and a focus on relative power may be less useful for understanding at least one important path toward war.

Second, there has long been a concern that countries may engage in aggressive foreign policies to divert domestic audiences (diversionary war theory, popularized as the "Wag the Dog" hypothesis).[12] This debate reached the media when journalists and politicians speculated about whether President Clinton used force against Iraq, Serbia, and other countries to divert Americans from various controversies at home, including the Monica Lewinsky scandal and his impeachment (Hendrickson 2002). Scholars have largely ignored the targets of diversion, so this study will help improve our understanding not only of when countries engage in aggression but also toward whom.

Third, scholars have considered under what conditions states intervene in other countries' conflicts (Regan 1998, 2000; Saideman 2001). Obviously, irredentism is a subset of this larger question—by understanding irredentism, we may get a handle on international intervention in general. Previous studies of intervention have tended to view the intervener as the actor and the target group as the target of intervention. Because we are looking at the interaction between the irredentist state (the intervener) and the kin group (the potential target), our work may help illuminate this larger discussion by illustrating the two-way nature of this relationship in the context of ethnic politics. Our hypothesis—that domestic politics and the complex of interactions between the mother state and its ethnic kin abroad drive irredentist decisions—may help intervention scholars understand why states intervene in their neighbors' conflicts in some cases but not in others.

Fourth, one of the plausible explanations of Hungarian cooperation and lack of international aggression (for example) is that economic interdependence and an improving economy have permitted leaders to pursue moderate policies toward kin in Romania, Serbia, and Slovakia (Linden 2000). Throughout our discussion, we examine whether economic ties and growing prosperity alleviate the forces that drive international aggression.[13]

Fifth, this book may serve as a counterbalance to the cottage industry that has developed touting the power of international organizations. Many have argued that the European Union and other organizations, such as the North Atlantic Treaty Organization (NATO) and Organization for Security and Cooperation in Europe (OSCE), have constrained the foreign policies of Eastern Europe, helping them to become normal European states. We are skeptical for a variety of reasons (Saideman and Ayres 2007), but the most obvious challenge is that some countries acted moderately before the membership pressures mounted while others continued to engage in aggressive ways after accession processes kicked in.

Sixth, if international organizations matter less than advertised, then significant questions remain about the course of Eastern European transitions. In a very short time, a number of countries made a quick transition from communism and authoritarianism to capitalism and democracy. But not all countries traveled at the same speed or even in the same direction. Irredentism, chosen or avoided, shaped these transformations for aggressors, victims and bystanders.

Seventh, this book moves beyond the debate between rationalists and constructivists by incorporating elements of each—material interests and identities both matter—rather than trying to remain within the boundaries of one approach or the other.[14] We start by focusing on the interests of politicians and their desire to gain and maintain high offices, a standard set of rationalist assumptions. Yet we then move on to consider not only the material interests of constituents but their identities—with and against whom do they identify—and identity is very much in the constructivist ballpark. The purpose of this book is not to recast the debate, but the effort to understand the question at hand—irredentism and its absence—has led us past the divide between the two camps to focus on both material and ideational factors that constrain and compel politicians.

Eighth, this study contributes to significant debates in comparative politics about minority rights. Scholars of Eastern Europe (Csergo and Goldgeier 2004; Csergo 2007; Deets 2006; Deets and Stroschein 2005; Jackson Preece 1997) have considered the problems of minority rights in the new democracies and the efforts by countries to address their kin abroad short of irredentism. While our focus is on the most violent efforts to deal with the grievances of kin, our chapters on Hungary and Romania focus on more moderate efforts, and, thus, help to place this debate about minority rights into a broader context.

Ninth, this book is part of a larger movement to unpack the meaning and consequences of identity (Abdelal et al. 2006; Chandra 2006; Posner 2004, 2005). We ask what it takes to be a successful nationalist, which requires a greater understanding of the contents of various nationalisms. Being more or less nationalist than another politician does not have meaning in and of itself without understanding the identities involved and their relative weightings. By taking seriously the content of nationalism and focusing on the contradictions between xenophobia and ethnic affinity, we hope to make an important contribution.

Tenth and finally, irredentism is and has been a cause of war. While not all wars are irredentist ones and not all irredentist temptations lead to war, this book may help us to understand the central question in international relations: under what conditions do countries go to war? Thus, this book focuses on a topic of interest to those who are interested in foreign policy, international conflict, nationalism and minority rights, the European Union, and Eastern Europe. Irredentism, it turns out, is relevant to much of international relations and comparative politics.

Room for Optimism? Less Irredentism Than Expected

Despite the very real dangers and costs, there has actually been less irredentist violence in recent years than one might have predicted. Given the costs of transitions, both economic and political, after the end of communism in Eastern Europe and the former Soviet Union, and given past grievances about various international borders, it is somewhat surprising that only a few countries have engaged in irredentist foreign policies since 1990. From this perspective, Armenia, Croatia, and Serbia may not be the anomalies; instead Hungary, Romania, and Russia become the interesting puzzles—the conflicts that did not occur.[15] This is particularly surprising given the regionwide uncertainty, both about power relationships and about the legitimacy of borders, brought on by the end of the Cold War and the near-simultaneous collapse of so many communist regimes. Collapsing empires tend to leave chaos in their wake; so, it makes sense to ask why, at least in some places, this one did not.

Given the numbers of Hungarians abroad and the plight that many of them face, it is surprising that Hungary has restrained itself. Certainly, the issue of Hungarians beyond the current borders of Hungary has been central in Hungary's politics, in its foreign relations, and in the politics of its neighbors. In many ways, Hungary seems to have found an optimal level of obnoxiousness—assertive enough about the plight of Hungarians abroad to satisfy the domestic audience, but quiescent enough to irritate but not antagonize the neighbors and other relevant audiences (NATO and EU members), or to spark more serious conflicts. By examining its blend of policies, assertion and acquiescence, we should be able to understand better how domestic politics interact with international pressures.

Romania has faced one of the roughest roads from communism to democracy. Ceausescu's regime left Romania poorly prepared for democracy and capitalism. The transition was the most violent of the Eastern European revolutions, and it was followed by a regime with dubious legitimacy and poor democratic credentials and habits. Moreover, Romania has an outstanding territorial grievance—the pact between Nazi Germany and Stalin's Soviet Union in 1939 removed Bessarabia from Romania and joined it with other territory to form Moldova. Yet Romania has been far less aggressive than one might have expected, given the prominence of the Greater Romania Party (an inherently irredentist label) and the strength of nationalism in mainstream parties.

Perhaps most surprisingly, Russia has generally acquiesced to its dismemberment.[16] When the Soviet Union disintegrated, Russia lost not only its former colonial territories in Central Asia, but also lands and peoples that had been integral to Russia since its creation.[17] Some twenty-five million Russians were left outside of Russia. While nationalists, most notably Vladimir Zhirinovsky, have focused on these issues at least superficially, Russia has been far more peaceful with regard to its neighbors in the Near Abroad than one might have expected, particularly given the economic and political dislocations of the post–Cold War period. Yet, one cannot become too complacent as the issue of the Russians in the Near Abroad was still relevant enough to appear in President Vladimir Putin's address to the Federal Assembly in the spring of 2005. Understanding why Russia has not pursued this issue in the past may be key to understanding whether it ever will in the future.

Explaining Restraint and Aggression

How can we explain the restraint demonstrated by Hungary, Romania, and Russia while accounting for the aggression by Armenia, Croatia and Serbia? Much has been made of the efforts by regional organizations, particularly the EU and NATO, to tie membership processes to good behavior (Ambrosio 2001; Cronin 2002; Kelley 2004a, 2004b; Linden 2000, 2002; Schimmelfennig and Sedelmeir 2005; Vachudova 2005). These authors and others are part of a larger trend, asserting the importance of international norms and organizations as constraints upon states, imposing costs on undesired behavior as well as increasing the benefits of cooperation. While there is no doubt that Eastern European countries have been very responsive to the recommendations (or demands) of these organizations, these arguments assert that international pressures are the primary drivers of foreign and domestic policy—in effect, that these countries are selling out policies they would rather pursue in exchange for admission to the club of Europe.

This begs a whole series of questions. Other countries have chosen not to embrace "the West," even at great cost (most obviously Serbia but Croatia and Bosnia as well for much of the post–Cold War era), so we still need to consider under what domestic conditions these international membership processes may matter. Further, even within the constraints of external demands, countries have varied in their behavior; Hungary has alternated between offending and accommodating its neighbors, for example. In addition, there are important questions to be raised about the sincerity of commitments made by countries as they seek membership. Are the measures taken to protect minorities merely cheap talk, promises that can easily be broken? Will membership prevent nationalist and irredentist conflicts in the future?

This book directly challenges those arguing that international factors such as relative power or membership in regional organizations deterred violence and caused peace in Eastern Europe (Kelley 2004a). We see a world in which states have engaged in irredentism despite the costs and the probability of failure. One of the fundamental assertions presented here is that politicians will do what may be extremely costly for their country if it benefits them in the short run.[18] Somalia in earlier decades suggests this pattern, as it engaged in aggressive irredentism toward its neighbors both when it was relatively strong and relatively weak (Saideman 1998). Somalia jumped through a window of opportunity presented by Ethiopia's regime change and civil conflict in the mid-1970s. However, it essentially tried to jump through a brick wall in the early 1960s. That is, in the earlier period, there was no window of opportunity: Somalia was weaker than both Ethiopia and the colonial powers governing Kenya (Great Britain) and Djibouti (France). Thus, to say that a country avoids doing something that is likely to be costly or risky is not good enough, as countries have engaged in extremely dangerous behavior in defiance of this logic. The cases of Croatia, Serbia, and Armenia demonstrate this quite clearly. We need to explain both the sources of restraint and of aggression—we address both the silent dogs and the pit bulls of the former communist world.

In this book, we consider various explanations for the causes of irredentism and of restrained foreign policies, including respect for international boundaries; pressures by the international community—especially NATO and EU membership processes; and the legacies of failed irredentist efforts. We then focus on domestic politics. What does it take for politicians to gain and maintain office in these countries? We posit a potential tradeoff between nationalism and economic integration, suggesting that politicians may be cross-pressured in some cases, but able to build irredentist, isolationist coalitions in others. We then consider the question of what does it take to be a successful nationalist politician. We suggest that not all nationalisms are the same—that the content of the nationalism matters. Some nationalists will privilege the lost kin in neighboring territories while others will focus on enmities with ethnic rivals inside the state. Nationalisms define who is "us" and who is "them," and we need to take seriously how these attitudes shape preferences.[19] We also consider the condition of the kin abroad, as that will impact their salience in both the domestic politics of the mother state and in the nationalist ideology.

Ultimately, we argue that domestic politics trumps international concerns; that the impact of EU and NATO membership conditions is far less significant than has been argued;[20] and that internal forces primarily drive irredentist foreign policy. We find that political imperatives cause elites to endanger their country because they are playing to a particular set of political forces, usually a narrow group of kin, in particular circumstances. In other cases, domestic politics causes politicians to take less aggressive stances, even when nationalism is quite strong, as the substance of the particular nationalism will point away from irredentism and towards less threatening foreign policy behaviors. This book, therefore, not only explains the irredentism that did and did not occur in Eastern Europe in the 1990s, but it also addresses the content of nationalism and its impact on foreign policy. In so doing, we reach some counterintuitive conclusions, including the possibility that xenophobia may actually be a force for stability between states in Eastern Europe and perhaps elsewhere.

How Irredentism Has Been Addressed

This is not the first time that scholars have considered the question of irredentism. Weiner (1971) raised this issue, arguing that the kin nearby had an important role to play. In earlier work (2000), we verified this intuition in quantitative analyses of Minorities at Risk Data from the 1980s and 1990s. The actions and behavior of an ethnic group's kin go a long way toward understanding what the group seeks to do—to join with a "mother" country or become independent. Weiner's article describes the phenomenon, but does not really address when a state will engage in aggressive efforts to "reunite" with its kin and when it will not. Brubaker (1996) focuses on what he calls the triadic nexus between nationalizing state, minority, and homeland to understand homeland politics, which he considers to be a broader topic within which irredentism fits. We depart from Brubaker in that we focus more on the homeland politics and less on the nationalizing state, which is his emphasis. Our question is more focused on foreign policy—what does one state do to another and why. Still, Brubaker shows that the host state, the ethnic group, and the homeland are interlinked. Jenne (2006) provides a powerful argument that the behavior of the three are tied together, as the more credible and powerful the external homeland state is (the potentially irredentist state in our terms), the more demanding the ethnic group is. Yet, her argument focuses mostly on the kin group and how it responds to different opportunities and constraints as it seeks to bargain with the host state. There are some difficult chicken-and-egg problems here. Do the ethnic groups that might be redeemed drive this process as their activities raise their salience in the motherland? Or does the homeland state manage their kin abroad, depending on how it suits them? We bet on the latter, with an important caveat. When the kin abroad actually play a substantial role (through votes, political positions or campaign finance) in the domestic politics of the homeland state, then foreign policy can become quite aggressive indeed on their behalf.

Others have focused more directly on irredentism. David Carment and Patrick James (1995) compare irredentist and nonirredentist crises, and they find that irredentist conflicts are likely to be more intense than others. In later work (Carment and James 1997; Carment, James, and Taydas 2006), they find that political competition is correlated with more irredentist crises, with regime type playing a stronger role than we would suggest.

McMahon (1998) also considers domestic politics, but argues that international constraints matter more. Chazan (1991) points to the importance of domestic politics, and particularly the composition of the decision makers' constituencies, but ignores key dynamics that we address here, including economic integration and the role played by xenophobia. Horowitz (1985) mentions that irredentism might be deterred by fears of upsetting domestic political balances, but he does not systematically explore this question. One of the purposes of this book is to take Horowitz's comment seriously. Indeed, one of the issues we face is that many analysts refer to domestic politics (including Linden 2000 and Kelley 2004a), but not in any systematic way.[21]

Somalia and Serbia supported some ethnic kin and not others, and this support varied over time (Saideman 1998). Serbia's assistance to Serbs in Bosnia and Croatia and Somalia's interventions into Ethiopia and Kenya waxed and waned with political competition within each country. When leaders depended on groups that had ethnic ties to particular "lost territories," then the politicians would support irredentist policies—invasion at the extreme. When elites did not depend on such groups, then there would be few real efforts to annex territory inhabited by kin. This work advanced the debate by focusing more attention on the complexity of ethnic ties, the nature of political competition (both in democracies and in authoritarian regimes), and the target of the efforts.

The problem is that these previous accounts best account for the attack dogs but not the dogs that did not bark—Hungary, Romania, and Russia, to name just three. Why have these countries not been irredentist thus far, given similar structural circumstances? There are a host of potential explanations, each one having important policy implications for both the United States and the community of international organizations. Consequently, this study will facilitate a better understanding of which explanations are most accurate, resulting in better policy recommendations.

Why These Cases?

This book is aimed at discovering the differences between irredentist and potentially irredentist countries. Quantitative analyses of irredentism have provided additional support for considering the kin state of ethnic groups. The data shows that groups are likely to be irredentist only if their kin dominate a nearby state, but even then, many such groups do not become irredentist (Saideman and Ayres 2000). Both for understanding what these groups eventually do and for understanding the foreign policies of states, we need to examine states that could be irredentist—that have kin nearby in territories that are seen as being historically theirs.[22] While there are many countries that fit into this category, we have decided to focus on the formerly communist states in Eastern Europe and the former Soviet Union to develop a set of controlled comparisons. These states have very similar histories, economic situations, and political conditions, yet have behaved differently.

Here we consider two sets of countries—those that have engaged in irredentism and those who did not, but could have been or were expected to do so in the 1990s. The former category includes Armenia, Croatia, and Serbia. The latter category of "silent dogs" focuses on Hungary, Romania, and Russia. To further our understanding of irredentism, we obviously need to consider the countries that have engaged in the most aggressive forms as well as those that did little or nothing.

Croatia and Serbia serve as an interesting comparison as their leaders seemed to be very different—Franjo Tudjman as a genuine nationalist and Slobodan Milosevic as a cynical opportunist—and because their efforts interacted with each other.[23] Indeed, it might be argued that these cases are exceptional because they fed off each other, but the real test is whether we find dynamics here that are similar or different from the other cases. Moreover, the Croatian case, in particular, raises important issues about deterrence and costs, as it deliberately chose to wage a war to take back "lost kin and territories" at the same time it faced an irredentist threat. Finally, most efforts to understand the power of conditionality ignore these two new states.[24] This is problematic, since they were among the most heavily conditioned—that is, threatened—states in Europe. As a result of their irredentism, they are at the back of the line for integration.

Armenia stands out as the one case of successful irredentism in the aftermath of the Cold War, although this effort has been extremely expensive and remains a source of conflict and instability. Some might consider this case not to be comparable, since it does not share the attributes of many Eastern European states, but rather was once part of the Soviet Union. There is something to this, for Armenia was never going to be at the front of the line for admission to Euro-Atlantic institutions. However, just like Croatia and Serbia, Armenia had a history as a distinct unit within a larger federation and of grievances about the intrastate boundaries. Also, Armenia, like Eastern Europe, faced the problems of regime change and economic liberalization. Indeed, a closer study of Armenia reveals many similarities, particularly to Croatia.

We then turn to the "silent dogs." Given the plight of Hungarians at various times in Romania, Serbia, and Slovakia, some expected more aggressive efforts by Hungary on behalf of their kin (Linden 2000). Hungary has engaged in a series of efforts that go beyond normal foreign policy but fall short of irredentism. This variation over time provides us with an interesting opportunity to determine what causes these shifts.

Moldova's territory so recently (1940) belonged to Romania, and there was some discussion within both Moldova and Romania about reunification in the early 1990s; yet Romania's passive approach to the issue is quite surprising, particularly given Romania's very troublesome transition. Despite the strength of nationalists within Romania, Romania's politicians have largely imitated Hungarian decision makers, developing very similar institutions and strategies. This is, at first, quite surprising, given how similar Romania seemed to be to Serbia at the outset of the 1990s, led by former communists with shaky credentials and nationalist pretensions.

Finally, Russia's loss of territory and the plight of the Russians left outside of Russia after the Soviet Union's disintegration made irredentism a live possibility. Russia has bullied its neighbors, but outside of sporadic (and ineffectual) efforts to reunify with Belarus, Russia has not engaged in any serious irredentism, despite severe economic problems and the rise of nationalist politicians. It also serves as a good contrast to the other countries, as Russia, in terms of military capabilities relative to its neighbors, has been in a much better position to act aggressively. Because of Russia's power position and its dominance over Eastern Europe and the former Soviet areas, it is almost impossible to ignore. This allows us to consider the role of power a bit more directly than the other cases. Finally, Russia's size (relative to the other cases) opens up a broad arena of complexity in determining who is "us" in nationalist terms, making it an excellent case to illustrate the importance of looking at the substance, not just the severity, of nationalism.

In each case, we determine which constituents mattered most, what their preferences were, the content of the country's nationalism, the condition and behavior of the potential kin to be redeemed and how politicians responded to the situation. We also assess both the credibility and the value of external promises, and consider how such efforts played in each political system.

Some might argue that the Western Balkans (Croatia, Serbia), Armenia, and Russia are not comparable to the countries in Eastern Europe (Hungary and Romania) because of different historical trajectories. Armenia might be seen as distinct because it was part of the Soviet Union, whereas the others had independent histories before the Cold War. Or Yugoslavia's successors may be seen as unfitting for comparison with the others as it was a federal system that broke apart. Still, the end of the Cold War confronted each of these countries with similar challenges—how to address the condition of their kin outside the country while facing the very difficult problem of transitioning (or not) to democratic competition and economic reform. Moreover, even if not all of the cases fit into the exact same box, pairs of the cases are comparable. Romania and Serbia were seen as being quite similar in most ways until 1996, when the incumbents in Bucharest stepped down after losing an election. Armenia and Russia face very similar circumstances, given their shared history, but only Armenia (the weaker of the two) has actually engaged in war to reclaim lost territory. Hungary and Romania are very similar, as both faced international pressures to settle their disputes, both faced a series of elections where incumbents were tossed, and their policies towards the kin abroad are reflections of each other's. Likewise, Croatia and Serbia are quite similar to each other. Finally, we selected these cases so that we have maximum variation in the outcomes—from the very peaceful to the very violent. One of the problems with the existing literature, with notable exceptions (Ambrosio 2001; Linden 2002; Vachudova 2005), is that it focuses either on the most violent cases (Gagnon 2004; Saideman 1998) or on the peaceful ones (Kelley 2004a).

In addition to the more extensive case studies, we also briefly consider a series of smaller case studies to show that the dynamics that play out in Eastern Europe and the Former Soviet Union are not unique to this region and not a creature of the case selection, but also matter in West Europe and South Asia. Our focus is on the aftermath of communism, but the dynamics at play and the risk of irredentist war are relevant beyond Eastern Europe and the former Soviet Union. We hope that this book helps to make sense of the post–Cold War landscape, but our primary goal is to understand the classic question: why war or peace?

We conclude the book by developing the implications for both scholarly debates and policy initiatives. To preview, if politicians are willing to bear international costs to pursue their policy preferences, then outside actors need to consider whether and how they can influence the domestic arena. Further, if nationalisms vary in how they value their kin and others, we need to understand the content of nationalisms, rather than merely focus on who is more or less extreme in their nationalism. Hate and intolerance may actually lead to less hostile international relations, and policymakers will have to face this possible contradiction.

NOTES TO INTRODUCTION

1. There is an extensive literature on identity and what constitutes kin. Here, we merely refer to those groups outside the country that are seen as belonging to the same nation—the same ethnic group that aspires to statehood. The most important works in this field are by Gellner (1983), Anderson (1996), Connor (1994), and Smith (1991). See also Hall (1998). We discuss identity more directly in chapter 1.

2. This omits cases of aggression based on historical claims, such as that of Iraq in 1990. Almost every country has an historic claim to territory beyond its current jurisdiction, either real or imagined. Irredentism, as we define it (and thanks to Miles Kahler for suggesting a clearer definition), is a specific, relatively narrow form of behavior, based on ethnic ties. To include all forms of territorial claims into the definition would stretch the concept of irredentism too far (Satori 1970; Collier and Mahon 1993).

3. Nationalism—the definition of who the nation is and what its goals are—does not always promote irredentism. Nationalism can lead to secession, which is the creation of a new state, rather than the union of pieces of existing states. Nationalism may produce changes in government, rather than changes in territory. This book, thus, examines nationalist dynamics of a certain kind, rather than the entirety of nationalism. We address the implications of nationalism scholarship for this book in chapter 1.

4. The term *irredentism* was derived from the successful effort that unified Italy in 1867. A second form of irredentism is when groups in multiple countries seek to secede from existing states and then merge, creating a new country. The Kurds are the most obvious modern example, since they reside in Turkey, Iraq, Iran, and Syria, and a po-

tential Kurdistan would incorporate territories from each. Because our focus is on the foreign policies of states, this second form of irredentism is less relevant for this book.

5. That is not to say that Russia has not engaged in either violence (Chechnya) or in coercive foreign policies towards the other parts of the former Soviet Union.

6. Not all politicians using nationalist claims are successful — they may not get into power — and not all successful politicians are nationalists as they can use other issues to appeal to potential supporters.

7. It is important to note that Toft's work focuses more on the importance of territory whereas we focus almost entirely on the relevance of the people sitting astride the contested pieces of land.

8. See Touval (1963), Selassie (1980), Laitin and Samatar (1987), and Saideman (1998).

9. For a thorough, though somewhat dated, analysis of support for irredentism in Ireland, see Cox (1985). We return to this case in chapter 7.

10. Scholarly interest in irredentism has followed current and recent events. See Carment and James (1995, 1997), MacMahon (1998), and Ambrosio (2001).

11. Other potential pipeline routes out of the region pass through Afghanistan and Chechnya, which has severely limited the alternatives to Armenian-Azeri cooperation on these issues.

12. Since Jack Levy's excellent review of this literature (1989), there has been a resurgence of interest considering this question, including Morgan and Bickers (1992), James and Hristoulas (1994), Miller (1995), Smith (1996), Gelpi (1997), Leeds and Davis (1997), and Clark (1998).

13. The debate about the impact of trade and prosperity on conflict has become quite lively as of late. For a good review of the literature, see Barbieri and Schneider (1999).

14. For an excellent survey of this debate, see volume 56 of *International Organization*, a special issue.

15. We are not alone in seeing this as a puzzle; Ambrosio (2001) and Linden (2000) have both considered the "dogs that did not bark."

16. For expectations of a more aggressive course, see Simes (1991), Goltz (1993), Brzezinski (1994), and Brubaker (1996).

17. For a relatively early assessment of these challenges, see Arbatov (1993).

18. Snyder (1991) crafts a similar argument to explain why countries expand beyond their means.

19. Fearon (1998) notes that nationalisms are not universalist, so that they have natural boundaries that limit their spread. Our intent in this book is to examine the substance of various nationalisms to illuminate where those boundaries are and whether they include or exclude irredentist policies.

20. We also consider the role of other institutions, such as the Council of Europe, the Organization of Security and Cooperation in Europe, and its High Commissioner for National Minorities. The EU and NATO, however, are central, since the others' influence largely depended upon the heavy hammer of membership into the big two.

21. Vachudova (2005) is exceptional in this regard. She develops a theory that incorporates both domestic and international factors into a single account, but her focus is not so much on ethnic conflict or irredentism as it is on the conditionality process.

22. For a discussion of what kinds of negative cases to select, see Mahoney and Goertz (2004).

23. Gagnon (2004) systematically compares these two cases and develops many insights for doing so, but he does not consider other cases, limiting how much his work might say about the less aggressive cases.

24. Vachudova (2005) is a notable exception.

Irredentism and Its Absence

International Pressures Versus Domestic Dynamics

In politics it is necessary either to betray one's country or the electorate. I prefer to betray the electorate.
— CHARLES DE GAULLE

C LEARLY, AN IRREDENTIST POLICY IS LIKELY TO be costly. Irredentism risks war with one's neighbors, and war is always a costly process, regardless of outcome. Any effort to (re)unify territories inhabited by ethnic kin will certainly antagonize neighboring states whose lands are sought. Further, such foreign policies are likely to alienate the neighbor's allies, and perhaps even other countries facing similar threats. As we will explore in subsequent chapters, irredentism has brought substantial costs—in deaths, damage, and economic hardship—to states that have pursued it. Our starting point, therefore, is this basic question: why would states do such an apparently irrational thing?

Several analyses of irredentism (MacMahon 1998; Ambrosio 2001) emphasize international constraints, so we need to consider the importance of external forces, particularly boundary norms (Zacher 2001) and the pressures of the international community. Similarly, there has been an outpouring of scholarly work asserting that efforts by the European Union (EU) and the North Atlantic Treaty Organization (NATO) to "condition" the behavior of the Eastern European states through their admission procedures are responsible for keeping peace in Eastern Europe after the collapse of communism.[1] However, one basic observation driving this project is that countries sometimes engage in policies that are counterproductive to the point of self-destruction.[2] That is, the international costs may be steep, but politicians pursuing their own individual interests—those that make the policy decisions—may be willing to have their country pay them. In some cases, the population may be quite willing to bear that burden. Armenia, Croatia, and Serbia pursued irredentism at tremendous costs, while Hungary, Romania, and Russia refrained.

Leaders frequently face a trade-off between what is best for the ethnic group and what is best for the country. The answers are often not the same, and, indeed, are frequently contradictory. We assume that politicians are most concerned with gaining and maintaining political office, as this is usually the prerequisite for attaining other goals via the political system (Mayhew 1974). Scholars of international relations have increasingly built their work on this assumption (Bueno de Mesquita et al. 2003). Chiozza and Goemans argue that war is not necessarily bad for politicians, since "the societal costs of war generally do not translate into political costs for leaders" (2004a, 605). We concur in the sense that the costs and benefits of war are borne unequally, so the key question turns on whose voice matters—those who pay or those who benefit.

Our second assumption is that a domestic audience is the primary actor in determining who governs and who loses office. Thus, we need to determine which members of the polity matter politically, since institutions and past patterns give more power and influence to some citizens than to others. In authoritarian regimes, individuals who matter most, the selectorate (Roeder 1993), reside in the coercive arms of the state—the secret police, the army, the party, and the like. In democracies, the key constituencies are the bodies of relevant voters for each party. For such systems, it is important to know which parties are in power, from which they receive support, and what their constituents' interests are. The greatest difficulty is understanding regimes in transition from authoritarianism to democracy, as the rules are not fixed, and it is not clear whether institutions really bind behavior. Still, leaders in such systems have relatively short tenures (Chiozza and Goemans 2004) so they must focus on the domestic scene as they scramble to remain in power.

Ultimately, this focus leads to two questions. Does one have to be a nationalist to gain and maintain power? And what does it take to be a good nationalist? Answering the first question will require specifying the interests of key constituencies in the relevant countries. To preview, we consider two sets of interests to be paramount: preferences concerning integration with the international economy, particularly regional organizations, and attitudes toward kin in neighboring countries. To answer the second question, we consider the treatment of the kin abroad and the content of the nationalist identities in play. Irredentism is far more likely if the "lost territories" are inhabited by ethnic brethren who are relevant politically in the homeland—and if the content of nationalism focuses on those kin. Irredentism will be much less likely if the kin are politically irrelevant and if national identity marginalizes the lost kin or includes them in a category separate from the domestic "us." The treatment of those kin—and how happy they are with that treatment—also matters. In other words, the key factors are not just where kin are located (Toft 2003) but also how much influence they have, how they view the status quo, and how their ethnic brethren in the "homeland" view them. For the purposes of addressing the foreign policy question of irredentism, we argue, with the exception of the treatment of the kin, that these are largely domestic dynamics that drive politicians in some cases to follow policies that harm their country even in the face of significant international incentives to do otherwise.

Still, we take seriously the arguments about external constraints. MacMahon (1998), Ambrosio (2001), Kelley (2004a, 2004b), Linden (2000, 2002), Schimmelfennig and Sedelmeier (2005), Vachudova (2005), and others have used different arguments to assert international constraints as the key to understanding moderate behavior. These arguments suggest that international norms and/or organizations played key roles in inhibiting states from engaging in irredentism. They also suggest that the transitions in Europe took place at a key point in history, as international norms limiting aggression gained strength via the Helsinki Accords and as regional organizations, especially NATO and the EU, had particularly strong leverage via their membership procedures.

In the next sections of this chapter, we address the impact of norms—especially boundary norms codified by the Helsinki Accords—and the influence of international institutions. Since both the academic literature and policymakers tend to stress the membership procedures of NATO and the EU, we dedicate much of the following sections to addressing that argument and raising several criticisms. We then consider concerns about military advantage and the balance of power. One might expect weaker states to refrain from aggressive irredentism aimed against their stronger neighbors, and stronger ones to be more willing to consider it, but we find this logic problematic. We also consider one additional set of arguments, focusing on history and the lessons learned from past aggression. We then move on to delineate our own argument, stressing the imperatives of political competition and the content of the nationalisms in play.

International Borders Matter, Intrastate Borders Do Not

The first and most obvious difference between the irredentist wars that occurred in the 1990s and the potential ones that did not is in their boundaries. Countries signing the Helsinki Final Act of 1975 recognized the existing boundaries of the time as the legitimate borders, regardless of their origins, including those separating Hungary from Romania and Romania from Moldova.[3] On the other hand, the Helsinki Final Act did not sanctify intrastate boundaries, and the boundaries within the collapsing states of Yugoslavia (including Serbia and Croatia) and the Soviet Union including Russia and Armenia) had less legitimacy attached to them. Therefore, one could argue that the difference between the silent dogs and the cases of irredentism is one of respected international borders and controversial intrastate boundaries.

Hypothesis 1: Irredentism will only occur over disputed formerly intrastate boundaries.

While this account might explain the lack of Hungarian irredentism and Romanian aggression, it does not explain why Russia has not altered the boundaries within the former Soviet Union.[4] Given the twenty-five million Russians outside of Russia, including concentrations near Russian borders in the Ukraine and Kazakhstan, we could have expected more aggression. Indeed, in the early 1990s, many analysts feared that Russia would engage in efforts to make its Near Abroad part of Russia again.[5]

The second difficulty this argument faces is that irredentism is and has been pursued by states elsewhere, aiming at territories beyond established international boundaries. Somalia repeatedly pursued a Greater Somali project, despite the legitimacy of its borders with Djibouti, Ethiopia, and Kenya (Saideman 1998). Pakistan's conflict with India now largely centers on its irredentist efforts aimed at Kashmir. While Pakistan has contested this boundary over time, it has lasted as long as many of the boundaries in Europe. Longevity, therefore, is not a sufficient explanation.

Third, the strength of international boundary norms cannot account for why some nationalist parties have performed better than others. How have international boundaries, legitimate or contested, been able to deter the rise of extreme groups? Romania and Russia have seen nationalist parties with irredentist programs gain significant numbers of votes and seats, while Hungary has not (Milkenberg 2002, 350–352). Irredentists dominated Armenia, Croatia, and Serbia for much of the 1990s. The causal mechanism between the existence of legitimate boundaries and extremist political success is not clear. It may be that collapsing empires facilitate the rise of nationalists, but again that does not account for why Slobodan Milosevic was successful for so long in Serbia while Vladimir Zhirinovsky and others fell short in Russia.

Fourth, if precedents and norms truly matter, then we should take seriously the implications of German unification. This event, which cemented the end of the Cold War, was also the greatest feat of European irredentism since the Anschluss—the unification of Germany and Austria before World War II. Potential European irredentists might have considered their unification efforts to be legitimate since Germany was allowed to become one state, despite the erasing of a Helsinki-era recognized international border.

Finally, it may be the case that strong boundaries surrounding weak states only breed more conflict. Atzili (2006, 145–146) argues that borders have four pernicious effects: perpetuating weakness; fostering intrastate violence; creating the conditions for spillover; and fostering "opportunities for neighbors to exploit weak states." Thus, while borders might seem to create stability, there are arguments that they may have unexpectedly nasty consequences.[6]

The differences between international and intrastate boundaries are significant and may be part of the causal story, but are not sufficient explanations, as they do not address the significant variation among irredentist efforts. Perhaps international boundaries matter more today than they did for Greece and Turkey thirty years ago (or today) or than they do for Pakistan, India, and China because of NATO and the EU, the institutions that currently shape European relations. On the other hand, as we will discover in the cases, boundaries may matter by shaping the meaning, the content, of nationalisms—who is "us" and who is "them."

The Lure of Europe: Conditionality and Integration

The Helsinki Final Act does not stand alone, but was part of a series of international institutions dominating the European scene. The Act led to the creation of the Conference on Security and Cooperation in Europe (CSCE), which became the Organization for Security and Cooperation in Europe (OSCE) after the Cold War. These organizations monitored compliance with the Helsinki Act, which included human rights and boundary norms. More importantly, both NATO and the EU have tied accession to compliance with European standards of good behavior, including respect for existing boundaries and resolving all outstanding territorial disputes. For instance, membership required bilateral treaties with neighbors, particularly between Hungary and Romania and between Hungary and Slovakia. Because these countries desperately desired to join NATO and the EU, they refrained from challenging international boundaries. Or so the argument goes.

The leaders of the newly democratic states of Eastern Europe desired membership in these organizations for both their intrinsic benefits and the grander implications of joining Europe. NATO membership significantly increases one's security, since outsiders such as Russia are less likely to challenge allies of the United States and Western Europe. Joining the EU is viewed as necessary for economic success, particularly as those left outside face significant barriers to trading with members (Vachudova 2005). Further, membership in these organizations may also be important for national identities (that one's country is European,[7] not Balkan, not second or third world), for domestic politics (leaders of successful applicants can claim the mantle of serious leadership), and the like. Indeed, given the demands made by the two organizations and the tremendous efforts made by applicants, one can only determine that membership means a great deal.

Binnedjik and Simon (1996, 1) assert that "enlargement has been successful in establishing incentives for aspiring members to resolve border and ethnic minority issues." Conditionality may matter both directly and indirectly (Zellner 2001). First, countries may constrain their foreign policies because they do not want to hurt their chances of joining European institutions, particularly NATO and the EU. Second, host countries may be treating their minorities better due to conditionality, making their plight less salient in their mother countries.[8]

Efforts by International Institutions

The most significant institutions involved in this region have been NATO, the EU, the OSCE, and the Council of Europe.[9] Each has played an important role, with the expansion processes of the first two making the latter two much more significant. Ironically, the OSCE had the least leverage because all the relevant states were already members, but it came to play the lead anyway, as it coordinated with the other organizations and sought to uphold the original Helsinki principles.

The OSCE created the office of the High Commissioner for National Minorities (HCNM) as Yugoslavia was disintegrating in 1992. Its role was to prevent conflict at its "earliest possible stage."[10] Former Dutch foreign minister Max van Der Stoel was the first HCNM, holding the office from 1993 until 2001, and emphasized early action, not just early warning (Zellner 2001, 271). Three instruments were most important—letters to state foreign ministries to recommend changes in laws or practices; "recommendations for the practical interpretation of OSCE norms"; and extraordinary efforts including roundtables, support for teacher training, publication of school books and more. In general, the HCNM advocated consociational techniques such as proportionality, coalition governments and autonomy (Wilkinson 2002, 3).

The Council of Europe was an exclusively Western club until the Cold War ended. Thus, it had some influence as it could determine whether Eastern European countries could join or not. Its strategy was somewhat different than other institutions, as it focused on "ex-post" conditionality—that new members committed to certain policies after they are admitted (Kelley 2004a, 2004b). The belief was that increased interaction with older members would influence the new ones. More significantly, it developed two of the more significant legal codifications of minority treatment: the 1992 European Charter for Regional and Minority Languages and the 1995 Framework Convention for the Protection of National Minorities (FCNM), which became the focus of Council of Europe activities.

The EU's attention was directed toward many issues at the end of the Cold War, including the negotiation and implementation of the Maastricht Treaty, and responding to the Gulf War and the disintegrations of the Soviet Union and Yugoslavia. The EU's first effort in promoting group rights, like its common foreign policy, failed in Yugoslavia. The Badinter Commission was given the responsibility of determining which former republics of Yugoslavia deserved recognition based on treatment of minorities, among other conditions. The commission was critical of Croatia and supportive of Macedonia. However, owing to intra-EU politics, particularly Germany's and Greece's respective obsessions with Croatia and Macedonia, the commission's recommendations were ignored.[11] The EU recognized Croatia but not Macedonia—showing that minority treatment was not the EU's key priority.

Even so, minority rights were an important part of the accession process. In June 1993, the Copenhagen Criteria clearly stated that eastward expansion was possible and what the applicants would have to do to join. This was a key turning point—it moved accession from a distant dream to a realistic possibility for most countries in Eastern Europe, but it tied admission to specific conditions. The Stability Pact, finalized in 1995, meant that the EU would not import border problems or domestic ethnic conflict, and combined with the Copenhagen Criteria, indicated that the EU was serious about the treatment of minorities and the prevention of conflict. Interestingly, the OSCE has the task of overseeing the pact.

In July 1997, the European Commission announced its "opinions" regarding the first ten applicants, recommending the opening of negotiations with Hungary, Poland, Estonia, the Czech Republic, and Slovenia, but not the others, including Romania. This occurred shortly after NATO announced its admission of Poland, Hungary and the Czech Republic. The opinions focused on the condition of Russian-speaking populations in Estonia and Latvia and on the plight of the Roma. Slovakia was singled out for its poor treatment of its Hungarian minority and for its slide toward authoritarianism (Avery and Cameron 1998, 46). Two years later, the European Commission recommended that negotiations begin with the remaining applicants— Romania, Slovakia, Latvia, Lithuania, and Bulgaria. The EU has relied upon the HCNM for monitoring the status of minorities. In Wilkinson's words, "the EU has used the HCNM and to a lesser extent the Council of Europe as the minority-rights equivalent of financial ratings agencies like Standard and Poor's or Fitch" (2002, 5).

NATO has also played a role in this process, starting with the Partnership for Peace (PfP) process, seen by many as a halfway house toward membership. PfP was viewed as both necessary for future membership but also a way to delay decisions about new members. In 1995, NATO released its *Study on NATO Enlargement*, which established conditions, including democracy and resolution of pre-existing conflicts:

> States which have *ethnic* disputes or *external territorial* disputes, including *irredentist* claims, or internal jurisdictional disputes must settle those disputes by peaceful means in accordance with OSCE principles. Resolution of such disputes would be a factor in determining whether to invite a state to join the Alliance.[12]

Thus, NATO made minority treatment and foreign policy specified conditions for admission and strengthened the role of the OSCE as the definer of norms.

Poland, Hungary, and the Czech Republic were widely viewed as the first ones likely to be admitted, although Slovenia and Romania also gained attention. In 1997, the decision was announced to let the first three into NATO in

1999. In November 2002, another set of countries was invited to join—Slovakia, Slovenia, Bulgaria, Romania, and the Baltic States.[13]

Clearly, membership to these various organizations mattered a great deal to the applicants, and these organizations made minority treatment and resolution of border conflicts key conditions for admission. Thus, we might expect:

Hypothesis 2: If countries seek admission to international organizations that stress ethnic and minority rights, then they will pursue moderate foreign policies.

However, many questions remain, including: did the conditions placed upon Eastern Europe force them to accede to the will of Western Europe? At what point did these pressures kick in, if ever? Would these countries have behaved much differently without these conditions? How much of the improvements in minority treatment are symbolic or temporary? In the next sections, we assess how scholars have considered these issues, and, in the subsequent chapters, we evaluate how these arguments apply to particular cases.

Limiting Bad Foreign Policies

Recently, scholars have focused on the demands placed by NATO and EU upon potential members as key constraints limiting the foreign policies of Eastern European countries. Ambrosio (2001) dedicates a book to the proposition that international pressures prevented irredentism in Eastern Europe.[14] While his concern is more about the outcome of irredentist efforts (whether they succeed or fail), his work is still relevant here. Ambrosio admits that ethnonationalism within the potential irredentist state may matter at the margins, but he puts nearly all of the causal weight on international pressures. He argues that if the state (not the politician directly) faces high costs, then it will not be irredentist. Ambrosio argues that Croatia was stopped in its efforts to absorb hunks of Bosnia by U.S. promises to support its integration into Euro-Atlantic institutions. This understanding of Croatian foreign policy is problematic, as Croatia only began to adhere, more or less, to the Dayton Accords after the death of President Franjo Tudjman in December 1999 and as his party, the HDZ, began to lose influence.[15]

Ambrosio also argues that Hungary altered its foreign policy in order to gain entry into NATO and the EU, focusing most directly on the series of bilateral treaties Hungary signed with its neighbors. However, his account of the timing of these treaties understates the importance of party politics in Hungary, which signed these treaties only after a change in governments.

Linden (2000) argues that regime type plays a crucial role in mediating between international pressures and foreign policy. He contrasts Hungary and Romania on one hand with Slovakia on the other to suggest that the transparency between the former facilitated a better relationship after the bilateral treaty was negotiated than was the case between Hungary and Slovakia. He argues that Hungary-Romanian relations improved only after NATO and the EU indicated that enlargement was going to occur and that there would be conditions attached with the EU's Copenhagen Criteria in 1993 and the *NATO Study on Enlargement* in 1995. Thus, Linden does a better job than Ambrosio of explaining the timing, but he leaves a crucial gap: why was there no irredentism in the early 1990s when democracy, particularly in Romania, was fragile and integration was a distant dream?

Kelley (2004a, 2004b) focuses on the same events, the bilateral treaties, but stresses EU pressures. The Stability Pact summit in 1995, under the aegis of the Organization for Security and Cooperation in Europe (OSCE) and the EU, set the stage as Slovakian Prime Minister Meciar apparently needed more progress on European integration for his domestic standing. Of course, the problem is that both Slovakia and Romania ran away from the bilateral treaties even as they were being signed. Moreover, Romania has been admitted to NATO and was admitted to the EU in 2007 without signing a border treaty with Moldova, which represents its best potential target for irredentism.

Cronin (2002) takes a different strategy, focusing on the socializing effort made by West Europe to increase the stability of Eastern Europe.[16] He argues that the leaders of Eastern European countries were likely to be socialized, internalizing Western norms, as long as they were in an uncertain environment, wished to join the group, and as long as they did not "hold strong beliefs that are in conflict with the persuader [NATO, EU]" (141).[17] This approach helps to explain both the commonalities and the differences in the region, as leaders faced an uncertain environment and nearly all wanted to join the Western club. Variation could be explained by different beliefs. This then raises a question which parallels our chief concern: why do some leaders have different beliefs (or preferences) than others?

In sum, Kelley, Linden, and even Cronin differ from Ambrosio in stressing the importance of domestic politics as part of the process by which international pressures get filtered into the foreign policy process. The key difference between those scholars and this book is that we consider domestic politics to be the primary cause. We therefore seek to explain shifts in the domestic forces that shape foreign policy, rather than merely identifying those shifts as important. Previous scholars are not entirely wrong, but their emphasis is misplaced.

Dampening the Fire: Improving the Condition of Minorities

A second causal argument is less direct: rather than conditionality constraining the foreign policies of states, international organizations may compel better treatment of minorities, thus reducing the pressures which leaders of mother countries face to engage in irredentism. If the European institutions compel host countries to treat their minorities well, then their plight will be less of an issue in the kin countries of these groups. There is little doubt that various European institutions have expended a great deal of effort to encourage and monitor better treatment of Eastern Europe's minorities, but questions remain about the efficacy of these efforts.

Kelley (2002, 3) argues that "the European institutions of the 1990s [Council of Europe, OSCE, European Union] were active and influential participants in the formulation of ethnic policy on the domestic scene." Using interviews and quantitative analyses, she indicates that incremental programs of rewards (the long road to EU membership) were very effective at imposing legislation to improve minority treatment, even when there was strong domestic opposition (Kelley 2004a). She found that incrementalism, credible promises of penalties or rewards, and coordination among key international actors were crucial.

The Center for OSCE Research (CORE) has focused on the effectiveness of the HCNM. Interestingly, CORE places somewhat less emphasis on international factors than Kelley. They find three sets of variables to be important—the chances of Western integration; the characteristics of the conflict; and the strength of moderate actors in each society.[18]

This indirect impact may actually be more important than the direct pressures.[19] Because the plight of kin is a key part of the irredentist dynamics that we specify in our theory, this form of conditionality may matter. By reducing the salience of the kin that would be the target of an irredentist effort, European institutions may have reduced the pressures politicians faced from their constituents. Still, as with other conditionality arguments, it fails to explain the restraint that existed before these efforts took place and also the failure of several states to act "appropriately" toward their minorities despite facing severe criticism.

Under What Conditions? Some Limits to International Pressures

Clearly, efforts by the EU, NATO, the Council of Europe, and the HCNM have been significant and have influenced Eastern European countries. However, we need to be careful not to overestimate the impact of external influences. If domestic politics or other factors are significant shapers of these countries' policies, an exclusive focus on the international pressures may lead to surprises and faulty policies. Furthermore, we need to figure out how international and domestic dynamics interact.

First, the processes for admission into the EU and NATO were quite complicated, with many conditions attached. Minority treatment and border issues were just a subset of many concerns members had about admitting Eastern European countries. Rather than focus directly on the issue, these institutions, particularly the EU, essentially subcontracted out to the HCNM to determine fitness on minority rights. Hughes and Sasse (2003) argue that the use of proxies, such as the HCNM, indicates that minority protection was a lesser priority. They go on to argue that the EU's conditionality is mostly talk, not sincere. Hughes and Sasse (2003, 17) use the word "charade" to describe the policy, arguing that the focus was mostly on appeasing Russia and avoiding a flood of Roma immigrants. Vermeersch concurs, arguing that "there is not a very strong connection between European pressure and policy change on minorities in Central Europe *except* when it concerns issues that are soft security priorities for EU member countries" (2003, 26).

Indeed, the decisions by NATO and the EU to admit some countries and not others are inherently political processes, driven by both domestic dynamics and international politics. The merit of each applicant may matter less than the agendas of the countries in the organization. Cyprus was admitted to the EU in the latest round of accessions despite the failure to resolve its conflict with Turkish Cypriots. If the EU had strong standards that genuinely applied, then it is hard to understand how Cyprus could be admitted.[20] Instead, a better explanation of which countries received invitations may focus on who one knows—which countries had friends within the EU. For Cyprus, this was obviously Greece. "If meritocracy did not prevail, a candidate with strong patrons in the EU could also expect special treatment" (Vachudova 2005, 113).

Second, not all countries have acted as if EU/NATO membership were the be all and end all of foreign policy. Several of Yugoslavia's successor states have been most reluctant to do what it takes to join Europe. The various factions in Bosnia refused for quite awhile to develop a single military (broadly defined), a step necessary for NATO membership. Croatia and Serbia spent most of the 1990s refusing to do what the Western community wanted—stop supporting nationalist factions in Bosnia, remove war criminals from significant political and/or military positions, significantly reform their economies, etc. Even after the death of Tudjman and the removal of Milosevic, Croatia's and Serbia's efforts to meet European demands have been slow, halting, and most reluctant. Even though Serbia faces steep budget problems and tremendous pressure from the West after Milosevic's extradition to The Hague, it still protects indicted war criminals, until recently it was still involved in Bosnia beyond what the Dayton Accord permitted, and it took much longer than expected to remove key individuals from the leadership of the armed forces.[21]

Third, though some have argued otherwise (Linden 2000), the presence or absence of democracy is not a sufficient explanation of the varying levels of irredentism. Somalia was most actively irredentist in its democratic period in the early 1960s as political competition pushed the major parties to seek the votes of those with irredentist agendas (Saideman 1998).

Fourth, in the very early 1990s, the magnetism of EU/NATO membership should have been at its weakest. How realistic, how credible was membership in 1991 or 1992? The EU admitted many of the new democracies only in 2003 (with Romania and Bulgaria having to wait until 2007). How could this distant possibility weigh so heavily in 1991? When Hungary's prime minister raised the possibility of joining NATO in 1990, it "shocked the Soviets, the Hungarian opposition, and the West" (Ambrosio 2001, 115). Likewise, during this time the European Union focused on deepening the single market, not broadening it. Indeed, most of the scholars focused on international institutions largely overlook this puzzle of the early 1990s.

Fifth, it is not clear how many of the reforms have been sincere. Both Romania and Slovakia signed bilateral treaties with Hungary, but then quickly passed laws against the spirit and perhaps even the letter of the agreements. These states and others may be paying lip service to the conditions, and then may regress once they are full members of the EU and NATO. Kelley (2004a, 194) asserts that implementation failure is not so problematic since it can both hurt and help minorities. However, given that the reforms demanded are more likely to be resisted by local officials than the previous policies of discrimination, Kelley's argument here is rather weak, compared to the rest of her book. As the chapters here on Hungary and Romania clearly demonstrate, the promises made to NATO and the EU seem to be both shallow and temporary.

There is no doubt that many of the countries in the region have shaped their foreign policies with admissions criteria of the EU and NATO in mind. However, this simple answer begs a whole series of questions:

- With so many different policies being "conditioned" besides minority protection, and with EU's own standards in question, how seriously did the EU constrain potential members?
- Why have some states responded strongly and sincerely to EU/NATO conditions while others have ignored or paid lip service to these demands?
- Why was there only irredentism in Yugoslavia in the early 1990s when democracy, particularly in Romania, was fragile?
- How much of the reforms have been sincere? Is implementation likely to occur after admission to NATO and the EU?
- Why has Russia refrained, given its noncandidacy?
- Why have nationalists done better in some countries but not others?
- Why and how can politicians be so focused on this one priority, membership, over all others? That is, how can politicians sell their soul for distant admission?

The point of this book is not to say that membership procedures and conditionality did not matter to Eastern European countries in the 1990s and early 2000s. Instead, we attempt to explain both the irredentism that did and did not occur at this time as well as the foreign policies in between. NATO and the EU are part of the story, but their role is not logically or empirically prior to domestic politics. A new explanation is needed—one that, we argue, should be focused on the domestic scene.

Power and Inhibited Aggression

Another set of external factors may also play a role—the relative strength of the various states involved. It may be the case that states are less likely to engage in irredentism when they are at a competitive disadvantage, but will attack their neighbors if the costs are not sufficiently high. Ambrosio (2001) focuses on the tolerance of the international community for irredentist efforts and the willingness to impose costs. While this largely focuses on the role of international institutions, it can be read in a second way. When the leaders of a state consider an irredentist project, if they are considering the costs of their actions, then they ought to be deterred if they face a relatively strong target.[22] We ought not to expect weaker states to attack stronger ones unless the leadership has some reason to expect success.

Hypothesis 3: States are more likely to engage in irredentism if they are more powerful than their target.

While Ambrosio might be right that the balance of power does greatly determine the outcome—that weaker states engaging in aggression tend not to be successful—relative power is not terribly helpful for predicting irredentist foreign policies. Again, Somalia serves as a salient example. Somalia launched its war against Ethiopia in 1977, when its target was weakened and distracted by revolution and its aftermath. Only outside intervention by the Soviet Union and Cuba saved Ethiopia at this time (David 1991). However, Somalia was even more aggressive in the early 1960s, simultaneously targeting Ethiopia and colonies of Great Britain (Kenya) and France (Djibouti). Not only did these efforts antagonize two great powers, but Ethiopia itself was far stronger than Somalia at the time.

Legacies of the Past

Before moving on to our argument, we need to address briefly an additional alternative explanation: history. Just as Germany and Japan are constrained by pacifism, which is a legacy of World War II, irredentism in the 1990s may have been difficult to imagine because of the costs borne in the past. Because Germany and Japan paid extraordinarily high costs for their aggressive foreign policies of the 1930s and early 1940s, they have constitutional limitations and pacifist publics (Berger 1998). These two were not the only ones to pay for their actions in the past. More importantly, other countries have histories of failed irredentism with high costs, such as Somalia, but pursued aggressive, self-destructive foreign policies anyway. Still, this approach suggests the following expectation:

Hypothesis 4: If a country has a history of failed (catastrophic) irredentism, it will be less likely to pursue irredentist foreign policies, and if a country lacks such a history, it will be more likely to engage in irredentism.

Obviously, the past does matter, largely by shaping the configuration of interests in the present and in shaping the identities in play. It is not the past itself, but its re-creation in present generations, that creates identities and interests (Kaufman 2003). By taking seriously the content of nationalisms in our study, history does make its way into our approach, but more systematically than simply that failed efforts in the past prevent aggression today.

Domestic Dynamics of Self-destruction and Unexpected Restraint

Our approach assumes that domestic politics matters, as it determines who governs, what their interests are, and what constraints or pressures they face. Most of the constraints said to be restricting irredentist foreign policies must somehow operate through domestic politics, as domestic dynamics most frequently determine whether leaders are removed or installed, what freedom they have to maneuver in domestic and international arenas, and what capabilities they can bring to bear. This does not mean that the politician always acts on behalf of the country to pursue the state's or constituents' best interests, or that he or she always supports conationals abroad. Instead, politicians will consider what their supporters want, the threats posed to them by their competitors, and their own interests in maintaining power (Chiozza and Goemans 2004), and go from there.

Institutions significantly influence who matters, as they determine whether coalitions are necessary to govern, whether minority groups are marginalized, which interest or ethnic groups tend to get representation and more. Obviously, stable democratic institutions provide a predictable battlefield, which then shapes the relative influence of different constituencies. Stable authoritarian structures have the same impact, but generally limit the ability of opposition groups to have influence. Systems in between, either long-lasting regimes with mixtures of institutions or systems transitioning from one regime type to another, are harder to predict or evaluate, as the rules are not necessarily binding. So, it becomes difficult for analysts and politicians to figure out who matters (Snyder 1999). Still, we can look at the emergent parties and institutions to suggest who may matter more. The relevance of this brief discussion is that it helps us understand the tendencies of different democracies, so that we figure out who matters and how their preferences turn into policy or not.

To understand the preferences of constituents, we need to focus on two sets of concerns that come into play when addressing irredentist issues: the impact of nationalism and material interests. These may interact to reinforce each other, providing politicians with clear incentives, or they may conflict with each other, challenging politicians to balance competing imperatives.

Nationalism: Who Is Us, Who Is Them, and Can You Live with Them?

Identity is a contested term in the social sciences, particularly as it relates to ethnic identities and to nationalism. Despite the existence of large data sets that code ethnic heterogeneity or the attributes of ethnic groups, scholars still do not agree on these concepts, in part because nationalism scholars and students of ethnic politics are not the same people, nor do they always talk to each other. We first present the latest thinking in the field of comparative politics and discuss how scholars think about nationalism. We then build on a recent work that takes seriously how to consider identity as a variable (Abdelal et al. 2006), and move on to focus on our conception of xenophobia.

There has been a long debate about whether ethnic identities are relatively fixed—primordial—or quite fluid where politicians can emphasize any identity at will.[23] The mainstream view, termed the constructivist approach, considers identities to be malleable but not easily so (Rothchild 1981; Horowitz 1985). Politicians and circumstances can alter which identities are most salient and what meanings they possess. Posner (2004, 2005) articulates this stance most clearly as he considers how institutions and group size interact, leading to variations in the relevance of particular identities. Chandra (2006) delineates a key property of ethnic identity—constrained change. Because ethnicity is based on attributes believe to be based on descent, it is sticky, she argues, in the short term. This allows for identity change over the course of time, but limits (but does not eliminate) the ability of politicians to manipulate identities. Her key challenge to the field is whether "the properties they take to be intrinsic to ethnic identity can actually be inferred" from her definition or a "better one" (Chandra 2006, 423). Below, we endeavor to do so, as an ethnic identity's nature and a country's willingness to engage in irredentism are inherently linked.

Scholars of nationalism, like those of ethnic politics, disagree about how much of the present day's nationalism is modern or fixed to the past (Smith

1995). Smith identifies views such as Anderson's (1983) as "gastronomic," where nationalisms are created by political entrepreneurs by mixing various available ingredients. In this approach, nationalisms are imagined and mythic. This is contrasted with "geologic" approaches (Gellner 1983) that claim that "the modern nation as an enduring descent group is in large part a precipitate of all the deposits of earlier generations of the community. The ethnic heritage determines the character of the modern nation" (Smith 1995, 12). Thus, any particular nationalism is essentially a reality or force that is not easily influenced by individuals. Smith ultimately argues that "the nationalist is a kind of social and political archaeologist . . . to rediscover and reinterpret the indigenous ethnic past" (1995, 15). This is not that different from the constructivist compromise familiar to students of ethnic politics. The relevance here is that identity, as discussed by scholars of ethnic politics and by nationalism students, is neither permanently fixed nor completely fluid, presenting politicians and their supporters with both constraints and opportunities.

Abdelal and his coauthors (2006) delineate two dimensions for all collective identities—content and contestation. Their specification does not precisely define how fluid these identities are, but the essential stance is a constructivist one—that identities are not fixed permanently in their meaning or relevance, but they are not easily created by individual politicians either. More importantly for us, the authors conceptualize the content of an identity, focusing on four nonmutually exclusive types: constitutive norms, social purposes, relational comparisons with other social categories, and cognitive models. That is, who belongs, for what purpose, as opposed to what other ways of identifying, thinking what? This focus and delineation of the content of identities is crucial since scholars have fallen into the habit of thinking in labels, such as Serb or Hutu or Romanian, without thinking very hard about what these labels entail.[24]

The usual distinction in discussions of national identity or nationalism is to contrast civic with ethnic; the former focuses on ties to the state, to the polity, while the latter stresses ethnicity.[25] As Abdelal et al (2006) assert, there is more to identities, including national ones, than that. In our work here, we focus essentially on two of the four key dimensions they develop: constitutive norms and relational comparisons. Or to put it another way, we care about definitions of us and them and tolerance of the other.

Any kind of identity distinguishes members of the group from nonmembers (Brewer 1991; Mercer 1995). While most analysts of nationalism take seriously the identification of who is the "us," identification of the relevant "them" is often overlooked.[26] Who is seen as the adversary to be opposed matters as it may determine who the targets of nationalist policies might be. Extremist politicians choose not only to favor the in-group but discriminate against the most salient out-group. Deegan-Krause (2004) documents the multiplicity of others that could be and were targeted by varying nationalists within post–Cold War Slovakia.[27] In our case studies in subsequent chapters, the existence of multiple "others" with varying salience will be quite significant.

Moreover, there is more to identity than us and them. There are shades of us and shades of them. To a group, another group may be seen as being kin under some circumstances and being the "other" under other situations (Brewer 1991).[28] Individuals within a given country will vary in how much they care about ethnic groups in other countries. Some will identify those outside of the country as being part of "us"—the same ethnic group—and therefore deserving of support. Some will identify the same group as being "them"—a rival group, undeserving of assistance and perhaps even a source of threat. Yet still others will simply not feel any kind of tie—amity or enmity—toward particular groups outside the country. For instance, all Somalis share a common race, religion, and language but are divided by a lineage system—a set of clan identities. The Somali identity may resonate much of the time, but the clan identities will be quite salient so that Somalis of other clans will be viewed as somewhere between completely "us" and completely "them." As a result, Somali irredentism has varied, depending on which clans and clan-families were in power, and, thus, which neighboring groups were viewed as us and them (Saideman 1998).

The second dimension is tolerance: how willing is the group to coexist with individuals of different identities?[29] An identity might have a very expansive definition of self and other but may be very intolerant of the remaining folks who are on the outside. Nationalisms will vary in how much homogeneity or heterogeneity is desirable. While this is difficult to express, the general point is that the definition of who is us and who is them is distinct from the varying of willingness or tolerance for interaction. To say a group is xenophobic means that they are less tolerant of coexisting with the other.[30] They do not want to live with the "other," they do not want to work with the "other," and they do not want their children marrying the "other."

Ironically, xenophobia, one aspect of nationalism, may contradict some of the other imperatives contained within the nationalism. For instance, in the Quebec provincial election in 2007, three parties competed. The Parti Quebecois was clearer than ever that its mandate would be to separate Quebec from

Canada. The Liberal party took a federalist stance, arguing for Quebec to stay in Canada. A third party, Action Democratique du Quebec (ADQ), gained much traction not by playing up the separatism debate, but by focusing on "reasonable accommodation" of immigrants. That is, the ADQ essentially became the party of xenophobes by focusing much attention on whether Quebec was endangering its identity by bending too much to the perceived demands of immigrants, particularly Muslims. There is more to the ADQ than xenophobia to be sure, as they present alternatives on a variety of issues. Still, this example is instructive as it clearly pitched one strand of nationalism directly against another. And the xenophobic appeal resonated more strongly than the separatist one, at least for this one election.[31]

Xenophobia matters for irredentism, since successful irredentist efforts will alter the composition of the state, bringing in competitors for jobs, additional claimants upon the state, and rivals in the political system (Horowitz 1985). The more xenophobic people are, the less interested they will be in including others in their society even if it permits the inclusion of more members of their group. While nationalism and collective identity suggest that people are other-regarding, that they tie their identities and their fortunes with imagined kin elsewhere, there is a self-centered component of identity as well. We need to take both the "us" and the "them" in any nationalist identity seriously. Ultimately, it becomes a question of relative passions: does a group feel more strongly about the kin or about the other? Another way to express this is: if the mother country is M, the kin in the neighboring country is K, and others who reside in the same territory as K are O, then the constituents in M may prefer $M > K > O$. Taking into account the intensity of the preferences, we might find that $|M| > |O| > |K|$. That is, constituents in the mother country may like the Kin more than the Others, but they may also hate or fear the Others more intensely than they like the Kin. Of course, they may not like the kin that much, either. For instance, in the aftermath of reunification, Germans became less interested in their kin, leading to a significant revision of immigration laws, sharply restricting the Right of Return (Cordell and Wolff 2007). The challenge, of course, is how to know whether a relevant constituency is relatively tolerant or xenophobic. We address how we operationalize our concepts at the end of the chapter.

It should be noted that tolerance or xenophobia can change over time, and in response to both material and ideational stimuli. As we will discover in later chapters, events on the ground—or the perception of them—can cause a shift toward intolerance, as can the revival of mythologies that demonize the other. Because we are interested in irredentist foreign policy choices, the concern here is how tolerant a constituent group is at a given time, and how changes in their view of the other are related to changes in policy decisions.

Table 1.1 illustrates how the dimensions of nationalism interact to create the strongest compulsion to irredentism, ironically, when people are the most tolerant of other groups. Intolerant nationalisms will only pursue irredentism if the new territories are homogeneous. Limited identification with the kin outside of the country will provide a weak foundation for assertive foreign policies on their behalf.

TABLE 1.1 Dimensions of Nationalism and Irredentist Inclinations

	Attitude Toward Other	
Identification with Kin	*Tolerant/ Heterogeneity*	*Intolerant/ Homogeneity*
Weak	Lack of interest	Hostile disinterest
Strong	Irredentism	Only irredentism if "clean"

Hypothesis 5a: If politicians depend on constituents who strongly identify with kin but are relatively tolerant of heterogeneity, then they are more likely to support irredentism.

Hypothesis 5b: If politicians depend on constituents who strongly identify with kin but are xenophobic, then they are likely to pursue irredentism only if the territory to be redeemed is relatively homogeneous.

Now, we need to consider a parallel set of interests that motivate constituents and, therefore, politicians.

Material Interests: Integration Versus Isolation

Irredentism, as a foreign policy, is likely to endanger the country's relations with its immediate neighbors and beyond. Economic ties matter here, as they are likely to be disrupted if war breaks out.[32] Consequently, individuals who benefit from positive relations with the international community, particularly economically, are less likely to lobby for irredentist foreign policies. Those who benefit from integration into the world economy will generally seek to reinforce openness (Milner 1988). On the other hand, integration is likely to hurt others. Increased competition will damage less efficient industries. Those who are likely to be hurt by international integration may be likely to support irredentism, as the backlash can delay or reverse integration. At the least, individuals who oppose integration will have common cause with nationalists interested in irredentism as both will not be concerned with its costs. This provides the potential for log-rolling coalitions, where disparate groups join, supporting each other's platforms as long as they are not directly in contradiction (Snyder 1991).

Nationalism and material interests may combine to constrain and vex politicians, or they may reinforce each other, pushing politicians to take clear stands. It depends on the mix of constituents a politician faces.

Table 1.2 summarizes the possible combinations of economic and ethnic interests. At this point, we do not want to say that one trumps the other always, but clearly when both push in one direction or the other, then politicians face pressure to follow that direction. Politicians in cell 1, depending on constituents with a weak interest in irredentism but strongly in favor of integration, will strongly oppose irredentist efforts. Politicians in cell 4 will support irredentism as their supporters will have strong interest in irredentism and do not mind being isolated. Two sets of mixed incentives may exist: weak interest in irredentism but seeking less integration with the international economy (cell 2); and strong ties to the "lost territory" and a strong interest in economic integration (cell 3). The former combination provides politicians representing this group with some latitude, as they are not compelled to help their kin, but domestic pressures for increased integration do not exist to compel them to cooperate more. In the latter situation, politicians face a difficult circumstance—their populations want competing foreign policies: cooperation and conflict. They want to integrate with the international economy while pursuing an aggressive foreign policy sure to antagonize the neighbors.

TABLE 1.2 Competing Interests and Support for Irredentist Foreign Policies

	Position Toward International Economy	
Interest in irredentism	Integration	Isolation
Weak	1. Opposes irredentism	2. Unmotivated
Strong	3. Conflicted	4. Supports irredentism

Hypothesis 6a: If politicians' constituents are interested in irredentism and prefer that the economy be isolated from external dynamics, then they will pursue irredentism.

Hypothesis 6b: If politicians' constituents are only weakly interested and if they prefer that the economy is integrated into the international economy, then they will oppose irredentism.

A key factor in any discussion of irredentism is the potential target population to be redeemed. They matter in three distinct ways: (1) their own separatist efforts may provide the mother state with opportunities to take action; (2) their plight may raise the salience of the irredentist issue in the mother state's domestic politics; and (3) they may have direct connections to the key decision makers in the mother state, giving them increased influence. Simply put, a country that has no ethnic kin to be redeemed will be unlikely to engage in efforts to reclaim historic territories.[33] A country having kin in neighboring states has a greater potential to engage in irredentism, but may not necessarily choose that as a course of action. The question in part depends upon the interests and conditions faced by the conationals in neighboring states.[34]

What Do the Kin Want? What Are They Doing About It?

Somalia's irredentism in the mid-1970s was sparked by the growing success of the Western Somali Liberation Front, which, in turn, was benefiting from the collapse of the Ethiopian government (Saideman 1998). The efforts of separatist kin justify the aggression—that the mother state is rescuing their brethren—rather than simply taking territory. If the kin are seeking union and having some success, this will make an irredentist foreign policy seem more likely to succeed.

The second, and related, dynamic focuses on the domestic politics of the mother state. Politicians within the mother state will face greater or lesser pressure to do something to help the kin, depending on the salience of their condition (Surhke 1975). The more visible their plight, the more likely it is that constituents will push politicians in the mother country to do something.[35] The less serious the threat facing the kin, the less likely it is that politicians will face pressure.

Politicians may have little choice if the kin are in trouble. The greater the threat faced by conationals on the other side of the border, the more visible their plight is to the domestic audiences of the decision makers in the mother country. Politicians will face greater pressure from their competitors to take more aggressive foreign policies if they can be accused of leaving their kinsmen in harm's way. If the kin abroad are satisfied with the status quo, then it will be harder to whip up nationalist feelings to "redeem" those who do not want redemption.

Who cares most about the plight of the kin on the other side of the border? The kin, of course. If they are politically marginalized in the mother country, we should not expect to see aggressive efforts made on their behalf. On the other hand, if members of the kin group are in positions of power, then we can expect to see greater efforts made. The example of Somalia is telling, as Somalis, inside and outside of the country, belong to various clans. When a particular clan was influential in Somalia, the country tended to give more support to its clan members across the border. In the early 1960s, when politicians competed for the votes of most clans, Somalia gave aggressive support to the different groups of Somalis in the various neighbors. In the mid-1970s, only one clan with significant numbers of clansmen on the side of the border, the Ogaden, were politically relevant, as they dominated the officer corps. Consequently, Somali irredentism was then much more selective, only focused on the Ogaden region of Ethiopia.[36]

Thus, when the kin themselves have a voice in foreign policy, aggressive efforts on their behalf become much more likely. Indeed, because this particular mechanism directly affects how decisions are made in the mother country, we expect it to matter much more than the kin's activities or plight in the neighboring country.

Hypothesis 7a: If the kin are actively irredentist, then the mother country is more likely to engage in irredentism.

Hypothesis 7b: If the kin face greater danger, then it is more likely that the state will give assistance.

Hypothesis 7c: If the kin are in positions of power in the mother country, then the mother country is more likely to engage in irredentism.

Our theory posits several conditions that jointly produce irredentism: politicians must rely on constituents who strongly identify with the kin in the "lost territory," these constituents are not opposed to the possibility of increasing the heterogeneity of the country, these constituents are less likely to benefit from economic integration; and the kin are salient through their activities, insecurity, and/or power. To be clear, an understanding of the relevant nationalism can clarify when politicians can be good nationalists without being irredentist. While the conventional wisdom has focused on the possibilities of success and the challenges presented by the international community, for this book's approach, the external conditions that matter the most are the treatment and behavior of the kin. This does provide an avenue for external influence, but we expect the power and impact of the international community to be much less than is currently believed.

The Way Ahead: Expectations and Concepts

This chapter has focused mostly on two sets of approaches to this question of understanding irredentist policy: those stressing international constraints (norms and international organizations) and those emphasizing domestic dynamics. Ultimately, we consider several of the conditions to be operating jointly—economic interests, attitudes toward kin and others, and the status of the kin. We do not expect relative power, the status of borders, a failed history of irredentism, or the efforts of international organizations through membership processes to matter as much. The key question then for the case studies to follow is, how do we measure our concepts? How do we know if a country was irredentist? How do we know that xenophobia exists as a restraint? Let us specify our concepts, starting with our dependent variable of irredentism and then moving onto our independent variables.

What Is Irredentism?

As we defined it in the introduction, irredentism in our book refers to territorial claims made by one state that are based on ethnic ties to a minority population that resides within another recognized state. For the case studies, we focus on activities by one country to gain a territory inhabited by ethnic kin—policies overt and/or covert to alter existing boundaries to bring in both desired people and territory. Somalia, again, is a good example, as its policies have covered the range of policies we have in mind, from giving arms to kin in neighboring countries to a conventional invasion of Ethiopia in 1977. Countries can do much to aid their kin short of irredentism, but merely supporting the rights of kin to organize and act politically is not necessarily irredentism.[37] Such efforts may still matter: they can be important as alternatives to irredentism and they can still antagonize the neighbors.

Policies short of irredentism may also be precursors to it, or may be perceived as such by neighboring states. Supporting the right to organize may be an alternative way for motherland politicians to support their kin abroad, but it may also be a way to support a nascent—or active—separatist movement under a "legitimate" guise. Thus, while we divide our cases into those that are irredentist (Serbia, Croatia, Armenia) and those that are not (Hungary, Romania, Russia), our analysis of the latter will show that irredentism may be more of a continuum than a binary condition. Indeed, one of the contributions of this book is to understand the range of behavior from doing nothing to full-out war, and policies that address neighboring kin short of war fall into this range.

Measuring the Competing Arguments

Scholars have asserted that irredentism does not occur that often because it is costly, focusing on the power of boundary norms, the possibility of denied admission to key international institutions, or the likelihood of defeat that is anticipated due to past failures or current inferiority. If boundary norms apply at all,[38] then we should not see irredentism across international boundaries but only across intrastate or interrepublican ones.[39] Because the Helsinki Act ratified all of the European borders that were established in the aftermath of World War II, it is quite clear for the case studies what is and what is not an international boundary. The concept gets fuzzier outside of Europe; the borders of Kashmir, for instance, have never been accepted. Of course, Somalia engaged in irredentism despite an explicit effort by the Organization of African Unity to ratify the existing boundaries, disregarding their tainted colonial heritage (Touval 1972). Still, the point here is that we consider all of Europe and the former Soviet Union's interstate boundaries prior to 1991 as clearly legitimate, and therefore (if the argument holds) potential constraints on irredentism.

When we consider the hypothesis regarding admission to international organizations, we focus almost entirely on the North Atlantic Treaty Organization and the European Union. While other organizations played significant roles, for our case studies, these two and especially the EU are the most important ones. The power of the Council of Europe and of the Organization of Security and Cooperation in Europe depended largely on the threat of possible exclusion from NATO and the EU. Like the boundary norm, this applies to all European countries, but unlike the Helsinki Accords, it does not apply to all former Soviet states, inasmuch as only those closest to Europe, the Baltic States, have been invited to start the process (and subsequently complete it). Neither Armenia nor Russia faced a serious chance of admission to either institution, although NATO did create some new institutions to try to satisfy Russia's concerns about encirclement.

Some countries have tried to unify kin-inhabited territories while others have not. Failure usually has a price, one that might cause others to refrain down the road. In the cases, we take into account the recent past—the twentieth century—and consider whether previous governments tried to revise existing boundaries and the consequences of such efforts. As with our definition of irredentism, we speak here of attempted foreign policies that range from giving assistance to separatists in the kin-state that aim at unification to conventional military operations with a similar goal. Again, to use Somalia as our model, it clearly had a history of failed irredentism before its 1977 invasion of Ethiopia as the early 1960s were characterized by aggressive efforts aimed at all of the neighbors, including attacking Ethiopia.

To consider the question of whether states might be deterred from acting against a strong state and that more powerful states are more likely to engage in irredentism, we need to assess how each potentially irredentist country stacks up against the state hosting the kin that might be a target. We focus here largely on military capabilities, because the basic concern here is whether an attack is more or less likely to be successful. While strategy, doctrine, technology, and other variables matter in shaping war outcomes, holding all else constant, we ought to expect countries with smaller militaries to be deterred from launching aggression at those with stronger ones. We use the best available data from the Correlates of War (COW) project, generated by EUGene (Bennett and Stam 2000) to create indicators that we use to assess relative military capability (and relative total capability as well) to inform our case studies. To be clear, in many cases, the balance of power is quite obvious: Russia is far more powerful than any of its neighbors, particularly after Belarus, Ukraine and Kazakhstan gave up nuclear weapons inherited from the Soviet Union. Still, we will use the COW data along with other information to evaluate the relative capabilities of potentially irredentist states and their targets.

Operationalizing Identity, Xenophobia, and Kin Status

The concepts that are key to our argument—identification with kin, tolerance versus xenophobia, economic preferences, and the kin's condition and influence—are harder to operationalize than those drawn from the various conventional wisdoms. The first two, dealing with the content of identity, are the most difficult, so in the cases, we triangulate, using interviews, evaluations by scholars, and where available, surveys, to determine how significant populations[40] of the relevant state view themselves, the kin and potentially relevant "others." Are the kin seen as belonging to the same group as themselves? Are there significant negative stereotypes about the kin? What role do the various inhabitants of the contested territory play in the nationalist discussions? We can also look at policy debates to figure out what the various politicians value or think that their constituents value. In the end, these are qualitative judgments about the content of different countries' politics—the basic stuff of comparative political study. The fact that these ideas are harder to operationalize than, say, balance of power goes a long way to explaining why they have been left out of the literature. We have tried to pull together as many sources as possible, to give as full a picture as possible.

The economic status quo and increased openness to the international economy affect people differently, so we assess in each case the general preference toward more or less integration by considering which groups are the key constituents of politicians. Certain classes of people will be hurt by significant economic reforms and international openness, such as pensioners, workers in obsolescent factories, and the like. Do politicians depend upon such people? Because they are material and rationalist, economic interests are easier to gauge from a distance than xenophobia or tolerance.

When considering the kin group abroad, three questions stand out: are they in danger, are they organized and engaged in an irredentist agenda, and do they have power in the mother country? Of course, identifying who the relevant kin group is comes first. This is not particularly problematic as, in each case, political upheavals (recent and more distant) clearly left some members of the national community on the "wrong" side of an international border. Still, some are more visible than others, and we rely on the particular country's discourse to identify the potential targets of irredentism. We consider the plight of each community of kin—are they facing severe discrimination and the threat of violence? We rely on the secondary literature of each case to assess this. Second, are there significant organizations within the kin community seeking to unify with the mother country? Again, the secondary literature along with news reports are useful for assessing whether there are irredentist desires on the part of the kin and what they might be doing about it. Finally, do the kin have power in the mother country? While personal connections are important but hard to document, financial flows in forms of campaign contributions, money for weapons, and the like are easier to track, as are voting rules that give the kin meaningful influence in the mother country.

In general, throughout the cases, we seek to triangulate, using as many sources as possible (including data sets, surveys, secondary literature, documents, and interviews), to determine the major actors and their preferences and strategies and to trace the causal process to see which factors are driving the outcomes.

Notes to Chapter 1: Irredentism and Its Absence

1. See Cronin (2002), Pevehouse (2002), Kelley (2004a, 2004b), Vachudova (2005), and Schimmelfennig and Sedelmeier (2005). Diez, Stetter, and Albert (2006) presents an argument that suggests that the EU has helped to limit conflict, but the article is somewhat ambivalent about its impact. Ted Hopf (1992) presents an early argument for conditions to be applied to the successors of the Soviet Union, requiring the creation of a regime to set forth rewards contingent on good behavior.

2. Snyder (1991) pursues a similar line of thought but focuses on the failed grand strategies of great powers, particularly their overexpansion. We focus on a particular form of foreign policy: irredentism.

3. Hungarians have noted, to their neighbors' displeasure, that Helsinki prohibits violent changes of boundaries but permits negotiated ones.

4. There has been much work (e.g., Roeder 1991; Bunce 1999; Hale 2004) examining how the contours of federalism within the Soviet Union generated conflict in some parts of the former Soviet Union and not others, but these works do not address the foreign policies of post-Soviet states.

5. For instance, see Binnendijk and Simon (1995), Brusstar and Jones (1995), Foye (1995), and Frazer and Lancelle (1994).

6. The stability of the boundary regime in Africa was largely explained by the common vulnerability of African states to secessionism and irredentism (Jackson and Rosberg 1982; Herbst 1989). See Saideman (2001) for evidence and arguments challenging this conventional wisdom.

7. Hungarians were quick to point out, in interviews, however, that they are European, so they need no additional proof or legitimacy from European institutions.

8. Vachudova (2005) argues that EU conditionality altered the balance of political forces within East European countries, empowering reformers and weakening those with authoritarian tendencies.

9. Individual countries have also mattered, such as the United States, which did considerable lobbying of its own.

10. See the HCNM website at www.osce.org/hcnm/mandate.

11. For somewhat contrasting accounts, see Crawford (1996) and Saideman (2001).

12. Chapter 1, paragraph 6. The complete text of the study can be found at www .nato.int/docu/basictxt/enl-9501.htm. Emphasis added.

13. One of the coauthors (Saideman) spent 2001–2002 on the U.S. Joint Staff in the Central and East European Division of the Strategic Planning and Policy Directorate. Other members of this division played a significant role in the U.S. decision-making process concerning NATO expansion. While much attention was given to whether countries were meeting the various conditions, there was a general feeling that the membership decisions were foregone conclusions determined by politics, domestic and international.

14. See Csergo and Goldgeier (2004) for a discussion of how integration processes affected the choices made by countries that sought to engage in nationalist foreign policies.

15. See chapter 2.

16. See also the contributions in Linden (2002).

17. See also Checkel (2005).

18. See www.core-hamburg.de/CORE_english/for_bee_minderh.htm, accessed August 23, 2007.

19. This discussion also suggests an additional hypothesis: If countries are seeking admission to NATO and the EU, then they will treat their minorities better. This hypothesis matters more directly further below when we consider the condition of the kin to be redeemed. However, the focus of the book is not to test this possibility—that is, we are not trying to determine whether NATO/EU admissions policies led to better treatment of minorities. This would require a somewhat different focus and a different set of cases—see Kelly (2004a) and Vachudova (2005). Instead, we raise this possible causal relationship since it does matter when we consider the role of kin in the irredentist equation.

20. George S. Yiangou, "The Accession of Cyprus to the EU: Challenges and Opportunities for the New European Regional Order," *Journal on Ethnopolitics and Minority Issue in Europe* 2 (2002); Thomas Diez, "Why the EU Can Nonetheless Be Good for Cyprus," ibid.; see also "A Derailment Coming," *The Economist*, April 17, 2004, and "An Ominous European Debut: Cyprus," *The Economist*, May 1, 2004.

21. These three conditions were significant "redlines" limiting American and NATO engagement with Serbia. In 2001–2, all discussion with the U.S. foreign policy bureaucracy of future interactions with Serbia centered on these three conditions, again based on Saideman's Joint Staff experience.

22. The classic debates on deterrence theory tend to differentiate between nuclear deterrence and conventional deterrence, finding the latter much less likely to hold up. See Jervis, Lebow, and Stein (1985), Huth (1988, 1999), and Morgan (2003).

23. The usual citations for these two extremes are Geertz (1963) and Brass (1991). For a critical view of the constructivist approach to identity, see Brubaker and Cooper (2000).

24. For typically egregious examples, see our previous work (Ayres and Saideman 2000; Saideman 2001; Saideman and Ayres 2000).

25. For instance, see Brown (1999), Snyder (1999), and Shulman (2002).

26. An exception to this has been Freudian psychoanalytic approaches, which regard us and them categories as intertwined; see Volkan (1987).

27. Petersen (2002) develops a logic where different sets of emotions leading to different sorts of targets, as fear leads to targeting the most threatening groups, resentment leads to a focus on higher status groups, and hate centers on historical rivals.

28. For a nuanced treatment of the "other," see Petersen (2007).

29. Brown (1999) makes a similar but not identical distinction between nationalisms that arise out of a sense of marginalization and rivalry with another versus those that arise out of a sense of self without direct and focused comparisons on others.

30. Wimmer (2002) asserts that xenophobia is inherent in the modern state, but our focus is on how it not only varies but also shapes the willingness of individuals and groups to enlarge their territories and take in "others."

31. As this book goes to press, Quebec politics continues to center on the "reasonable accommodation" debate, sidelining the long-running conflict over sovereignty or separatism.

32. On the other hand, those engaged in illegal activities may favor irredentism, as it disrupts regular policing and creates porous boundaries and new economic opportunities. We are grateful to Jim Church and Tom Eisiminger for pointing this out.

33. In Saideman and Ayres (2000), we found that groups that are not near states dominated by ethnic kin are unlikely to desire union with their kin.

34. A growing literature has focused on the relationships of neighbors that have ethnic groups straddling borders, including Davis and Moore (1997), Petersen (2004), and Woodwell (2004).

35. Cetinyan (2002) argues that the status of the ethnic group will not increase the chances of intervention. Rather, he asserts that stronger ethnic groups will receive more support. Jenne (2004, 2006), using similar analytical techniques, argues that the possibility of outside support will increase the demands that an ethnic group will make as their relative bargaining power is stronger. Van Houten (1998) applies similar approaches, arguing that the outcome largely depends on whether the kin state is strong and highly irredentist. What he takes as a key independent variable—whether the kin state is irredentist or not—is the focus of our book.

36. This discussion is based on Saideman (1998).

37. There is a significant literature on the politics of minority rights, particularly as part of the transitions in Eastern Europe. See Csergo (2007), Deets (2006), Deets and Stroschein (2005), Jackson Preece (1997), McIntosh (1995), Mihailescu (2005), and Stroschein (1996).

38. See Saideman (2001) for a skeptical view of the impact of boundary norms.

39. Indeed, it can be argued that the lines dividing subunits of federal states have developed their own legitimacy, at least at the top level. The republics of Yugoslavia all received recognition, yet Kosovo has been far more problematic since it was not equal in status to Serbia, Croatia, and the others before the events of 1991.

40. The entire society does not need to share these views, just those portions that are politically relevant. That is, they are constituents of the leading parties or otherwise provide support to decision makers (campaign contributors, strategists, muscle, and the like).

2

Dueling Irredentisms

Greater Croatia and Greater Serbia

Better to reign in hell than serve in heaven.
—JOHN MILTON, *Paradise Lost*

I RREDENTISM EXACERBATED THE CONFLICTS IN THE aftermath of the Yugoslavia's disintegration, as efforts to unite all Serbs in a Greater Serbia and Bosnia's Croats in a Greater Croatia prolonged the conflict and produced atrocities as part of a strategy of ethnic cleansing. While Czechoslovakia and Yugoslavia differed on other dimensions, a key distinction between the Velvet Divorce of the former and the brutal disintegration of the latter is the role of irredentism. The dueling irredentisms not only prolonged the Bosnian conflict but also have made progress slow and hardly steady even after the demise of the leaders responsible for the conflict.

Croatia and Serbia are important cases for our understanding of irredentism for several reasons. First, they are an important contrast to the relatively modest foreign policies emerging contemporaneously in Hungary and Romania. Second, they demonstrate the critical dilemma at the center of this book: that sometimes what is good for politicians may be quite bad for the country. Franjo Tudjman and Slobodan Milosevic led their respective countries into disaster, but they were both able to outlast many of their opponents. "While, from the perspective of the well-being of Serbia and of Serbs throughout Yugoslavia, this strategy was disastrous," writes V. P. Gagnon,

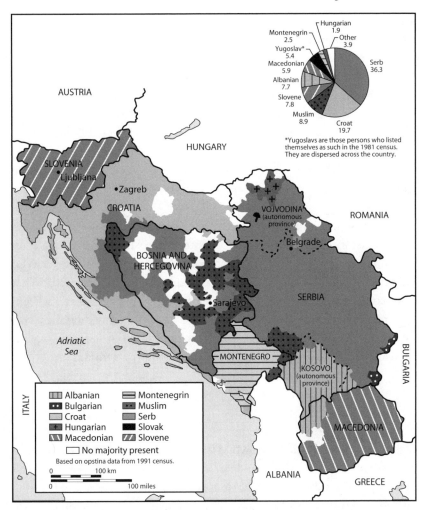

FIGURE 2.1 Ethnic Composition of Yugoslavia, 1991
Courtesy of the University of Texas Libraries

"from the perspective of conservative elites, it was strikingly successful, enabling them to maintain control long beyond the time when conservative elites in the rest of Eastern Europe had lost power" (2004, 88–89). Third, the two leaders seem to present very different kinds of politicians, one a diehard nationalist and the other the epitome of opportunism, respectively. They thus pose a challenge to any effort to think systematically about irredentism. Finally, because both countries caused tremendous damage to both their own societies and neighboring ones, they present an important policy problem that needs greater understanding.

While more attention has focused on Serbia's irredentism,[1] Tudjman was Milosevic's partner in crime in two senses.[2] First, Tudjman's hostile policies toward Serbs in Croatia reinforced Serb fears, legitimating Milosevic's claims. Second, before Yugoslavia began to fall apart and as it did so, the two leaders discussed the division of Bosnia between them, which would facilitate both Greater Serbia and Greater Croatia; their talks included a widely reported meeting in Karadjordevo in March 1991. These efforts not only failed to reach fruition but also did so at great cost to the entire region, especially for the people of Bosnia.

Because so much has been written about these cases, we do not present a detailed history of Yugoslavia and its disintegration.[3] Instead, our focus is on several key issues: What aggressive steps did Serbia and Croatia take? Who were the key constituents of Serb and Croat elites? What did they want? What is the content of Serbian and Croatian nationalisms, and how did these identities matter? How do rival explanations perform? By comparing these two cases of irredentism to each other and to the nonirredentist states, we can understand better the forces pushing countries to or away from war.

Serbia's Self-destruction

Serbia's irredentism gained the world's attention more than any other country's as it provided both overt and covert assistance to Croatia's and Bosnia's Serb populations. What is less obvious is that Serbia was selective, focusing on Serbs in parts of Croatia and on Bosnian territory, but not in other Yugoslav republics.

Serbian Irredentism

The pursuit of a Greater Serbia was never as consistent as many commentators have portrayed it, and it became less so over time. Even at the outset, Serbia's elites did not target all republics inhabited by Serbs. In 1985 (and leaked in September 1986), the Serbian Academy of Sciences drew up a blueprint of a Serb-dominated Yugoslavia that would include Serbia, Montenegro, much of Bosnia-Herzegovina, the predominantly Serb areas of Croatia, but would exclude Macedonia, Slovenia, and most of Croatia and would cede part of Bosnia-Herzegovina to Croatia as compensation (Bennett 1995, 81). Slovenia easily broke away from Serbia-dominated Yugoslavia.[4] The Yugoslav armed forces provided only a token effort and gave in quickly. Similarly, Serbia largely ignored the departure of Macedonia despite a small but significant Serb minority.

On the other hand, Milosevic and his allies had a strong role in helping to organize and arm Serbs in both Croatia and Bosnia. The emergence of irredentist groups in Croatia and Bosnia seeking union with Serbia was hardly accidental or spontaneous. In both republics, Serb parties formed as elections approached, and in each, radical members of the party eventually took over. Milan Babic was able to take over the leadership of the Krajina Serbs, with help and instructions coming from Belgrade (Gagnon 2004, 149).[5] More infamously, Radovan Karadzic rose to lead the Bosnian Serb Democratic Party, imitating the strategies of his Croatian kin and working closely with Belgrade until, again, it became inconvenient for Milosevic.

The assistance was much more than rhetorical. Belgrade not only provided planning but also armed and directed the paramilitaries and other armed groups operating in Croatia and, later, Bosnia.[6] These paramilitaries played an important part in the war, causing much of the violence and perpetrating many atrocities (Mueller 2000). According to Vojislav Seselj, a leader of one of the most prominent paramilitary groups, the Chetniks, "Milosevic organized everything. We gathered the volunteers and he gave us special barracks, Bubanj Potok, all our uniforms, arms, military technology and buses. All our units were always under the command of the Krajina or Republika Srpska or the JNA. . . . Nothing could happen on the Serbian side without Milosevic's order or his knowledge" (Judah 2000, 188).[7]

As Slovenes, Croats, and other non-Serbs went AWOL or dodged the draft,[8] Serbs increasingly dominated Yugoslavia's armed forces (Gow 1992, 2003). After the de facto departure of Slovenia, the military's essential mission of preserving Yugoslavia's unity became obsolete. The Yugoslav Army, increasingly dominated by Serbs, intervened in Croatia and then in Bosnia. It proclaimed neutrality and a larger mission to maintain Yugoslavia, but acted in favor of the Serbs. Indeed, the armed forces became an instrument of Serbia, assisting Croatia's Serbs and fighting against the Croats.[9] Most notably, the Yugoslav People's Army (YPA) leveled Vukovar and Dubrovnik. In accord with international agreements, the army withdrew from Croatia, leaving behind equipment and personnel. Trying to dodge international recriminations, Serbia followed the same strategy in Bosnia, with the creation of two supposedly distinct armed forces, the Bosnian Serbia Army (VRS) and the Yugoslav Army (VJ). This division was largely cosmetic, since the Yugoslav Ministry of Defense paid the salaries of VRS officers and personnel were rotated to and from Bosnia. Indeed, the head of the JNA (and later VJ), General Veljko Kadijevic, asserted in his memoirs, "The command and units of the JNA were the spine of the army of the RS complete with arms and equipment."[10]

Despite these efforts, Milosevic's nationalism was quickly revealed to be insincere, as he accepted a variety of plans offered by the West and by the United Nations which the Bosnian Serbs rejected. Lord David Owens (1995, 144) concludes that by April 1993, Milosevic was looking for a way out, and "the interests of Serbia and Montenegro from then on were the decisive factor." Indeed, Milosevic even engaged in sanctions against the Bosnian Serbs to force them to the table. Richard Holbrooke (1998) clearly makes the case that Milosevic forced the Dayton Accords down the throats of Radovan Karadzic and the other Bosnian Serb politicians. Even more striking, Serbia stood aside in 1995 when Croatia reconquered territories the Serbs had held since 1991.

Explaining Serbia's Irredentism

This case suggests that economic decline, the weakening of the authoritarian regime, and federal institutions provided incentives for Milosevic to engage in nationalist policies (foreign policies once Yugoslavia was, in reality, defunct), as well as support for such efforts by enough of the population.[11] Yugoslavia's economy was in deep trouble as it suffered from high unemployment, increasing debt, and international pressures such as IMF conditions and oil shocks (Woodward 1995b, 253–254).[12] This was particularly dangerous for Yugoslavia as the economic suffering was not evenly distributed. Rather, Slovenia and Croatia were much better off than Macedonia and Kosovo (and, therefore, Serbia). Consequently, responding to these economic problems caused the republics to prefer radically different solutions. The federal government, Serbia, and external creditors wanted to give the federal government more control over the economy, while Slovenia and Croatia wanted less federal control so that they would not be dragged down by the weaker republics. This economic crisis not only worsened relations among the republics but also weakened the existing set of institutions and ideologies; communism promised jobs, if nothing else.[13] Here we consider the patterns of competition over time and the content of Serb nationalism, which facilitated rather than inhibited irredentism.

Patterns of Competition

Milosevic was among the first to seize nationalism as an alternative basis of support after visiting Kosovo, where strife between Serbs and Albanians was accelerating.[14] Because of the design of Yugoslavia's institutions, Milosevic only had to play to the Serbs to gain power in Serbia. His constituency included those who would be hurt by serious economic and political reform: party officials, farmers, the elderly, elites who ran state-owned factories, unskilled and semiskilled workers, and junior Serb army officers.[15] "He and the socialists were perceived as the only guarantors of existing social benefits, pensions and jobs" (Malešević 2002, 182).

Milosevic created a coalition of these conservatives, who feared losing power and benefits if Serbia and Yugoslavia truly reformed economically or politically, with nationalists, who focused on the condition of Serbs within the federation. Both groups sought recentralization of Yugoslavia under Serb leadership, as this would both protect Serbs and delay economic and political reforms. Few, if any, of these constituents would care much about the lost opportunities for international engagement, since membership in the European Union and other international organizations would only endanger their positions.[16] Indeed, the plight of Serbs in Kosovo became "the conservatives' main weapon against reform forces within Serbia and in the wider federation" (Gagnon 2004, 67).

Elections came to Yugoslavia in 1990 and 1991. How real political competition was remains hard to determine, since Milosevic could have tried to stay in power had he lost then, as he tried to later on. Still, there were multiple parties and candidates taking competing positions.

Milosevic's Socialist Party of Serbia (SPS) competed with the Serbian Renewal Movement (SPO), and the Democratic Party, as well as a coalition of moderate parties. Vuk Draskovic led the SPO, which began as a nationalist, anticommunist party. During the campaign, Milosevic was not positioned as a radical nationalist (Kaufman 1994, 290). This stance is somewhat surprising, given his desire to appeal to Serb nationalists, yet he accused Draskovic of being too extreme on this issue. Milosevic did lose some votes to the SPO as a result. By playing the role of the moderate nationalist, he could promise to defend Serbs while seeming to present a lower likelihood of war. It is quite interesting that Draskovic moderated his own stances in 1991, arguing that Milosevic was risking war (Gagnon 2004, 102). This is quite revealing, for the issue was not really who was better at protecting the kin in Croatia, but who would do so with less cost to the people of Serbia.

Importantly, the existing institutions favored Milosevic. The electoral system was one of majority districts, meaning that a candidate had to win not just a plurality but a majority of votes within a district to gain a seat in parliament. In Yugoslavia's elections, this electoral rule gave disproportionately large numbers of seats to the strongest, best-organized parties.[17] Since Milosevic's party, the SPS, inherited the organization of Serbia's Communist Party, it was able to compete throughout Serbia and win many districts against divided competitors. Also, Milosevic controlled the media in Serbia, giving him a greater ability to set the political agenda and to define his opponents as he wished (Thompson 1994). Finally, Milosevic was able to plunder the Yugoslav and Serb treasuries to give money to pensioners and other important constituents before the election. Consequently, Milosevic and the SPS received more than 45 percent of the vote in the first round, resulting in nearly 78 percent of the seats in the parliament.

The political crisis between and within the republics continued, leading to protests in Belgrade in March 1991. Yugoslav and Serb leaders refrained from declaring an emergency, although this was considered. Simultaneously, violence in Croatia escalated as Serb paramilitary forces started to attack elements of the Croatian police. Two months later, Milosevic and Serbia blocked the normal rotation of the federal presidency, leading to the final breakdown of Yugoslavia.

The initial focus of the war was the Krajina and Slavonia regions of Croatia, largely inhabited by Serbs. At no point was there an effort to take Zagreb, which had a significant population of Serbs. The war's initial stages polarized the military and Serbian public opinion. Not only did Slovenes and Croats defect from the military, but officers and conscripts from other ethnic groups also deserted, leaving the military even more dominated by Serbs (Cohen 1995, 230–231, 266; Silber and Little 1996, 167, 242). The SPS began to lose support, mostly to Seselj's more extreme Serbian Radical Party but also to the more moderate Democratic Party.[18] The SPS, in fact, lost support from all sectors of its coalition. The moderate competing coalition disappeared, the SPO lost support, and the Serbian Radical Party now became a major player (Milic 1992, 132). The next major election in Serbia pitted Milosevic against Milan Panic, an émigré executive who had returned from the United States, presenting a clear choice between nationalist conflict and a more peaceful approach. Since the previous election, Serbia had aggressively and successfully supported Croatia's and Bosnia's Serbs. Panic had pushed for more accommodative foreign policies. On December 20, 1992, after a year and a half of conflict, the Serbian people reinforced their support for irredentism, as Milosevic won over Panic but lost votes to Vojislav Seselj.[19]

Serbia's enthusiasm for irredentism declined over time. The economic sanctions levied against Serbia and Montenegro in May 1992 eventually laid waste to the Serb economy. "Although the embargo took a serious toll on the civilian population, it did have positive effects. . . . It made Milosevic readier to make compromises" (Djilas 1995, 100–101). In December 1993, Milosevic's competitors criticized ongoing negotiations, but they changed their tune by the summer of 1994. Milosevic even went so far as to impose his own sanctions on the Bosnian Serbs, which led to the lifting of some international sanctions.

Political competition has also changed over time, declining over the course of crisis, though it intensified again after the Dayton Accords. It is difficult to determine how and whether elections matter in political systems in the process of transition. However, Milosevic's behavior from 1990 to 2000 suggests that he preferred to win elections than lose them, though he tried to stay in power after losing the last election. After the 1992 election, Milosevic built an alternative basis of support—a police force that was larger than the army. Milosevic has paid special attention to Serbia's police, greatly increasing its size, trying to attract potential defectors within the military with higher salaries (Gow 2003, 79–89). At the same time, Milosevic and his allies enriched themselves and their supporters by privatizing government assets in opaque, biased ways. Ironically, this created a wealthy class of "tycoons" who were deeply embedded with both organized crime and Serbia's security apparatus, but who became less dependent on Milosevic as they gained more state assets and as Milosevic then had less to give. Ultimately, challengers to the government promised these oligarchs that they could continue enrich themselves after Milosevic left the scene, creating the conditions that led to his fall (Gagnon 2004, 129–130).

Tolerant Nationalism?

In Serbia in the 1990s, one had to be a nationalist to do well politically.[20] Milosevic was among the first communist leaders to see the power of Serb nationalism to divert attention from the failed economy. In each election, competitors played up their nationalist credentials, largely disagreeing about whom would threaten the highest costs, but largely agreeing that the defense of Serbs was very important.[21] This raises the next question: what does it take to be a successful nationalist in this context?

Most of the discussion about Serbian nationalism focuses on Kosovo—that this territory plays a large symbolic role with many myths that play important roles in today's politics. For our purposes, the more important question is one of tolerance—the conception of Serbia, even Greater Serbia, as a multiethnic state. Certainly, this may seem a bit puzzling, given the use of ethnic cleansing as a wartime strategy in Bosnia and then as a potentially final solution in Kosovo's endgame. Yet, it is very significant that Serbian politicians have been most focused on trying to keep lands that are largely inhabited by other groups, particularly Kosovo and Vojvodina. Why is this the case?[22]

"Why would I want to be a minority in your country when you can be a minority in mine?"[23] This question reflects a key component of Serb nationalism—not the desire to eliminate other groups, but the expectation that Serbs would rule over minorities.[24] Dimitrijevic (2000, 639) asserts that Serbia wanted the world to acknowledge its legitimate and historical "mission to dominate their territory." Judah's work suggests that Milosevic and Serb elites would have been satisfied with a Greater Serbia inhabited by other ethnic groups.[25] Before the breakup, Serb elites in Bosnia and elsewhere had tried to "woo the Muslims" (Judah 2000, 196). Indeed, there was even an expectation that the Bosnian Muslims would opt to remain in Yugoslavia, despite the predicted departure of Croatia and Slovenia, since the Muslims of Bosnia, Albania, and the Sandzak region of Serbia would be a very large minority in a Greater Serbia (Judah 2000, 197). It is easy to forget in the aftermath of a bloody civil war, but the fundamental difference that drove Slovenia and

Croatia apart from Serbia was that Milosevic and Serbia wanted to recentralize the Yugoslav federation. This would have given Serbia greater influence within the federation, but the federation would have remained multiethnic. It is also important to remember that the rhetoric before and during the conflict was not about eliminating "the other" from Serbia or from its surrounding territory, but to protect and unify the Serbs from these various territories. Moreover, there was little evidence of xenophobia before the conflict. While the rates of intermarriage among the ethnic groups of Yugoslavia have been exaggerated, it is notable that Serbs were most willing to marry outside of their ethnic group (Botev and Wagner 1993). Similarly, when Serbs were asked whether they minded various groups as their neighbors, they provided more tolerant responses than ethnic groups in other countries.[26]

Despite the polarizing dynamic produced by the conflict, behavior during the war indicated that a significant degree of tolerance remained, even as ethnic cleansing was occurring. There were plenty of deals struck between Croats and Serbs over the allocation of towns, depending on their composition (Judah 2000, 206). Most notably, Bosnian Serbs were more than accommodating when it came to Fikret Abdic, who ran the Bihac pocket for much of the war and who had significant differences with the Bosnian government in Sarajevo.[27]

Serb irredentism presents some confusing contradictions. In the course of the conflict, violence was used strategically to expel Croats and Bosnian Muslims so that Serb control could be assured.[28] Yet, before the conflict, there seemed to be a willingness to incorporate more minorities as long as Serb dominance was guaranteed. The constant here is not hatred or violence, but of the domination of Serbs and Serbia over others.

Croatia's Ignored Irredentism

Croatia, which has laid claim to parts of Bosnia, continuing to undermine the Dayton Accords, has been nearly destabilizing as Serbia. Its irredentism, largely overlooked in the shadow of Serbia's, not only facilitated the rise of Milosevic but also prolonged the war in Bosnia. Croatia's efforts cost up to $3 million per day, hundreds of thousands of displaced Bosnian Croats, and more than seven thousand dead Croats (Hoare 1997, 121). Yet the government responsible for these efforts was only defeated after its founder, Franjo Tudjman, died.

Seeking Herzegovina

Clearly, Croatia's obsession was with Herzegovina, the southern part of Bosnia and Herzegovina, with Mostar as the most important city in the region. Croats in other parts of Bosnia generally did not seek union with Croatia, nor were they seen as particularly important in the eyes of the mother country. Efforts to unite Herzegovina with Croatia took several paths, focusing on cooperation with Serbia, manipulating Bosnia's politics, and the use of force against the Bosnian government. The pursuit of a Greater Croatia at the expense of Bosnia preceded the war, exacerbated the bloodshed, and continued after the Dayton Accords were signed, although the strategies varied.

The first, and perhaps most revealing, efforts came in the form of a series of meetings between Tudjman and Milosevic. Widely reported after the fact, these discussions apparently focused on dividing Bosnia between the two republics. Despite Milosevic's support for potential rebels within Croatia, Tudjman cared enough about Herzegovina to work with his adversary. Uniting the lost territory was apparently more important than the taboo of "sleeping with the enemy." Seeing war with Serbia as being very risky, given its superior armed forces, Tudjman sought to bargain, with Bosnia providing the chips (Hoare 1997, 124).

The second and most enduring effort has been Croatia's meddling in Bosnian politics. The principal Croatian vehicle for influencing events was Bosnia's Croatian Democratic Union (HDZ) party. Croatia changed the leadership of the HDZ several times, depending on whether it was trying to seek Greater Croatia more aggressively or trying to limit the costs of its irredentist policies. Croats in Bosnia were divided between the strongly nationalist population of Herzegovina and the more moderate groups, living in Sarajevo and central Bosnia.[29] As a result, the political outlook of the leadership of Bosnia's Croats was not a foregone conclusion—there was a real division among Bosnia's Croats. Accounts lay responsibility for the leadership of the Bosnia's Croats on Tudjman. Mate Boban, leader of the Croat nationalist faction within Bosnia during much of the war, replaced more moderate HDZ leaders, declaring the region to be independent in July 1992. Boban, in turn, was replaced in February 1994, coinciding with a cease-fire between Croats and Muslims.

After the conflict, Croatia continued to encourage separatism in Bosnia. As late as 1999, Croatia misappropriated funds that were supposed to be for demobilization of elements of the Bosnian Croat military. Instead, these funds ($175 million) almost certainly found their way into the hands of the local HDZ, which shortly thereafter launched a referendum drive to create a third, Croatian, entity to parallel the Serb one.[30]

Third, most significantly and most destructively, Croatia created an armed challenge to the Bosnian government in the pursuit of the partition of Bosnia. Cooperation between Bosnian Croat and Bosnian Muslim forces ended in the fall of 1992. Large scale fighting between Muslim and Croat forces in Bosnia broke out in early 1993, including most notably the bombardment of Mostar. The Croatian forces bombed both the Muslim quarters of the city and the historic bridge that was the chief architectural treasure and tourist attraction of Herzegovina. The bridge's destruction served symbolically to divide Croats and Muslims, but it did more to rally the international community.

The connection between these events and Croatia are quite direct. Croatia armed the Croatian Defense Council (HVO), which was essentially the military arm of the Bosnia HDZ (Goldstein 1999). "No one has ever doubted that the HVO was simply a branch of the regular Croatian Army, which for diplomatic reasons used a slightly different appellation" (Judah 2000, 207). The Bosnian Croats supplemented this by renting and buying arms from Bosnian Serbs to use against the Muslims (Udovicki and Stitkovac 1997, 191). The United Nations reported that between three thousand and five thousand Croatian troops were operating in Bosnia as late as 1994.

In the aftermath of Mostar, domestic and international audiences criticized Croatia's role in Bosnia. Tudjman's response to the news that Muslims were being held in Croatian camps was that "the others had camps as well" (Silber and Little 1996, 299). The United States, along with the mounting casualties in Bosnia, pushed Tudjman to relent. In exchange for U.S. support for efforts to regain Croatia's territories conquered by the Serbs in 1991–92, and with the possibility of receiving assistance from Islamic countries, Tudjman and Bosnia's Croats made peace with the Bosnian government, agreeing to ally against Bosnia's Serbs.[31] Tudjman was able to cash in these promises, receiving enough support to arm and train his army and to retake the lands lost at the outset of the wars of Yugoslavia's disintegration.[32]

Throughout the 1990s, Croatia sank a huge amount of political capital in the irredentist effort to unify Herzegovina with Croatia. As a result, it is in the back of the queue for admission to the European Union, it still faces problems with meeting international requirements for the extradition of war criminals, and its economy was severely battered by years of war. Yet, from the standpoint of domestic politics, the Herzegovina "obsession" was not irrational.

The Sources of Croatian Irredentism

There is some debate among scholars as to whether Croatia won or lost the wars of Yugoslavia's disintegration. Lord David Owen (1995, 353), who tried to facilitate agreements between the various actors during the conflict, asserts that "the victors in the Yugoslav wars of 1991–95 have been the Croats and President Tudjman." On the other hand, Tanner (2001, 301) avers, "the price of the thousand-year-old dream had been enormous. Apart from Bosnia, no state in Eastern Europe had suffered such material destruction and loss of life to win its independence." There is much more consensus on the causes of Croatia's policies than on the sum of the consequences: a coalition of nationalist elites, well-funded Croats abroad with a strong interest in the irredentist project, and conservatives seeking to maintain their status despite liberalization and democratization.

Franjo Tudjman, winner of Croatia's first elections, and in his mind, "the Father of the Nation," had a history of trumpeting the nationalist cause.[33] He tried to have Croatian declared a separate language in 1967. He was active in the Croatian Spring episode of 1971[34] and engaged in other efforts in the 1970s and 1980s. As a result, he was arrested and jailed several times. We therefore should not be surprised that when political space opened he quickly rallied around Croatian nationalist symbols that tended to focus on the Fascist Ustashe period during World War II (Bartlett 2003). Indeed, some argue that there was no content to his ideology besides the nation (Prelec 1997, 82).

To be clear, Tudjman was not a lone voice in the wilderness. There was an audience for Croatian nationalism,[35] including very significant ones abroad. Writes Lenard Cohen, "Tudjman also traveled extensively abroad, where he established a network of contacts and sources of financial support within the large Croatian diasporic community (over three million people) that was later to prove vital to the success of the HDZ" (1997, 75–76). Croatian émigrés had fled after World War II, and tended to be ultranationalists (Udovicki and Torov 1997). These émigrés in the West—the United States, Canada, Germany, Austria, and several nations in Latin America—also tended to be wealthier than Croats in Croatia, so they were an important source of campaign contributions and other funding (Goldstein 1999). The "Herzegovina lobby" funded Tudjman, the HDZ party Tudjman created, and the wars Tudjman fought (Udovicki and Stitkovac 1997): "The Herzegovina lobby—Croatian emigrants from Herzegovina as well as their kin in the country—formed an important pillar of Tudjman's support. In return for financial and political backing, he was beholden to this clique. They openly advocated the annexation of Herzegovina, the southern part of Bosnia-Herzegovina" (Silber and Little 1996, 86).

Notable among these returning émigrés, Gojko Susak was a Croatian-Canadian. Originally from Herzegovina, he emigrated to Canada. He returned to Croatia in 1989, playing an important role in raising money from the émigrés for the HDZ, "adept at tapping the purses of the tight-knit Herzegovinian community in the Americas, delivering millions of dollars' worth of contributions to Tudjman's campaign (Tanner 2001, 222). This money played a crucial role, for the HDZ's crucial advantage over the opposition was its superior finances (Gagnon 2004, 137). For these efforts, Susak became Croatia's first Minister of Defense, which again involved fund raising. Once in this position, Susak acted as a catalyst for conflict, firing missiles in Serb-majority areas in April 2001 (Gagnon 2004, 150).[36]

This, of course, raises a critical question: Why was the Croatian diaspora in the West, or enough of it, so supportive of the Greater Croatia project? First, expatriates may be more extreme than the citizens of their homeland.[37] They ultimately do not pay the costs for the policies they advocate—their homes are not destroyed, their economy is not damaged, their lives are not at risk. As a result, they are less inhibited by the risks.[38] Second, it matters who left their home country and why. While it would be unfair to paint all Croats who fled Yugoslavia after World War II as Ustashe fascists in league with Nazi Germany, a significant number were (Silber and Little 1996, 82). Furthermore, many of the émigrés fleeing from Herzegovina had been radicalized by the violence during the war (Burg and Shoup 1999, 66). So, the active members of the Croatian diaspora tended by quite nationalist and committed to the cause of Greater Croatia.[39]

The kin in Herzegovina also played a crucial role in Croatia's politics. "From the start of the conflict they were more interested in unification with Croatia than with becoming part of an independent, Muslim-dominated Bosnia" (Tanner 2001, 286). While Croats in other parts of Bosnia were focused on Yugoslavia and Bosnia, those in Herzegovina sought union with Croatia. They even served as labor for Croatia's nationalist project—extremists from Herzegovina were brought in and entered the Croatian police force in various hot spots to confront Croatia's Serbs (Gagnon 2004, 150). Many Herzegovinian Croats fought for Croatia during the first days of the war. Politically, they played an increasingly important role, as they gained the right to vote in Croatia's elections.[40] In the 1994 election, the Croatian diaspora was allocated twelve to fourteen seats in the Sabor, Croatia's 164-seat legislative body, significantly larger than its share of Croatia's population. Of course, Croatia's HDZ won all of these seats (Gagnon 2004, 159).[41] The important point here is that a key political constituency in Croatia's political system had a direct interest in the irredentist project.

A third force in Croatia's politics supported aggressive stances to defend Croatia from Serbia and to annex Herzegovina, made up of those who would be harmed if there was genuine democratization and economic liberalization—the elderly, less well educated, and the poorest sectors, as well as elites who would lose power and privileges (Gagnon 2004, 171; Bartlett 2003). The HDZ played well among the poor and uneducated, since it promised much but did not seem to be asking for sacrifices in the name of economic reform. As in Serbia, Croatian elites sought to redefine the political space so that reformers challenging the government would appear to be rejecting the Croatian nation (Gagnon 2004). With the focus on the Serb threat, Tudjman and his allies were able to defer real political reform and instead engaged in a privatization effort that enriched friends of the party.

We must note that the Croatian irredentist project was not universally popular. Indeed, most parties, as well as the Catholic Church, opposed it.[42] Even the HDZ split on this issue. However, this opposition was ineffective for four reasons. First, Tudjman was difficult to challenge since he was not alone in considering himself as largely responsible for Croatia's independence. Second, the political system gave disproportionate power to the HDZ, which consistently won only pluralities in votes but gained significant majorities in seats.[43] Third, the threat of Serbia, the potential one before July 1991 and realized at that time, did serve to demobilize opponents to the government (Gagnon 2004). It was very difficult to criticize the self-anointed "Father of the Nation" when the country was at war, and the government did its best to paint such critics as traitors. Finally, there was a party more extreme than the HDZ: the Croatian Party of Right (HSP), with irredentist claims far

outreaching Tudjman's that sought a Greater Croatia from the Austrian border to Bulgaria (Hislope 1996). Like the extreme nationalists in Serbia, this
party allowed Tudjman to appear more centrist than otherwise would have
been the case.

Croatian Nationalism Versus Strategic Behavior

Because Herzegovinian Croats played such an important role in Croatia's
politics—as voters, as government officials (among them the minister of defense), as fundraisers for Tudjman and the HDZ, and as members of the diaspora in the West—the question of the content of Croatian nationalism is less
crucial here than in the other cases. In this case, individuals and groups in
power had a direct interest in the irredentist project. Still, the content of Croatian nationalism helped to motivate politicians and constituents who did
not have these direct ties.

In short, to be a good nationalist in the Croatian context meant emphasizing Croats as Europeans, and the others, Serbs and Muslims, as Others—less
civilized non-Europeans. Indeed, Serbs serve as a focal point for Croatian
identity: that Croatian nationalism is defined by its opposition to Serbs and
Serbia (Biondich 2004; Ceh and Harder 2004). While not all Croats are intolerant, there is a stream of thought within Croatian nationalism that is
quite exclusivist, where Croats are a nation and minorities are barely mentioned as having a role. Biondich (2004) delineates the development of different Croatian nationalisms and charts the emergence of the more exclusivist
variant. Surveys of public opinion back this up, as Croatians are likely to say
that they would not want immigrants or Muslims as their neighbors.[44]

Tudjman's willingness to embrace symbols of the genocidal Ustashe regime, while unpopular abroad and among the Serb community, did not meet
with as much criticism at home as one might have expected. Indeed, he was
tapping into sentiments in the population and among elites (Cohen 1997).
Significantly, the definition of the Croatian nation strongly identifies with
territory—and this territory includes not only Croatia but significant portions of Bosnia (Uzelak 1997). "Greater Croatia as envisaged by Tudjman was
likewise conceived as an ethnically pure state, to be realized for this so-called
humane exchange of populations that would also entail the removal of most,
if not all, Serbs from Croatia" (Magas 2006, 120).

In this case, it is difficult to separate the genuine from the strategic. Given the wealth and interests of the Herzegovinian lobby and the Croatian diaspora in the West, if Tudjman had not existed, he probably would have been created. There is little doubt that Tudjman was a true believer, given his past imprisonments for nationalist statements, but it is also abundantly clear that the nationalist course of action served domestic political purposes. It was very difficult to criticize a government during wartime, and the HDZ-led regime did not hesitate to use the war to stifle criticism and engage in authoritarian practices. The government went so far as to launch offensives to gain more support, which resulted in the HDZ's making significant gains in the February 1993 elections (Moore 1993).

Ultimately, Tudjman had to compromise on his goal of a Greater Croatia. The attacks on Mostar produced more criticism than had been previously received. It raised the possibility of NATO planes bombing Croatian troops. At the same time, the United States became deeply involved in the conflict, trying to bring the Bosnian Croats and Muslims together to facilitate a deal with the Serbs. Unless the three-sided war became two-sided, it would be impossible to reach a settlement. The U.S. government promised support for the return of the Serb-conquered parts of Croatia in exchange for cooperation in Bosnia. However, Croatia continued to meddle in Bosnia's affairs until the death of Tudjman and the fall of the HDZ from power in the late 1990s.

Comparing Balkan Irredentists

While Croatia and Serbia engaged in war over parts of Croatia, their irredentisms were reinforcing. Serbia's efforts caused Croats to throw more support to Croatian nationalism, which strengthened the appeal of a Greater Croatia. Likewise, Croatian nationalism gave greater legitimacy to Milosevic's claims. Further, there was room to cooperate, despite the ongoing conflict in Croatia, as both were tempted by the division of Bosnia. What can we learn from studying Serbia's and Croatia's irredentism? In general, we find evidence for our arguments about the imperatives of domestic politics, nationalism, and xenophobia, while those who argue that costs, as determined by other states or international institutions, find less support. The following table summarizes our findings.

TABLE 2.1 Hypotheses and Findings from Croatia and Serbia

	Hypothesis	Croatia	Serbia
1:	Interstate boundaries limit irredentism	Confirmed: Aggression only across intra-Yugoslavian borders	Confirmed: Aggression only across intra-Yugoslavian borders
2:	Admissions processes limit irredentism	Disconfirmed: Aggression before process started, resistance to pressures of IOs	Disconfirmed: Aggression before process started, resistance to pressures of IOs
3:	States will be deterred by stronger targets	Confirmed: Croatia only attacked a weaker Bosnia, but from balancing perspective, this was counterproductive	Mixed: Serbia attacked weaker Bosnia and Croatia, but not other weaker parts of Yugoslavia
4:	History of irredentism	Disconfirmed: World War II was negative experience	Disconfirmed: World War II was negative experience
5:	Tolerance of homogeneity/ xenophobia	Disconfirmed: Relevant irredentist audience was exclusivist	Confirmed: Constituents were tolerant of diversity
6:	Economics/ irredentist interests	Confirmed: Constituents identified with kin, did not seek integration	Confirmed: Constituents identified with kin, did not seek integration
7a:	Actively irredentist kin	Confirmed: Some kin sought irredentism	Confirmed: Some kin sought irredentism
7b:	Danger	Confirmed: Kin at risk in Bosnia	Confirmed: Kin at risk in Bosnia, Croatia
7c:	Kin in positions of power	Confirmed: Expatriate Herzegovina lobby was very powerful, had a significant number of seats, and was very interested in irredentism	Disconfirmed: Kin did not have substantial influence in homeland

Boundaries

These two cases give some evidence to the boundary-norms argument, as neither Croatia nor Serbia transgressed beyond Yugoslavia's old borders. Instead, the irredentist efforts aimed at revising the boundaries between the republics. One could argue that the aggression should have diminished once the international community recognized the various parts of Yugoslavia as independent states. This was certainly the intent of those giving recognition, but it is not reasonable to expect that the sudden transformation of intrastate to interstate boundaries to stop a war in its tracks.

Despite the vulnerability of each to boundary altering efforts, Croatia and Serbia engaged in policies that challenged the status quo and the norms that might have maintained their own territorial integrity. Croatia, most obviously, faced an irredentist threat from Serbia, yet tried to unify Herzegovina with itself. This hypocrisy was widely noted—that Croatia was entitled to its entire territory but also that of a neighbor. Serbia faced its own separatist problems, most notably in Kosovo but in Montenegro and Vojvodina as well. Again, Serbia has faced problems in arguing for the sanctity of its territorial integrity in the aftermath of its efforts to alter the boundaries of the other republics. We should not find this hypocrisy to be terribly surprising (Krasner 1999), but the more important point here is that leaders of neither were restrained by the potential or actual claims that could or would be made against their own territories.

Admissions

Efforts by the European Community to prevent the outbreak of violence and then to manage it failed spectacularly.[45] The EC threatened to cancel credits and other arrangements with Yugoslavia in the spring of 1991 if the Yugoslav military intervened (Salmon 1992). As the conflict accelerated in late May 1991, EC leaders Jacques Santer, chair of the European Council of Ministers, and Jacques Delors, chair of the European Commission went to Belgrade, met with leaders from all sides, promising that the EC would help Yugoslavia get loans from the International Monetary Fund as well as associate membership in the EC. The next month, the EC then agreed not to recognize Slovenia or Croatia if they unilaterally seceded. As events revealed, none of the actors in Yugoslavia was deterred by these threats or swayed by these promises.

International pressures did matter—but only when the actual costs accrued. Threats did not move Tudjman or Milosevic. Instead, it was the actual impact of sanctions over the course of time that wore down Milosevic. At first, international sanctions served as a convenient excuse for a failing economy. Only as the costs of war piled up and antagonized Serbia's population did Milosevic reduce support for Bosnia's Serbs, ultimately engaging in his own sanctions to force them to the bargaining table. Indeed, enthusiasm for the kin waned when the refugees from Croatia and Serbia became a burden for the Serbs of Serbia proper.

External efforts to condition Croatia and Slovenia continue to this day, but with limited success. Progress in the European Union accession process has largely been held up because neither Croatia nor Serbia has complied sufficiently with the required conditions. The most notable one is the extradition of indicted war criminals to the International Criminal Tribunal for the Former Yugoslavia. NATO has not allowed Serbia to join the Partnership for Peace, a necessary step toward membership, as Ratko Mladic, former commander of Bosnian Serb military forces, is apparently still free in Serbia. While Serbian President Boris Tadic showed more interest in the EU,[46] the domestic political costs of doing what the EU wants are steep. Serbian Prime Minister Zoran Djindjic was assassinated in March 2003. While it might have been his campaign against organized crime that led to the killing, Djindjic's leading role in the arrest and extradition of Milosevic to The Hague almost certainly contributed. Moreover, in Tadic's win in the 2004 presidential election, the competitor was Tomislav Nikolic of the Serbian Radical Party, who received 45 percent of the vote. While some of Nikolic's support was a protest vote, much of it came from the nationalist part of Serbia's population. Surveys show that even supporters of EU integration are opposed to extradition of indicted war criminals (Batt 2005). Thus, the domestic base for significant reform and accommodation with the EU is not particularly strong.

Neither former Yugoslav republic seemed sensitive to potential costs of their future behavior, but both changed the policies in the face of mounting costs. That is, promises and threats did not constrain irredentist behavior, but the costs incurred by such behavior eventually reduced the willingness of the people and the governments to bear these costs. The pattern here is one of resistance to the threats and promises of outside actors, whether it is NATO or the EU. Before the war broke out in 1991, the EC issued threats, and even sent observers. This failed. Tudjman and Milosevic altered their strategies only after the costs accumulated, risking their positions. Yet their accommodation only went so far as both continued to try to meddle in Bosnia's affairs, even after the Dayton Accords included restrictions against this behavior. Their successors continue to resist complying with the conditions set forth for integration and cooperation.

Power and Deterrence

We do not expect weaker states to attack stronger states, since the likelihood of failure and significant costs would be quite high. Because of the way Yugoslavia collapsed, with more of the military falling into the hands of Serbia, power imbalances favored the irredentists. According to the 1992 figures for the Correlates of War data, Serbia was almost two times more powerful than Croatia, and Croatia was about one and a half times more powerful than Bosnia.[47] Thus, deterrence logics might account for the pattern of aggression, except neither Macedonia nor Slovenia was particularly powerful, either. Thus, relative power cannot account for the selective nature of Serbia's efforts. Croatia's behavior is also puzzling from a realist perspective, since it engaged in a war against a potential ally at a time of grave threat. Croatia gave up its efforts in Bosnia only after U.S. pressure accumulated, but Croatia should never have supported the dissolution of Bosnia if it had focused on the defense of its own territory rather than aggrandizing at the expense of its neighbor.

History

It is quite striking that the World War II experience did not deter Croatia or Serbia. Despite its extreme bloodiness, the war and the failed efforts to create a Greater Croatia did not serve as salient lessons to deter this generation of nationalists. Indeed, rather than serve as a reminder of the costs of nationalist programs, the events of the war were remembered in ways that exacerbated present-day conflicts. Because the Ustashe was able to create a Croatian state, Croats could "view the wartime experience as a legitimate political experience and defense of Croat national rights" (Biondich 2004, 70). The past would serve as no deterrent here.

Interests in Kin Versus Economy

In each case, the leading politicians were able to create logrolls of groups that had interests in the kin and those that were not in favor of increased international integration. While there may have been more sincere nationalists supporting Tudjman than Milosevic, both relied on the groups that were threatened by the world economy and by economic reform. Both Milosevic and

Tudjman anticipated the power of the nationalist card, building political networks that would provide crucial support. Existing political institutions and the new ones that they created provided incentives to engage in irredentism. Milosevic relied on nationalists and conservatives, so he did not have to worry much about the opportunity costs of Serbia's policies; his supporters were not going to benefit from reform and international economic ties. He was able to weather two failed irredentist campaigns and stay in power as he diverted the assets of the state to his supporters.

Tudjman's campaign finance came largely from wealthy Croat émigrés, who could call for extreme defense of Croatian national interests from the comfort of their homes in the West. While some of supporters within Croatia and Herzegovina had direct interests in the irredentist projects, others supported Tudjman as the best apparent protector of Croatia from Serbia and the best apparent chance to defer economic and political reform.

The most striking aspect of the recent histories of Croatia and Serbia is that Tudjman died before he could lose office, and Milosevic lasted much longer than one would have expected. Given Serbia's poor economic performance and the wars Milosevic lost, and given the price Croatia paid for independence and its failed effort at a Greater Croatia, one might have expected greater opposition earlier on. Instead, serious challenges developed only after the Dayton Accords were signed.

Experts disagree about how much nationalism there was (Gagnon 2004). For the approach here, it is not necessary to argue that the majority identified with the kin across the borders in Croatia and Bosnia. The key is whether the most important constituents considered the Croats and Serbs on the other side to be "us" enough to be worthy of sacrifices to be paid by others. Clearly, in the case of Croatia, between the Herzegovinian Croats and the members of the HDZ, Tudjman had a constituency that did define Croatian nationalism as inclusive of the Croats in Bosnia. It was an exclusivist nationalism that saw little room for Serbs (not so much concern about Muslims) in a Greater Croatia. This does not provide support for the xenophobia hypothesis, but the willingness to commit ethnic cleansing meant that xenophobia and irredentist inclinations could go together.

In Serbia, this is not quite as obvious, since Milosevic did not appear to be as sincere in his nationalism. He gathered a winning coalition through a series of elections and crises with groups that had varying interests, including the desire for Serbs to remain in the same country. Indeed, the key here seems to be that Serbs tolerated others in their midst and did not mind a multiethnic Yugoslavia or a multiethnic Serbia. Rather, the content of the nationalism allowed for others to coexist as long as Serbs were protected and favored. Still, there are more extreme, more xenophobic nationalists in Serbia, but these individuals and groups seemed to be convenient for Milosevic, rather than important drivers of policy.

The Role of Kin

These cases demonstrate that the role played by the kin can become complicated quite quickly. Croatian Serbs and Bosnian Croats and Serbs did engage in the irredentist project, providing manpower and political cover for the policies of their mother countries. However, in the case of the Croats of Herzegovina, we can say that they were quite significant, a critical constituency for Tudjman and his party. In the case of the Serbs, the kin outside of Serbia proper seemed to be the object of Milosevic's manipulations. While it seemed at times that the Bosnian Serbs might have slipped outside of Milosevic's control, he ultimately was able to negotiate on their behalf and end the war when it no longer served his interests.

The other factor that makes any clear assessment difficult is that Serbs and Croats outside of their titular republics did not share the same goals. Bosnia's Croats were split between those who supported the Greater Croatia project and those who sided with the government of Bosnia. The same was true for Serbs. Still, there were active groups engaging in both politics and war that supported the irredentist projects in Bosnia and Croatia, assisting and legitimating the efforts made by Croatia and Serbia.

Clearly, in Bosnia and Croatia, the relevant kin were in harm's way. Our second hypothesis, that irredentism is more likely when coethnics face danger, is supported here. In Croatia, the Serbs faced a new regime built on anti-Serb rhetoric, symbols, and behavior. Tudjman and the HDZ did little to reassure the Serbs, giving meat to Milosevic's claims. In Bosnia, there was great fear and uncertainty faced by all groups, with these fears finding a basis in reality once the war broke out.

Finally, the hypothesis concerning the power of the kin finds support in the Croatian case, but not in Serbia's experience. The Herzegovinian Croats, as well as the diaspora elsewhere, clearly had influence through both their campaign contributions and their votes. While Tudjman would have probably acted as he did, the kin in Bosnia helped get him and his party into power and stay there despite some serious reverses in the various wars. For Serbia, the kin mattered, but not through their influence on Milosevic or Serbia's political system. There has been no mention of their ability to influence via campaign contributions, and Serbia never gave the coethnics seats or votes in Serbia's political system.

In sum, these two cases alone provide inconclusive results. The argument centering on the content of nationalism and its interaction with economic interests finds support in the experiences of Croatia and Serbia, as do arguments about borders and activist or endangered kin. Scholars focusing on the importance of international organizations and the restraining impact of bad previous experiences with irredentism find little support. Deterrence arguments, xenophobia, and the power of kin find mixed support. Indeed, it seems likely that xenophobia is relevant if the kin are not in a position of power, but that their desires overwhelm the restraining impact of fears and dislike of others when kin are able to sway the course of events. To understand the sources of irredentism better, we need to move to another case to see if the arguments that seem to apply here are or are not specific to Yugoslavia's collapse.

Notes to Chapter 2: Dueling Irredentisms

1. For a sample, see Popov (2000), Djilas (1993, 1995), Gagnon (1994), Gow (2003) Miller (1994, 1997), and Judah (2000).

2. Gagnon (2004) is one of the rare efforts to compare Serbia and Croatia systematically.

3. For a thorough background of the conflict, see Silber and Little (1996).

4. Judah (2000, 173), among others, alleges that Milosevic made a deal with Slovenian leaders to allow Slovenia to secede without much resistance.

5. Indeed, Babic held his position as long as it was convenient for Belgrade. As soon as he became an obstacle to Milosevic's plans, he was removed (Silber and Little 1996, 204).

6. For more on the paramilitaries and their relationship to Serbia, see Ron (2003).

7. For more details of Serbia's influence over the Bosnian Serb army, see Gow (2003, 76–78).

8. Gagnon (2004) expertly details the demise of the heterogeneous Yugoslav army.

9. Gow (2003) documents the role of the Yugoslav military quite extensively.

10. Judah (2000, 230). See also Gagnon (2004, 92–93).

11. Gagnon (2004) asserts that much of the population did not favor nationalist policies, using surveys to show support for Yugoslavia and the patterns of desertion to show the unpopularity of the wars.

12. See also Bookman (1994).

13. Hence the name of Woodward's book: *Socialist Unemployment* (1995b).

14. Cohen (2001, 62–65) discusses this "epiphanal moment," which served as a turning point for not just Milosevic but also all of Yugoslavia.

15. See Pecujlic (1992), Cohen (1995, 156), Woodward (1995a, 93), and Pavlakovic (2005).

16. Indeed, in a survey taken in 2004, 42 percent of Serbs were either Euroskeptics or Europhobes, providing a significant base for nationalist opposition to reform (SMMRI poll for the Serbian Government Office for EU Integration, September 2004, cited in Batt 2005, 67).

17. This electoral system produced disproportionate outcomes in Croatia as well (Goati 1992, 171; Cohen 1995, 157–158).

18. For more on Seselj and the Serbian Radical Party, see Hislope (1996).

19. Andrejevich (1993, 24). See also Miller (1994).

20. This remains true in the first decade of the twenty-first century as well (Pavlakovic and Ramet 2005).

21. Milan Panic is a notable exception, but his defeat, admittedly overdetermined, suggests that one could not avoid positioning oneself as a good nationalist if one wanted to win. Gagnon (2004) argues that Milosevic used violence to demobilize the population and that the nationalist cause was actually rather unpopular. The problem, however, is that most politicians seemed to act as if taking nationalist stands was necessary or desirable or both.

22. Ron (2003) argues that it has more to do with state capacity than with the nature of the nationalism, so that violence tends to occur along the state's periphery, where there is less oversight.

23. Woodward (2005a, 108), citing Yugoslav political theorist Vladimir Gligorov. Isakovic (2000, 132–133) suggests that this phrase "understates a ferocious nationalism."

24. This contrasts sharply with the rhetoric of the Greater Romania Party, for instance. See chapter 6 for how xenophobia elsewhere makes Serb nationalism appear tolerant by comparison.

25. To be clear, others, including Gow (2003), argue that ethnic cleansing was not merely a means to unify lost territories but a goal in itself.

26. World Values Survey, www.worldvaluessurvey.org, accessed August 23, 2007. The dates of the survey are 1999 (Croatia) and 2001 (Serbia). Indeed, only 8 percent mentioned that they would not want to have immigrants as their neighbors. Approximately 14 percent mentioned Muslims as undesirable neighbors, again quite low by European standards. Ron (2003, 31) does cite polls that showed increasing hatred toward others once the war was underway, but the larger argument and other polls cited in his book suggest that Serbs did not mind living with others as long as they maintained political control.

27. In personal communications, Stuart Kaufman raises doubts about how meaningful this might be; the Nazis made a variety of deals for the sake of expediency during World War II. Still, it fits a larger pattern here of willingness to live with and dominate Bosnia's Muslims rather than expel them all.

28. Indeed, several authors do assert that an "ethnically cleansed Serbia" was the goal (Banac 2006).

29. This is widely reported. See, for example, Silber and Little (1996).

30. "Former Bosnian president sentenced to 10 years," International Relations and Security Network, www.isn.ethz.ch/news/sw/details.cfm?id=13072, accessed October 18, 2005.

31. Again, this was widely reported, but Silber and Little's (1996) account details these events quite clearly.

32. Military Professional Resource, an American-based organization often funded by U.S. government contracts, entered Croatia shortly before the decisive battles of 1995. Many suggest that this was not a coincidence, although MPRI representatives deny planning or running the operations.

33. For a content analysis of Tudjman's speeches and their nationalist content, see Uzelak (1997).

34. This was an effort to gain more autonomy for Croatia, much to the ire of the Tito regime.

35. For an argument focusing on the imperatives of domestic political competition, see Hislope (1996).

36. Gagnon (2004) presents an argument where the aggression in Bosnia was more of a diversionary tactic to unify Croatia behind the HDZ and to unify the HDZ itself. While this may have been the motivation on the part of some members of the HDZ, the history of both Tudjman and the Herzegovinian Croats suggests a more sincere interest in the irredentist project.

37. For more on the Croatian diasporas, see Hockenos (2003).

38. This criticism of diasporas was frequently voiced during interviews in Hungary when the Hungarian diaspora was discussed.

39. See also Bartlett (2003, 44–45).

40. The new citizenship law was passed early in the HDZ's administration and applied to all Croats abroad, with the greatest impact on Herzegovinian Croats. On the other hand, the law made it harder for non-Croats to gain citizenship (Bartlett 2003).

41. There is some confusion about the total number of reserved seats for the Croats in Herzegovina. Bartlett (2003) indicates that there are twelve, but Gagnon (2004) uses fourteen.

42. For more on the development of the various parties in Croatia, see Zakosek and Cular (2004).

43. Indeed, the HDZ reformed the electoral system early in its regime to divide the opposition (Bartlett 2003).

44. See note 26.

45. The European Union was emerging from its previous organization as the European Community during the conflict.

46. *RFE/RL Balkan Report* 8, no. 40 (November 12, 2000).

47. We used EUGene, a software package that generates data from the Correlates of War project. See Bennett and Stam (2000) and www.eugenesoftware.org.

3

Reunification at Any Price

Armenia and Nagorno-Karabakh

> *However badly the people live, there are holy things, there are positions that they will never surrender under any circumstances.*
> —ARKADY GUKASIAN, THE SELF-STYLED PRESIDENT
> OF NAGORNO-KARABAKH

IN ALL CASES OF ATTEMPTED IRREDENTISM IN THE last twenty years, the Armenian seizure of Nagorno-Karabakh has been the most successful. Armenia's drive to incorporate cut-off kin and the territory they live on resulted in the de facto (if not de jure) moving of Armenia's international boundary to cover the Karabakh region and assume control of that area's Armenian population. In the process, Azeris living in the territory and the corridor between it and Armenia proper were largely driven out, solving the problem that xenophobic nationalists often want to avoid — the incorporation of Others. Armenia's campaign stands as the greatest irredentist success of the late twentieth century, though it came at great cost.

Because irredentism is generally quite costly and because scholars have argued that these costs deter states (Ambrosio 2001), we need to examine what the costs of irredentism are, particularly the relative impact of international and domestic costs. The overarching argument of this book is that domestic calculations trump international ones. If a particular foreign policy is costly to the country but advantageous to politicians' political careers, they will chose the dangerous path regardless of costs to the state. On the other hand, perhaps states have engaged in irredentism precisely when the international costs have been low. We need, therefore, to have an accounting of costs to enter into the irredentism equation. Specifically, do states engage in very costly behavior from the standpoint of their international situation? Can and do states anticipate the consequences of their aggressive behavior? It would be one thing if leaders did not expect that their states would bear much in the way of international costs, but another if they do expect high costs and go ahead anyway. Put another way, this book's argument is that irredentism occurs in spite of traditional expectations that foreign policy will maximize a state's security or welfare interests (Waltz 1979; Keohane and Nye 2001). Armenia, as irredentism's great success, is an ideal case to examine this question.

To account for costs, we need to specify what sorts of costs we are looking for. Based on the logic suggested here, we should be most interested in those costs that will affect a state's domestic or international situation—that is, those costs which can have a significant impact on the state's (and therefore, the leader's) political condition. These can be divided into two categories:

1. Domestic political costs. These include costs to a leader or ruling group within society that might affect that actor's access to power, ability to succeed in factional power struggles, or costs that contribute to the overall instability of the domestic political situation.

2. International costs. These are costs to the state as an actor in the international arena, as well as to its overall welfare. They include: loss of allies; loss of influence in international forums; and loss of the benefits of cooperation with other states or IGOs, such as denied or delayed membership. In addition, foreign policies may endanger the economy as well as members of the society—that is, basic threats to a state's welfare and the well-being of its citizens.

Irredentism is costly, and known to be costly, but leaders engage in it anyway. Armenia's drive for irredentism first began in 1987 prior to the breakup of the Soviet Union and flowered into full-blown war after 1991. In that war, it achieved its strategic objectives on the ground—control of the Nagorno-Karabakh territory and incorporation of its Armenian population into the Armenian state, along with the cleansing nearly all Azeris from the area. But even in triumph, irredentism has been enormously costly, so much so that Armenia is (from a standard self-interest standpoint) noticeably worse off than it might have been otherwise.

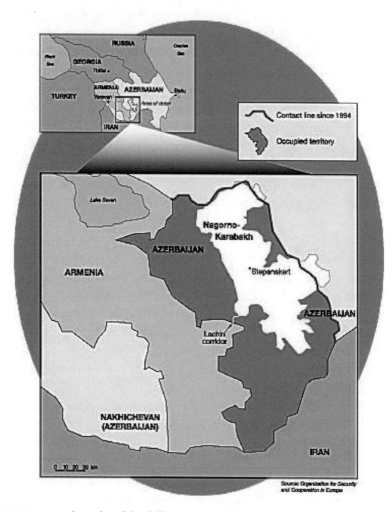

FIGURE 3.1 Armenia and Azerbaijan
Source: Organization for Security and Cooperation in Europe

Reuniting the Nation

Armenia is the only successful irredentist state after the fall of communism. Croatia and Serbia lost the territory they sought, but Armenia gained not only the desired territory but also a land bridge to connect Nagorno-Karabakh to the rest of Armenia.

Armenian irredentism toward the region of Nagorno-Karabakh, contained within neighboring Azerbaijan, predates the creation of the modern state of Armenia and the collapse of the Soviet Union. Armenia was born an irredentist state in 1991, and it has yet to experience a nonirredentist history. Indeed, the conflict over various bits of land in the Caucasus—including the Nagorno-Karabakh region—had a history going back a century or more and is closely tied to Armenian national identity.

Russia first gained control of the Caucasus territories in the early nineteenth century, initially by treaty with the Persian Empire in 1813 and then by a Russian annexation fifteen years later of territory including much of what is now Armenia (LeDonne 1997, 16). The turmoil of the early twentieth century, as the Ottoman Empire turned on its Armenian subjects, brought massive additional Armenian migration into Russian-held lands. It also brought the first major waves of violence between Armenians and Azeris in Karabakh, as the collapse of Russian authority in 1918 created (briefly) a chaotic situation involving three new states in the region: Armenia, Azerbaijan, and Georgia (Kaufman 2001, 51). With the help of first Turkish and then British troops, the newly created Azerbaijani army asserted its control over Karabakh, taking its then-capital city Shusha in March 1920 and killing or expelling that city's entire Armenian population (Goldenberg 1994, 159).

The emerging conflict stopped when the Soviet army, having asserted Communist Party control over Russia, annexed first Azerbaijan and then Armenia later in 1920. Throughout the Soviet years, however, Karabakh remained an issue, with periodic attempts by Armenians both in the Karabakh region and elsewhere to petition Moscow to return it to Armenia. These occurred in the mid-1920s, 1936, 1945, 1949, and on several occasions during the 1960s (Kaufman 2001, 51). Despite years of Soviet repression and various attempts to deal with its "nationality issues," in the 1980s Karabakh remained the "single most volatile issue" for Armenians (Fowkes 1997, 133).

As General Secretary Gorbachev's policy of *glasnost* began to take effect in the outlying, non-Russian republics, ethnic groups largely denied a voice for decades began to discover it again. Moreover, many of the areas outside Russia contained a mishmash of borders created by the varying ethnic policies of Stalin, Khrushchev, and Brezhnev. As the political system opened up, so too did the opportunity to complain more loudly about long-held grievances and injustices. In Armenia and Azerbaijan, these grievances continued to center around the status of the enclave of Nagorno-Karabakh, a region of Armenians contained within the borders of the Azerbaijan SSR. An official state census of 1989 showed the region to be about 75 percent Armenian and 25 percent Azeri (Rieff 1997). In addition to the region's pre-Soviet history of violence (well remembered by both sides), Armenians in Karabakh were substantially disadvantaged even by Soviet Caucasus standards. There was little opportunity for Armenian language education, job discrimination was a common problem (as all hiring went through officials in the Azeri capitol of Baku), and underinvestment in basic infrastructure and development was significant (Kaufman 2001, 58).

Demonstrations petitioning Gorbachev to change the republic lines to rejoin Karabakh to Armenia proper began in August 1987, and continued to increase through 1988 (Croissant 1998, 26). Mass-level movements took advantage of the new openness to renew calls for Karabakh's return to Armenia. In late 1987, the first sporadic outbreaks of violence began, generating Azeri refugees who would play a crucial role in later rounds of escalation (Kaufman 2001). In January 1988, Politburo member Alexander Yakovlev received a petition with 75,000 Karabakh Armenian signatures—roughly 60 percent of the Armenian population in the region (Fuller 1988, 2). When this petition was summarily rejected, protest rallies broke out. In response to popular pressure, on February 20 the Soviet of People's Deputies for the Nagorno-Karabakh Autonomous Oblast (NKAO, a political structure largely unique within the USSR) formally requested transfer to the Armenian SSR (Tolz 1988). This set off a spate of violence, and refugees began crossing in both directions, with Armenians fleeing Azeri-dominant areas and Azeris fleeing Karabakh (Croissant 1998, 28–29). At the same time, the previous party boss in Karabakh—Boris Kevorov, who was loyal to his Azeri superiors in Baku—was replaced by Genrikh Pegosian, who was more willing to press the Armenian cause to the Soviet leadership (Kaufman 1998, 20–21). In June 1988, under pressure from a growing ground-level nationalist movement, the Supreme Soviet of the Armenian SSR passed a resolution calling on the USSR government to transfer NKAO to Armenia.

Thus, the first instance of "official" Armenian irredentism began more than three years before the collapse of the USSR and the creation of an independent Armenia. This is significant, insofar as in 1988 leaders in Armenia (and a number of other Soviet republics) had begun to question the longevity of the Soviet system and the borders it had created within itself. However, before 1991, none of these boundaries constituted *international* borders of the sort that might be recognized and reinforced by the international system. The expectation that intrastate boundaries are more likely targets for irredentism (see chapter 1) is thus borne out here.

Intercommunal violence, started by the clashes in Askeran and Sumgait of February 1988, increased in frequency and intensity throughout that year and into 1989. Peaceful rallies in Yerevan in response to the Sumgait violence led to the organization of what became known at the Karabakh Committee, an organization that largely bypassed the existing, Soviet-installed leadership and drove Armenian mobilization throughout 1988. The success of these efforts, coupled with the failure of Armenian Communist Party First Secretary Demirchyan to keep order or any semblance of control over events, led to Demirchyan's replacement with a new leader, Suren Harutiunyan, in May (Kaufman 2001, 65). It also led the Armenian SSR to endorse the February call from Karabakh for unification (Herzig 1990, 156). By the fall of 1989, the Armenian legislature had adopted a fairly hard-line nationalist position, recognizing a National Council elected by the Armenian Nationalist Movement Party as the official representative of the NKAO region. In December, that Council and the Armenian Supreme Soviet, now dominated by Armenian Nationalist Movement members and sympathizers, issued a joint statement proclaiming a "United Armenia Republic" (Croissant 1998, 33–35).

The two governments immediately began work on a unified budget structure, first implemented in 1990. These actions set off another wave of Azeri-Armenian violence, including an anti-Armenian pogrom in Baku that led to the expulsion of nearly all Armenians from the city, followed by a Soviet occupation of the Azerbaijani capital in January 1990 (Kaufman 2001). While this action accelerated the movement of refugees, particularly Armenians fleeing Azerbaijan, it did little to stop the creation of Armenian and Azeri militias, which continued to play out the conflict with escalating force.

In August of 1990, the first noncommunist government in seventy years was created in Armenia with the election of Levon Ter-Petrosyan, leader of the Armenian Nationalist Movement, to the chair of the Armenian Supreme Soviet. Ter-Petrosyan, who had been one of the members of the Karabakh Committee in 1988 and 1989, immediately declared his intention to secede from the USSR, and changed Armenia's name to the Armenian Republic, citing the earlier proclamation of a "United Armenia" as justification for including Nagorno-Karabakh in his new state. As the violence in and around the Karabakh region escalated into open warfare in 1991, Armenia stepped up its diplomatic, financial, and military support for the Nagorno-Karabakh militias, with many volunteers from Armenia itself.

In the aftermath of the failed August 1991 Soviet coup, both Armenia and Azerbaijan became independent states. On the ground, both states were essentially already at war with each other over the Karabakh region, although Armenia officially renounced its claim to Azerbaijani territory at a Russian-Kazakh-mediated peace conference in September 1991 (Croissant 1988, 44). From that point, while the Republic of Armenia continued to give military support to the militias fighting to free the Karabakh region from Azerbaijan's authority, its official diplomatic position remained simply support for self-determination for the people of Nagorno-Karabakh (Croissant 1988, 69; Cornell 1997). Thus, while its actions on the ground helped create what was in effect a union of the two territories, Armenia's diplomatic strategy was to put pressure on Azerbaijan for denying Karabakhis their rights to self-determination.

The coup, and subsequent collapse of the Soviet army, fueled the fighting with new armaments, particular heavy weapons, as various units either sold their weapons or joined in the war (Kaufman 2001, 73). This war escalated rapidly over the year following independence. In late November 1991, Azerbaijan initiated a full-scale rail blockade of Armenia, cutting some of the latter's most important trade links to the outside world (Croissant 1998, 45–46). In early 1992, Azerbaijani forces launched a series of offensives designed to retake territory and/or reassert Baku's authority. Most of these led to Armenian counteroffensives that put still more territory under control of Armenian militias, culminating in the successful creation of an open ground corridor (the Lachin corridor) between Karabakh and Armenia proper in the spring of 1992, with the capture and ethnic cleansing of the cities of Khadzhaly and Shusha (Croissant 1998, 80–82; Kaufman 2001, 73). This corridor expanded throughout 1993, but the fighting otherwise stalemated, and by May 1994 all parties had agreed to a cease-fire mediated by the Organization for Security and Cooperation in Europe (OSCE). Since that time, there have been intermittent talks sponsored by the OSCE, by Russia, and by the United States, none producing an agreement. The Nagorno-Karabakh region has continued to operate as an independent ministate and has received support from Armenia, but no other state has formally recognized its independence. The 1994 cease-fire continues to hold, broken only occasionally by sporadic clashes. Thus, Armenia largely succeeded in a de facto kind of irredentism (the governments of the two territories work in very close concert), but appears stalemated on its original objective of legal incorporation of the Karabakh territory, for which no other world power was willing to express support.[1]

Since the creation of the 1994 cease-fire, the region has continued a kind of political and military stalemate. Armenian leaders in both Armenia proper and in Karabakh have had little room to bargain, given the strong nationalism of the territory's population and the likelihood that, like previous leaders, they too could be tossed out for not representing their constituents' demands loudly enough (Rieff 1997). Sporadic attempts to resolve the conflict by negotiation and outside mediation have produced no results; attempts in 2001 by the United States, and throughout the 1990s and up to 2006 by the OSCE (under the auspices of the "Minsk Group," chaired by the United States, France, and Russia), did not bring the conflict any closer to a resolution. Armenia's irredentism, while undoubtedly more successful than any other in the post-Soviet period, appears unlikely to be ratified in the international arena, and seems set to remain a unification on the ground only.

Costs of Irredentism

It is not difficult to trace the outlines of the sacrifices that Armenia has borne because of its policy choices. Costs are accounted here in two areas: domestic political costs, and costs to the welfare of the state both within and on the international front. The supposition of this book is that irredentism is driven by domestic political calculations for leaders, not by considerations of "state interests"; we should therefore not be surprised to see high costs to the state, but relatively lower costs, and, more likely, significant gains to the irredentist politicians themselves.

Domestic Politics Dominated by Irredentism

During the initial and active phases of the conflict—from 1987 until the cease-fire in 1994—the Karabakh issue dominated Armenian politics. As noted earlier, in 1988 and 1989 the communist-appointed heads of both the Armenian

SSR and the Karabakh region were sacked for failure to keep order and re-solve the fundamental problems. Given the political forces they faced from mobilized masses, failure in these areas was synonymous with failing to ad-vance the Armenian nationalist cause (including, in particular, unification with Nagorno-Karabakh). That an informal grouping of cultural and intellec-tual elites, the Karabakh Committee, was effectively able to pressure the Arme-nian SSR's Supreme Soviet into supporting annexation was testament to the domestic political forces in play. During the active portions of the conflict, the dominant political costs (especially after independence) were borne by those who did *not* support an irredentist agenda, leading some authors to de-scribe the period as one of mass-driven ethnic mobilization in which political success was conditioned by the ethnic politics of the street (Kaufman 2001).

Although the 1994 cease-fire stabilized the situation on the ground largely in Armenia's favor, Karabakh continued to be a live issue in Armenian domes-tic politics. In part, this is due to international pressure from outside forces (the United States, Russia, OSCE) to resolve the conflict permanently, but it also stems from the continued use of Karabakh as a domestic political card (and the interactions between these two). By 1997, the politics of both Arme-nia proper and the Karabakh region had become extremely radicalized on the irredentist issue, leaving very little room for political maneuver or compro-mise by any Armenian politician (Rieff 1997). In 1994, Robert Kocharian, who had been head of the Karabakh State Defense Committee, was elected the region's first "president"; he was reelected to that post by popular vote in 1996. In March 1998, Kocharian was named prime minister of the Republic of Armenia under President Ter-Petrosyan—perhaps the clearest demonstra-tion of Karabakhi political access in Armenia. Ties between prominent Kara-bakhis and the Armenian power structure also extended to the military. In 1994, the prominent Karabakh military leader Samvel Babayan was made a major general in the Armenian Army; he later helped organize the political party "Right and Accord" to contest the Armenian parliamentary elections of 1999 (de Waal 2003, 256–257). This ensured the dominance of the Karabakh issue and of a hard-line stance on that issue, at the highest levels of the Arme-nian government. It also served as a signal to less nationalist politicians that political futures could hinge on having the "correct" position on this issue.

Ter-Petrosyan's first serious political troubles came in 1996, when he stood for reelection against Vazgen Manukian, a former supporter of the president who had turned against him as the government's popularity began to fall.

With the economy doing poorly, Manukian sought to capitalize on widespread disillusionment and appeared to be garnering significant public support, especially after three other candidates stepped down in support of him (de Waal 2003, 257). After an apparently manipulated first round of voting, however, Armenia's Central Electoral Commission declared Ter-Petrosyan the outright winner, an outcome contradicted by most international observers. An uprising by Manukian supporters was put down by military and security forces, putting Ter-Petrosyan in debt politically to the military—which was strongly pro-Karabakh (Laitin and Suny 1999, 155). Defense Minister Vazgen Sarkisian, a leader in the Karabakh Party (which was composed of prominent proirredentist Armenians as well as Karabakhis), bluntly claimed in the midst of the political crisis: "Even if they [the opposition] win 100 percent of the votes, neither the army nor the National Security Service, nor the Ministry of the Interior would recognize such political leaders" (de Waal 2003, 258). With the resolution of the 1996 crisis, it became clear that pro-Karabakh forces held the balance of political power in Armenia.

In 1997 and 1998, in response to international pressure from the CSCE's Minsk Group (chaired by Russia, the United States, and France), Ter-Petrosyan began to pursue a policy of conciliation toward Azerbaijan, to be marked by "mutual compromise and direct talks between Baku and Stepanakert." Citing the Dayton Accords over Bosnia, he suggested that Armenia would have to settle for what it could get, while protecting the Karabakhis' most fundamental interests (de Waal 2003, 259). While this produced favorable responses on the international front, it immediately created a crisis in Armenian politics, as opposition leaders rose up to call Ter-Petrosyan's policy "treason" and "capitulation" (Croissant 1998, 122). Political battles immediately broke out within the government between various ministers, with President Ter-Petrosyan and Prime Minister Kocharian on opposite sides. The crisis came to a head in February, when several of Ter-Petrosyan's allied ministers and a large bloc of his party's members of parliament resigned or withdrew their support, forcing the president's resignation (Croissant 1998, 122–123; de Waal 2003, 260). Kocharian was appointed interim president, then elected to the post in March with the help of the nationalist Dashnak Party, assuring that Armenian policy would continue to be strongly irredentist toward Karabakh (de Waal 2003, 262). It was Ter-Petrosyan's switch from ardent irredentist to attempted peacemaker, therefore, that led to his government's collapse, as his earlier actions had tied his hands from pursuing any other policy.

International Isolation: The Price of Irredentism

Throughout Armenia's recent existence, its most important relationships have been those with Russia, the United States, Azerbaijan, and Turkey. Although early in the conflict the Soviet Union and then Russia provided some aid to Azerbaijan, Russia has generally sided with Armenia in subsequent relations, signing a joint military basing agreement with the Armenian government in 1994, and transferring substantial amounts of weaponry to Armenia in the years following (Croissant 1998). In 1995, Armenia agreed to maintain the existing Russian military base at Gyumri for another twenty-five years, effectively insuring a continued significant Russian presence in Armenia for the foreseeable future (de Waal 2003, 261). Armenia was likewise the only Caucasian Republic to join the Commonwealth of Independent States at its inception, and has remained a member since—binding it still more closely to Russia (Laitin and Suny 1999, 155). Relations with the United States have also been good. Although there have been some attempts in the U.S. Congress to restrict aid to Armenia to punish it for its support of the Karabakh war, these have been successfully defeated by skillful lobbying by the Armenian diaspora, which serves as an important source of international support. Through the 1990s Armenia was the largest per capita recipient of U.S. foreign aid among all post-Soviet states, while Azerbaijan was denied any direct aid from the United States in the 1990s, another sign of the diaspora's sway on American policy (Cornell 1997; Laitin and Suny 1999, 155).

As for its relations with the rest of the international community, Armenia's position went from good to poor over the course of the 1990s. Because its initial postcommunist transition was dominated by anticommunist nationalists, the new Armenian regime won favor in the West. But with the 1994 cease-fire, and the stalemate that followed, Armenia looked less and less like the underdog and increasingly like the victimizer. Occupying 15 percent of Azerbaijan's territory and having driven hundreds of thousands of Azeris from their homes, Armenia lost the international high ground on the Karabakh issue (Laitin and Suny 1999, 163). At the same time, its internal political problems in 1996—marked by manipulated elections, outlawed opposition parties, and the use of force to suppress dissent—reduced Armenia's standing as a member of the new wave of democratizing states. This took a toll on Armenia's ability to argue its position in international forums. At an OSCE summit in December 1996, every state except Armenia accepted a resolution supporting Azerbaijan's territorial integrity—essentially an international repudiation of Armenian irredentism (Laitin and Suny 1999, 164).

In the immediate regional context, Armenian relations with Azerbaijan and Turkey have obviously been very bad. Both of Armenia's neighbors have tried to impose punishments on the Armenian economy, mostly by cutting off road and rail access (Croissant 1998, 87; de Waal 2003). There has been some border tension between Armenia and Turkey, but no shooting, and the forces of Armenia proper have generally avoided direct and large-scale conflict with the army of Azerbaijan. Clearly, pursuit of the irredentist path has made enemies of both Azerbaijan and Turkey.[2]

Given the geopolitical and historical realities of the region, it is clear that a certain amount of tension between Armenia and its neighbors was likely in any case. Armenia's relations with Turkey are substantially driven by past perceptions of the genocide, but here the conflict of Nagorno-Karabakh has fanned those flames on both sides. Certainly, the early violence in the late 1980s raised the specter for Armenians of a new, Turkic (Azeri) genocide of Armenians, which increased the salience of the older genocide stories for Armenian policy (Kaufman 2001). A nonirredentist Armenia might have had to start with tense relations with its neighbors, but would have had an opportunity to improve on them; a violently irredentist Armenia, in possession of what Azeris (and Turks) regarded as part of Azerbaijan, had no such chance.

Armenia's largely complete isolation from Azerbaijan has been more sharply felt as the United States and the West in general have grown closer to Azerbaijan. Even before 9/11, American businessmen—particularly in the oil industry—became interested in Baku as a gateway to what was estimated to be a very large untapped Caspian oil reserve (Laitin and Suny 1999, 164). This trend continued in the aftermath of the terrorist attacks on New York and Washington. On September 12, Azerbaijan offered the United States its unconditional support in tracking down Islamic terrorists, with which the Baku government had had its own difficulties.[3] A substantial increase in U.S. aid to Azerbaijan followed,[4] as well as a new relationship of military cooperation that brought U.S. military aid to Azerbaijan even with that given to Armenia.[5] And in 2005, Armenia missed out on the largest foreign investment opportunity in the Caucasus since the fall of the Soviet Union, as a new oil pipeline opened to transport Caspian Sea oil to Western markets via Azerbaijan, Georgia, and Turkey—bypassing Armenia entirely.[6] By the early twenty-first century, therefore, Armenia had begun to lose its edge in support from the outside world as strategic and economic considerations provided a counter-weight to traditional ethnic diaspora politics in Washington, and to fall far-ther behind in both political and economic integration with wider world structures.

The international cost to Armenia of its irredentism has therefore been complete isolation from its two most important neighbors, as well as lost op-portunities to forge better relations and economic ties with the West, particu-larly as 9/11 changed the balance of forces acting on U.S. policy. A closer rela-tionship with Russia has helped offset this isolation a little—though not nearly enough, as the discussion of economics below demonstrates—but it has also made Armenian policy more subject to Russian interests than most independent states would like. Appeals to states with strong Armenian dias-poras, like the United States and France, have likewise been enough only to keep Armenia and its plight from being ignored altogether, but not enough to bring the Armenians any significant leverage or offset the disadvantages of having become a pariah in their own corner of the world.

In addition, the human costs of the battle over Karabakh have been sub-stantial, for both Armenia and the other players in the region. By the end of the fighting in 1994, it is estimated that 25,000 soldiers and civilians (mostly the latter) were killed (Rieff 1997). While there are no reliable estimates of the balance of these deaths between the two sides,[7] it seems reasonable to assume that the 1989–94 fighting cost thousands of Armenian lives. The fighting also caused some 400,000 Armenians to flee from Azerbaijan to Armenia during 1989–91 (Rieff 1997); total refugee estimates for the entire conflict run up to one million for both sides, indicating that Armenia was forced to incorporate hundreds of thousands of refugees into a weak economy. The human costs of irredentism were, therefore, quite high, although apparently not high enough to cause either Armenian leadership or the public to rethink the strategy.

Armenia's apparently victory on the ground is surprising, but its losses are not, given the structural disadvantages it faced against Azerbaijan. Azerbai-jan's population is more than twice Armenia's, and its land is more than twice Armenia's size. Azerbaijan enjoyed economic advantages with more neigh-bors, access to the Caspian Sea (and its oil), and a highly desirable commod-ity that it could sell, at least northwards to Russia. By most standard measures of available state power, Azerbaijan held the advantage. Comparing Corre-lates of War (COW) data for the two countries for the period of the 1990s, Armenia tended to have roughly one-half of Azerbaijan's aggregated mea-sured power resources; in the early years, during the active phase of the war, the ratio was closer to 3:1 in Azerbaijan's favor (Bennett and Stam 2000). While it is easy in hindsight to assume that in the late 1980s Armenian victory was assured, this was clearly not the case based on the objective factors of the day.

These disadvantages in structural power seem to have been countered by a combination of Armenian willingness to take casualties and to fight as volunteers, some early assistance in armaments from the collapse of the Soviet Union and from Russia, and the tactical advantages of fighting in mountainous territory that was their home turf—in other words, the measurable strategic power advantages that Azerbaijan enjoyed were overridden by idiosyncratic factors on the ground, including the strength of Armenian nationalism and its ability to mobilize men to fight. These advantages were to a great degree intangible and subject to change: if Armenians did not have the willingness to take losses that they did, they might have changed course.

But while these intangible advantages were sufficient to bring Armenia success in terms of control over territory, they were not enough to prevent substantial losses and damage in the process. Armenians were willing to bear these costs, indicating that standard deterrence forces based on rational calculations of power held little sway. In recent years, as Azerbaijan has increased its income from oil and Armenia has fallen farther behind, the aggregate power situation has shifted even farther in Azerbaijan's favor—with no concurrent shift in Armenian policy toward Nagorno-Karabakh.

Armenia's economy has likewise done very poorly since independence. It is easy to point to actions taken because of the conflict that have had a substantial impact on the Armenian economy—the blockade by Azerbaijan beginning in 1989, or by Turkey in 1993, and the bypassing of Armenia in building a pipeline from Baku to the Black Sea, which carries a very substantial opportunity cost in lost revenue (Croissant 1998, 132–133, 139). Indeed, it has been argued that "without resolving the Karabakh issue the region's security and economic development may be permanently threatened" (Laitin and Suny 1999, 145). At the time Azerbaijan's blockade was imposed, the rail and road lines across that border carried 90 percent of Armenia's imports of fuel and supplies from other republics (Curtis 1995, 21). In 1991, the Armenian national income fell 12 percent, and 1992 and 1993 were marked by high inflation, large drops in productivity and income, and large budget deficits (Curtis 1995, 41). The blockade coincided with severe energy shortages, and unemployment was running above 50 percent by 1997 (Rieff, 1997). By the dawn of the twenty-first century, some observers estimated that 80 percent of the Armenian population was living in poverty on less than $25 a day (Daniszewski 2001). Finally, Armenia's poor economic performance has contributed to domestic political instability, including the political crises of 1996 and 1999, and has made it difficult for Armenia to negotiate with other states on a host of issues. Thus, irredentism seems to have taken a serious economic toll.

Armenian irredentists hoped to offset these economic losses with help from the Armenian Diaspora around the world, which did contribute generously—though often to projects of their own choosing. A new, modern road to link Armenia to the Karabakh capitol of Stepanakert was completed in 1999 at a cost of $10 million, mostly raised by Armenians around the world (de Waal 2003, 256). But there was dispute about whether such aid was sufficient to offset the other problems with Armenia's economy; in 1997, President Ter-Petrosyan estimated that Armenia was getting no more than $10 million per year from diaspora members, far less than it needed even to meet basic needs (de Waal 2003, 259).

With the collapse of the Soviet Union, Armenia's economic realities suggested that, quite apart from any conflict, it would likely struggle in a post-Soviet world: it is the smallest of the former Soviet republics, landlocked, and with no significant resources of energy or minerals that might boost its export earnings. Armenia's economic hope clearly rested on its ability to trade on its location, as a crossroads between Russia, Turkey, the Caspian Sea, and the Persian Gulf. But that strategy depends on Armenia's ability to forge cooperative trade and transportation links with its neighbors, which were all but destroyed in the conflict over Karabakh. To add to this situation, a great deal of Armenian infrastructure was destroyed by a large earthquake late in 1988; by the time of independence, much of this damage remained, in no small part because Azerbaijan's response to the Karabakh conflict (the rail cutoff of 1989) severely hampered Armenia's ability to recover and rebuild. In recent years, Armenia has managed to turn in a positive growth rate, aided by an IMF-sponsored development plan; by 1999, real growth had reached 5 percent, and by 2005 it had reached an estimated 8 percent rate. But recent growth has represented simply an effort to dig out of the very deep hole that Armenia put itself into the early 1990s. Finally, while Armenia has continued to receive some significant economic backing from its diaspora population abroad, this backing comes at a price (continued irredentism and a lack of flexibility toward Karabakh), though it has helped to alleviate some of the economic suffering brought on by the combined effects of war, earthquake, and the collapse of the USSR (Rieff 1997).

The effect of much of this economic pain—in terms of expected impact on Armenia's irredentist policies—was mitigated by the fact that most of the costs were opportunity costs, not direct ones. Western economists pointed out time and again the advantages that Armenia *would* gain from integration with the global economy. But Armenia had never been well integrated even into the Soviet economy, and its people were used to living in an economic backwater. Unlike the Russian case (see chapter 6), the collapse of the Soviet Union created no new class of Armenian capitalists and wealthy oligarchs eager to profit through Armenian ties to the world economy. As we will see below, Armenian irredentism was a substantially mass-driven phenomenon, and while the masses might have had an interest in economic integration in the abstract, they neither understood that nor expressed it. The political and economic benefits of diaspora Armenians made things worse, since those in the diaspora (in this case, many in the United States) already benefited personally from global economic integration, and had little interest in seeing Armenia itself do so if it meant selling out the nationalist dream.

Counting the Costs

Armenia has clearly suffered substantial human losses, and its economy did very poorly in the early 1990s. Its relations with its neighbors—which would likely have been tense but not necessarily destructive because of past conflicts—have been plunged into mutual hostility and deep distrust. Its status in the international community, while initially strong in the immediate aftermath of independence, has gradually slipped as intransigence over the Karabakh issue, along with domestic political instability, have eroded favor for Armenia, particularly in the West. After 2001, as the oil market tightened and Washington looked increasingly for Muslim states as allies in its war on terror, Armenia's diplomatic leverage vis-à-vis Azerbaijan slid further still. Irredentist success (the de facto joining of the Karabakh region to Armenia), combined with continued reliance on diaspora Armenians, has imposed a very restrictive set of policy constraints on present and future Armenian governments, leaving them very little room to maneuver or compromise. In essence, irredentism has boxed the Armenian government into a corner domestically, which restricts its freedom of movement internationally—a classic problem of two-level games (Putnam 1988). This may eventually hamper Armenia's ability to sustain its economic growth, or to integrate itself further into the globalizing world of IGOs and economic and political agreements. It may also mean that a future settlement of the Karabakh issue will go against Armenian interests, and that as with Serbian gains in Bosnia and Croatia even the successful irredentism of Armenia will be lost.

"Sacred Cause": Explaining Costly Irredentism in Armenia

The previous discussion begs the question, why? Why would Armenia subject itself to these costs in an attempt to unite with the Karabakh territory? Why, seeing those costs in the late 1980s, did Armenians not back away from war? Why, as the 1990s dragged on and prospects for a resolution on Armenian terms dimmed, did the Armenian government not become more flexible in its search for a solution? The answer, as this book argues in other cases, lies in the nature of domestic politics within Armenia. In particular, the nature of Armenian nationalism and the mass-elite dynamics in the late 1980s and early 1990s generated a situation that has led Armenia into a tragic and costly stalemate, even as it achieved its immediate military and territorial goals in the early 1990s.

The Three Forces of Armenian Identity

Several observers have disputed the popular characterization of the Armenian-Azeri conflict as one fueled by ancient, primordial hatreds (Kaufman 1998, 2001; Laitin and Suny 1999; de Waal 2003). Nevertheless, the nature and content of Armenian nationalism as it emerged in the late 1980s and through independence played a substantial role in pushing the conflict, in particular in the rigid demand for unification with Karabakh. Three forces have driven Armenian national identity throughout this period: the image of martyrdom, the belief in antiquity, and the relationship to territory.

It is no accident that the escalation of the Karabakh conflict from territorial dispute to full-scale war began with the killing of significant numbers of Armenians in Sumgait, an Azerbaijani city, in early 1988. Those killings had as much to do with the frustration of Azeri refugees as anything else, and the fact that they were not followed by more widespread anti-Armenian violence soon thereafter suggests that there was no broad plan for the "ethnic cleansing" of Azerbaijan of its Armenian population. Nevertheless, the attacks touched a nerve within Armenians' image of themselves as a "martyr nation." This image had its roots in early Armenian history, with the defeat of the first unified Armenian nation at the hands of the Persians in AD 451 (Kaufman 2001, 53). The defining moment of modern Armenian nationalism is the Turkish genocide of 1915, an event whose effects can still be seen in the pattern of Armenian nationalism around the world (Laitin and Suny 1999, 147; Panossian 2002, 136). One prominent Armenian author and historian put it this way: "To curse at Muslims and especially at Turks, to talk much about the Armenian Genocide, and to remind others constantly of the brutality of the Turks are all regarded as expressions of patriotism. Among the leaders of the past we consider those who curse Turks and killed Turks to be the most patriotic. Our most recent heroes are those who assassinated Turkish diplomats in European cities" (Ishkhanian 1991, 10).

The Sumgait killings thus reinforced this image in the minds of Armenians, and convinced them again that living safely under Azeri (which they equated with Turkish) rule would never be possible (Cornell 1997; Laitin and Suny 1999). In this sense, Armenian nationalism is similar to Israeli nationalism: the belief that one is surrounded by enemies that intend your extermination, and that no outside force can be counted on for your defense—that survival depends on the ability of the nation to defend itself from otherwise bloodthirsty enemies (Laitin and Suny 1999, 152). In this regard, Karabakh was seen as important in part simply because of its location between Armenia and the Azeri heartland—a bulwark against potential Azeri aggression. These beliefs quickly spilled over into local press reporting in 1988 and 1989, with one Armenian report of riots in Azerbaijan arguing that they showed "the true nature, the psychology of the Azerbaijanis. There is nothing in their souls besides murder and bestiality" (Kaufman 2001, 68).

This image of Armenia as the martyr nation has been undergirded by a belief in the antiquity of Armenia, and therefore its "rightful" place among the nations of the world and in the Caucasus in particular. Particularly strident Armenian nationalists have claimed that Armenians "were the aborigines of the Armenian plateau who have been living there continuously since the fourth millennium BC at the latest" (Astourian 1994, 47). Others have suggested that the population of Greater Armenia (including Karabakh) was speaking a unified Armenian language by the second century BC (Laitin and

Suny 1999, 146). More objective scholars agree that Armenians constituted a coherent ethnic group by the fifth century AD (Kaufman 2001; Panossian 2002). The purpose of reinforcing these claims of antiquity, of course, has been to establish the rightness of Armenian prior claims to territory—including the territory of Karabakh.

Tying all of this together with the Karabakh conflict is the role that the Armenian territory (including Karabakh) plays in Armenian identity. There is something ironic in this, for the elements of the name Nagorno-Karabakh come from Russian (*nagorno*, mountainous), Turkish (*kara*, black), and Persian (*bagh*, garden) (Kaufman 2001, 50). The dominance of Armenians in the region in modern times dates primarily to the nineteenth century, when the expanding Russian empire brought Christian Armenians out of the Ottoman and Persian empires and under the protection of the Russian Tsar (Goldenberg 1994, 157–158). By the end of the twentieth century, Armenians made up between 70 and 80 percent of the Karabakh population (Laitin and Suny 1999; Melander 2001). A substantial portion of Armenians' claims to the Karabakh territory is this demographic dominance, tied to the beliefs (outlined above) that the presence of Armenians in the area dates back centuries, at least to the period of the Roman Empire (Rutland 1994). That territory and people were linked in Armenian minds can be seen in the Armenian rejection, in mid-1988, of a plan to give Karabakh autonomous republic status, on the grounds that the plan would expand the borders of the Karabakh territory to include too many Azeris—an indicator of the strong anti-Turkish (and therefore anti-Azeri) xenophobia of Armenian nationalism (Melander 2001, 60).

The modern creation of Armenia as a diaspora nation marked by the genocide of 1915 made territory a fundamental concept in Armenian nationalism, since to be in diaspora—to be a "scattered people"—is to envision a return to the "homeland." Hence, "Armenians who deny the fundamental historical role of Karabakh in Armenian *national* history are . . . held to be traitors to the Armenian nation" (Laitin and Suny 1999, 147). Reunification of Karabakh was thus held to be a "sacred cause" against which it was unacceptable to consider the material costs or consequences (Kaufman 2001, 60).

Linking these three together, the widespread Armenian support for Karabakh irredentism becomes clearer. If Armenia is a nation defined by genocide and diaspora, with an ancient history and therefore "prior claim" on lands that have historically been Armenian, then a reunification of those lands becomes the patriotic duty of Armenian nationalists. Likewise, if Armenia's self-image rests on a story of persecution and victimhood, with Turks and Turkic peoples defined as the relevant Others, calls for ethnic cleansing of Armenian lands make sense within the larger narrative. Thus, Armenian Defense Minister Serzh Sarkisian (born in Karabakh) argued, "The most important thing is not the territory. It's that one ethnic group is left in Armenia. . . . Our cultures are not compatible. We can live side by side but not within each other. . . . There are very few of us" (de Waal 2003, 273). Unlike Russian nationalism (discussed later in chapter 6), Armenian nationalism had within it a built-in, exclusivist rationale for irredentism, as well as a framework with which to marginalize as "traitors" those who would compromise on the "sacred cause." This dynamic laid the groundwork for the events of 1988–92, creating a political environment in which "ethnic outbidding" by rival elites was extremely likely and moderation extremely difficult.

Mass Movements and Ethnic Outbidding

It is clear from the events of 1988–1992 that these feelings of nationalist sentiment ran deep among Armenians. Despite the real and growing costs of escalating violence and war, thousands of Armenians were willing to risk death in the name of their nationalist narrative (de Waal 2003). The story of Armenian irredentism is, therefore, first and foremost, a story of mass nationalism, which shaped the political landscape of what could and could not be done by political elites who sought positions of power (Kaufman 2001; de Waal 2003). In the immediate aftermath of the Sumgait violence of 1988, as the martyr and genocide dimensions of Armenian identity were strengthened, the long-standing demand for Karabakh took on a much larger significance, and the ground was thus laid for would-be political leaders, in the environment of collapsing Soviet authority, to engage in nationalistic outbidding (Kaufman 1998, 2001).

This mass sentiment was initially met by the existing, communist power structures in both the Armenian SSR and the Nagorno-Karabakh Autonomous Oblast within the Azerbaijan SSR. Leaders in the Soviet apparatus were not generally chosen for their nationalist views, and these were no exception. In fact, Boris Kevorkov, the party boss in Karabakh—who answered to the party leaders in Baku, not Yerevan—was so intent on supporting the status quo that he fired a young Armenian official in 1975 for mentioning "lost Armenian lands" in a poem—even though the lands referred to were in Turkey (Kaufman 2001, 59). All connections between the Karabakh Armenians and their kin in the Armenian SSR—including Armenian-language education, cultural ties, and even routine hiring—were directed through the existing Azerbaijan SSR structure. This tended to create resentment over time across a host of issues, the solution to which seemed (to Armenians) to be reunification.

In the Armenian SSR leadership, the situation seemed to be little better through 1987. Armenian party officials, though possibly sympathetic to the claims of Karabakh Armenians, did little to advance the cause, mostly keeping a low profile on the issues and attempting to maintain order without resorting to force (Rutland 1994, 845; Melander 2001, 52). This traditional Soviet bureaucratic desire for stability was, however, overwhelmed by events on the ground, as the demonstrations of early 1988 shifted legitimacy away from existing government structures and toward new movements outside the existing Communist Party hierarchy: the Karabakh Committee in Armenia, and the Krunk and Dashnak movements in Karabakh itself (Rutland, 1994; Kaufman, 2001). These movements quickly either toppled or sidelined the existing leadership through a series of protests, street demonstrations, and petitions. Though for the most part peaceful, these were surprisingly effective. Kevorkov was ousted in Karabakh in February 1988, replaced by Genrikh Pegosian, who was much more willing to represent the masses' demands to the Soviet structure (Kaufman 2001, 60). District Soviets and then the Supreme Soviet of Karabakh bowed to the growing mass pressure and passed resolutions demanding the transfer of the territory to Armenia; in the middle of 1988 and again late in 1989, the Armenian Supreme Soviet followed suit (Cornell 1997; Kaufman 2001).

This shift in power from the official structures to mass movements with leaders outside the Communist Party apparatus became apparent as the drive toward independence unfolded. Ter-Petrosyan, an academic born in Syria who had never been a significant Communist Party player, became Armenia's first president after the Karabakh Committee organized itself into the Armenian Nationalist Movement (Rutland 1994). In Karabakh itself, authority devolved initially to the strongly nationalist (and irredentist) Dashnak Party, later passing in 1992 to a Defense Committee headed by Robert Kocharian, who also had no Communist Party ties. After independence and after the war had stabilized itself, mass movements continued to drive Armenian politics in both Karabakh and Armenia proper. In early attempts by the OSCE to fashion a resolution, Kocharian—originally put forward in contrast to the more hypernationalist Dashnak Party—continued to maintain a hard line (AFP 1993), while Ter-Petrosyan faced political pressure from harder-line nationalists in Armenia intent on scuttling any attempts to make concessions (Liloyan 1993). Ultimately, the power of these movements was demonstrated in 1998, with the toppling of Ter-Petrosyan's government and the ascension to power in Armenia of Kocharian—backed by the Dashnak Party he had once been brought in to replace. Mass political pressures thus continued to define Armenian politics well past the origins of the conflict, through independence and the stabilization of the front lines that led to the stalemate of the mid-1990s.

This dominance over Armenian foreign policy has continued despite an apparent weakening of nationalist electoral strength on the domestic front within Armenia. Parliamentary polls in May 1999 saw the Dashnak Party earn only 7 percent of the vote, with a coalition including former Communist Party leader Karen Demirchian taking the largest bloc of seats on a program of economic reform (Interfax 1999). Kocharian, as president, remained in control of negotiations with Azerbaijan, which have continued to show no progress. Despite disagreements on domestic and economic issues, political parties across the spectrum have continued to support a strong position on the Karabakh issue, suggesting that politicians had learned their lessons from the 1998 crisis: support for serious compromise on Karabakh or the corridor linking it with Armenia was tantamount to political suicide (Demuryan 2000). Armenian politicians across the political spectrum continued to call for either recognition of Karabakh's union with Armenia or its independent status; Karabakh leaders have consistently echoed this position (Liloyan 2001). Given the unlikelihood of the independence option, this has essentially amounted to a continued call for formal irredentism to solidify the de facto union of 1994. A dozen years after the cease-fire, political talks have deadlocked, and there are no public signs of substantive compromise by any Armenian politicians.

Armenia as the "Perfect Storm" of Irredentism

From the preceding discussions above, it is clear why Armenia represents both the most successful, and in some ways most violent and intractable, case of postcommunist irredentism. The Armenian case represents a "perfect storm" of irredentist factors: all of the forces hypothesized in chapter 1 to contribute to irredentist foreign policy were present in Armenia in the late

1980s and through the 1990s. In that sense, Armenia represents the most violent and aggressive end of the spectrum. A look at our hypotheses, applied to the Armenian case, is as follows:

TABLE 3.1   Hypotheses and Armenia

	Hypothesis	
1:	Interstate boundaries limit irredentism	Confirmed: Aggression began across intrastate, not interstate, borders, and the later interstate boundary was never recognized as legitimate
2:	Admissions processes limit irredentism	Mixed: Admission to major European institutions (NATO, EU) not relevant; other IO attempts to influence behavior were ineffective
3:	States will be deterred by stronger targets	Disconfirmed: Azerbaijan was structurally stronger than Armenia throughout 1990s
4:	History of irredentism	Confirmed: Armenia had no history of costly failed irredentist efforts
5:	Tolerance of homogeneity/ xenophobia	Mixed: Armenian nationalism was both strongly supportive of irredentism and strongly xenophobic, leading to ethnic cleansing of captured regions (homogenization)
6:	Economics/irredentist interests	Confirmed: Strong support for irredentism combined with indifference to economic integration
7a:	Actively irredentist kin	Confirmed: Karabakhi Armenians were active from very early on in mobilizing and demanding reunion
7b:	Danger	Confirmed: Karabakhi Armenians were subjected to substantial discrimination prior to irredentism
7c:	Kin in positions of power	Confirmed: Karabakhi Armenians were heavily involved in Armenian politics at the highest levels

One possible explanation, that irredentism is more expected along disputed intrastate borders rather than interstate ones, is certainly true of Nagorno-Karabakh. While the Soviet Union had a vast array of often bewildering internal boundary disputes and a complex system of different levels of autonomy to try to deal with them, the NKAO territory was one of the longest and most consistently contested of these cases, even under otherwise stable Soviet rule. This suggests that Armenia is a good support case for the notion that the status of boundaries can be a contributing factor in the complex equation of irredentism. Even this argument, however, must take into account the complex modern history of the situation. Armenian irredentism toward Karabakh began in 1988, well before anyone knew what the future of the USSR would be—indeed, at a time when the continued existence of the USSR was not seriously in question. As the union broke up in 1991, the republic's borders quickly became internationalized—yet Armenia's irredentist policy did not change. If irredentist processes were determined solely by the status of borders, one might have expected the Armenian government to back off when the border between the Armenian and Azerbaijani republics became recognized by the international system. But rather than retract its irredentist demands, Armenia escalated the conflict and hardened its position.

The involvement of international organizations and the "lure of conditionality" also failed to sway the outcome, as we predicted, though the conclusion here is not so dramatic as in Serbia and Croatia, which had a realistic expectation of being able to join Western institutions. Across the 1990s and into the early twenty-first century, as numerous other Eastern European and former Soviet countries were lining up to join Western-led international institutions, Armenia continued to stick to its irredentist guns, even when this led to isolation in those same forums (as when it stood alone against the OSCE in 1996). Membership in the EU was not at stake, but the ability of Armenia to have a voice in the international arena—through the OSCE, in the Council of Europe, and at the UN—was, and in this Armenia chose to let its influence wane rather than give up on its irredentist dreams. Throughout its irredentist struggle, the Armenian economy has suffered—a condition that better relations with Western Europe would likely have helped alleviate. But whatever promise there might have been has not been enough to shift Armenian foreign policy.

Armenian irredentism is likewise not explainable by reference to rational power calculations. Throughout the conflict, Armenia has been at a measurable strategic disadvantage vis-à-vis Azerbaijan, in terms of geography, population, and economic size and structure. To be sure, Armenians were able to overcome these disadvantages to win their objectives on the ground—reminding us of the difficulty of predicting outcomes based on structural power alone—but only at tremendous cost. Yet even as these costs mounted and became increasingly apparent, Armenia did not waiver in its commitment to the irredentist cause. Even the Serbian population, weary of war, eventually turned on Milosevic; so far, the Armenian population has shown no signs of doing likewise to its nationalist leaders.

A major part of the explanation for Armenia's violent irredentism is its own past, as understood and interpreted in the postcommunist era. Constructed Armenian nationalism emphasized connections to the land, and to the Karabakh region in particular. However, there had been no cases in the past in which Armenia had tried but failed to regain Karabakh. Indeed, the greatest disaster of Armenian modern history was not a result of Armenian policy, but of Turkish actions: the Armenian genocide. Far from acting as a brake, therefore, historical precedent for Armenians provided an accelerator by demonstrating the dangers of *inaction* against neighbors presumed to be implacably hostile. But as with the status of borders point, here the reality is more complex than a simple explanation might suggest. Armenia had no real experience with irredentism, failed or otherwise, and had certainly never in modern history made a land grab of the sort it has attempted in Karabakh. While the costs of this effort were therefore foreseeable by outsiders, those costs would likely have looked very different to Armenian decision makers at the outset of the conflict. Indeed, the "sacred cause" language was used specifically to justify "irredentism at any price," a stand justified not so much by the objective history of the region but by the highly nationalized version of that history held by the Armenian population. Our argument from chapter 1—that history matters, not because it offers simple lessons but because it shapes contemporary interests and perceptions—is therefore well supported by the Armenian case.

Because the territory of Karabakh was largely Armenian—and, owing to the early rounds of ethnic cleansing violence in 1988 and 1989, quickly became almost exclusively so—it presented a very tempting irredentist target, particularly to elites who had risen to power on the basis of Armenian nationalism. These elites—and their supporters—were undoubtedly xenophobic and intolerant toward Azeris, who were equated with the hated Turks. This xenophobia had the perverse effect of forcing politicians to pass up early negotiated solutions that might have brought more Azeris—those not yet driven from their homes—under Armenian control. And while the violence that began in 1988 undoubtedly cemented exclusionary feelings on both sides, the rapidity with which the conflict escalated suggests that those views—the sense that Armenians and Azeris could not live peaceably together—were already well entrenched at the very beginning. Had the Karabakh territory been less homogenized, therefore, irredentism would have been much less likely; as it was, it presented the perfect target for Armenian leaders wanting to build and maintain domestic power.

Perhaps the most puzzling dynamic, to Western eyes, has been Armenia's continued insistence on a hard irredentist line despite the significant and ongoing economic costs. Many Western observers expected that societies like Armenia's, finally given the opportunity to join with the dynamic capitalist economies of the West, would gladly eschew whatever old notions of nationalism they had in favor of economic integration. Because of its location, however, Armenian economic integration with the global economy would mean economic cooperation with both Turkey and Azerbaijan. For Armenian nationalists, this was unthinkable. Economic cooperation requires mutual trust and the belief in mutual benefits, neither of which was present in the Armenian population, or Armenian elites. Had Armenia had the opportunity for economic integration by cooperating with some other, non-Turkic partner—if it had direct access to Western Europe, for example, as Hungary does—calculations might have been different. As it is, there has been no way of separating the question of economic integration with the West from the nationalist question, and thereby playing the one off against the other. The Armenian case thus represents a condition where the choice suggested in our sixth hypothesis—irredentism and isolation, or restraint and integration—was constrained, and only one option was politically feasible.

The condition of Karabakh's Armenians also contributed, as we expected it should. Unlike Russians in the near abroad (see chapter 6), Armenians in Karabakh were structurally disadvantaged under the Soviet system of republics, in an already resource-poor part of the USSR. Moreover, Karabakhi Armenians were both concentrated geographically and mobilized to advance their own interests. In this sense, the peculiar status of Karabakh in the Soviet system—an "Autonomous Oblast" that nevertheless had to answer to the Azeri Republic government in Baku—provided the worst possible set of conditions: it simultaneously gave Karabakh Armenians a structure through which to channel grievances and mobilize support, while guaranteeing that that structure would (because its authority went through the Azeri-dominated government in Baku) create inequalities and grievances around which to mobilize. Armenian irredentism was therefore made much more likely by the existence of a highly mobilized, well-organized group of kin, clamoring to change their status and "return" to the Armenian fold.

In lining up all of these criteria, Armenia represents the "perfect case" for our theory—a case we should expect, if we are predicting anything at all, to get right. The irredentist outcome is predicted and reinforced by an entire host of factors—a case, perhaps, of overdetermination, which may help explain why it has been so difficult to resolve. Having examined the hardest case, we can now move on to consider cases where "the dogs didn't bark"—Hungary, Romania, and Russia—to see if these same forces work in the opposite direction.

NOTES TO CHAPTER 3: REUNIFICATION AT ANY PRICE

1. Indeed, this situation in some ways parallels that of the Turkish part of Cyprus. See chapter 7.

2. Most of Armenia's international border is shared with these two countries. Its relatively small border with Iran offers little help in an economic development or strategic sense, in part because of complicated relations involving Iranian Azeri populations and Iranian policy in the region, and in part because Iran is itself a pariah to the West and therefore a poor conduit to Western markets. Likewise, Armenia's northern border with Georgia offers access only to another relatively poor Caucasian republic, one that has had difficult relations with Moscow and its own share of political instability. Poor relations with Azerbaijan and Turkey thus present very serious costs to Armenia in both economic and strategic terms.

3. "Azerbaijan offers to help hunt down organizers of US terror attacks," Associated Press report, September 12, 2001.

4. "US boosts aid to Azerbaijan for fighting drugs, encouraging small business," Associated Press report, January 25, 2002.

5. "US, Azerbaijan forge new military cooperation," Associated Press report, March 28, 2002.

6. "Giant Caspian oil pipeline opens," BBC report, May 25, 2005.

7. Conflict data sets feature varying estimates: Licklider (1995) lists more than 10,000 casualties; Regan (1996) estimates 7,000; and Ayres (2000) estimates 25,000.

Pushing the Envelope

Hungary's Assertive Attention to Kin

Aggression and help are two different things.
—FERENC KALMÁR, HUNGARIAN MINISTRY OF FOREIGN AFFAIRS

I N ANY DISCUSSION OF IRREDENTISM IN EASTERN
Europe, Hungary figures prominently both for what it has done and for
what it has not done. Because it lost roughly two-thirds of its territory
and a third of its population at the end of World War I, Hungary faces a set of
challenges that risk irredentism. How does Hungary safeguard Hungarians in
the neighborhood? Before and during World War II, the answer was irredentism, as politicians and parties promised to regain the lost territories. Hungary
sided with Nazi Germany and was successful, in the short run, incorporating
lands and peoples primarily from Czechoslovakia and Romania. However, this
Greater Hungary was temporary, for it lost the war and the territories it had
conquered.[1] The plight of Hungarians abroad was pushed into the background
during much of the communist period, but gained saliency in the first days of
the post–Cold War democracy. Indeed, Hungary has consistently spent considerable effort and significant political capital to address the situation of the
Hungarians abroad, but it has refrained from naked aggression.

Because of Hungary's history of irredentism and its assertive but not quite
aggressive foreign policy, it is an inherently interesting case. Hungary has
been a key case for scholars studying irredentism (Ambrosio 2001) and/or internationally induced stability (Linden 2000). These arguments fail to cap-

ture two key aspects of Hungary's foreign policies—that it has been more assertive than one might otherwise expect and that it has varied over time. To explain both its extraordinary assertiveness as well as its variance, a focus on Hungary's domestic politics is necessary. The two major wings of Hungarian domestic politics have both shown interest in the issue of Hungarians abroad, but the center-right parties (the Hungarian Democratic Forum and then the Alliance of Young Democrats, Fidesz) have been more assertive than the center-left parties (particularly the Socialists).

As in the rest of the book, the key questions are: Does one have to be a nationalist to win political office in Hungary. If so, what does it take to be a successful nationalist? The behavior of parties and the resulting foreign policies suggest that Hungarian politicians do have to be concerned about Hungarians abroad, but carefully so. The place of Hungarians abroad in Hungarian identity is more complicated than one might expect, as there are shared ties, particularly of language, but also divisions based on differing historical experiences.

History of Failed Irredentism

As one of the losers of World War I, Hungary was compelled to sign the Treaty of Trianon at Versailles in 1920. Hungary went from being one of the great powers of Europe and a key element of an empire to a weak state, surrounded by countries where Hungarians lived at risk. Millions of Hungarians were left outside of Hungary due to this treaty, largely in Romania, Czechoslovakia, the Soviet Union (in Ukraine) and Yugoslavia. In the 1990s, the number of Hungarians outside of Hungary (5 million) was half of those left inside (10 million). As in many other countries in the region, in the 1920s and 1930s, despair combined with resentment about the war produced the rise of right-wing parties promising order and restoration.

The Arrow Cross fascist government aligned itself with Nazi Germany, a relationship from which it profited greatly. Hungary regained territory from Czechoslovakia after it was dismembered. Much of Transylvania, the largest territory containing the most "lost" Hungarians, was returned. However, these gains were only temporary, and defeat on the battlefield led to the *status quo ante*. Once again, Hungary lost historic lands, but this time, Hungarians in these areas were targeted for retribution for the crimes, real and alleged, of Hungary during the wartime occupation.

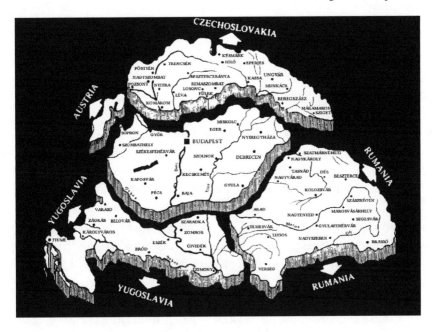

FIGURE 4.1   Hungary After Trianon

During the Cold War, the communist regime did not and could not pay much attention to the plight of Hungarians outside of Hungary. The focus of the regime and of the population was on events at home, including the 1956 revolt and the increased repression that followed. Thus, the issue of Hungarians abroad was largely dormant until the end of the regime, when it became one of the three most important foreign-policy priorities of the new democratic governments.

The Plight of Hungarians Abroad

The issue of the kin abroad has been salient in Hungarian politics because there has been much hostility and government-led discrimination against them, particularly in Romania, Slovakia, and Serbia.[2] This concern was evident at the outset of democracy in Hungary, since most Hungarians were of the opinion that the kin abroad were likely to stagnate or decline in the neighboring countries (Csepeli 1997, 214). The problem was particularly acute, for most of the Hungarians abroad were in states making difficult transitions from communism.[3]

Romania's Hungarians: Low Expectations Are Exceeded

From early on, the focus was largely on Romania's 1.5 million Hungarians, both as a legacy of the Ceausescu era and the violent nature of the transition (Oltay 1992a, 1992b). Following past positions, Romanian leaders insisted on keeping Romania a unitary state, maintaining that Hungary had no responsibility for the condition of its kin. The riots in Tirgu-Mures in 1990, particularly the apparent complicity of the government, signaled to Hungary that their kin were in danger. Even though the violence subsided quickly, the presence of nationalist and xenophobic parties, the Greater Romania Party and the Party for the National Right, in informal and then formal coalitions with the governing National Salvation Front (NSF) caused Hungarians to be most concerned about the plight of their kin in Romania.[4] The presence of nationalists within all major parties and particularly those in the first governments made it very difficult to reach a bilateral treaty. Romania also refused for quite some time to allow a Hungarian consulate in Transylvania, where most Hungarians resided. The use of minority languages in courts and government affairs was restricted.

While the laws changed slowly, the atmosphere significantly improved in 1996 when the Democratic Alliance for Hungarians in Romania (UDMR) joined a coalition with the rest of the opposition parties to govern from 1996 until 2000. This government issued decrees that eventually gave Hungarians some rights in the use of their language in administration as well as some growth in Hungarian education. While there is some debate about the progress made at this time,[5] the UDMR was a key party in the coalition, and had some influence. In 2000, the NSF, now named the Party of Social Democracy (PSD), returned to power, this time relying on an informal alliance with the UDMR instead of the nationalist parties. Again, Hungarians achieved some improvements, and the threat of violence declined. Finally, in the 2004 election, the UDMR became a coalition partner with the center-right parties.

While anti-Hungarian nationalism still exists, and there is some controversy over the inclusion of the UDMR in government even in 2004, the climate has substantially improved, with Tirgu-Mures in 1990 standing out as the sole significant outbreak of anti-Hungarian violence. Efforts to provide collective rights for the Hungarian minority have created tensions within Romania and between Romania and Hungary, but not more than that. The UDMR has softened its stand over the years, no longer asking for significant autonomy,[6] making them a viable coalition partner. The presence of anti-Hungarian politicians in positions of power and influence has kept the condition of Hungarian Romanians alive and visible in Hungary's domestic politics. Yet the threat has been low enough that other priorities have generally mattered more in Hungary.

Hungarians in Slovakia: Restrained Resistance

The 560,000 Hungarians in Slovakia opposed the breakup of Czechoslovakia, knowing that Slovak nationalists would target them. Vladimir Meciar and his allies have been the key threat to them. Meciar led Slovakia when it seceded, governing from 1993 to 1998. He frequently scapegoated the Hungarians while governing in an authoritarian manner (Kettle 1996). Indeed, he was viewed as being relatively insensitive to international pressures since he had other priorities than integration (Kelley 2004a, 127, 135–136).

When in power, Meciar sought to undermine the Hungarian community and its identity. His government passed laws to restrict the use of the Hungarian language in 1992, signs were removed, and names were regulated. He proposed changing the districting of the country so that the administrative regions would run from north to south, dividing and marginalizing the Hungarian communities (Nas 1996). Indeed, in most interviews, discussion of Slovakia focused almost entirely on Meciar. The consensus essentially is that there are always nationalists in Slovakia, but the threat to Hungarians is significant when Meciar is in power.[7]

Events in Slovakia paralleled those in Romania. The various Hungarian parties formed the Hungarian Coalition, which eventually gained a role in the governing coalition in 1998. Meciar threatened to come back in 2002, just as Iliescu did in Romania in 2000, but found no willing coalition partners, despite the plurality of votes his party gained. Thus, despite close calls during the each of the last elections, Slovakia's Hungarians are more secure, particularly, as they, like the ones in Romania, have been able to get seats in parliament and serve in governing coalitions. As in Romania, policy moved slowly but somewhat favorably toward the Hungarians once Meciar was out of power.

Hungarians Held Hostage: Vojvodina Under and After Milosevic

The Hungarians facing the greatest physical threat have been the more than 300,000 who reside in Vojvodina, a formerly semi-autonomous territory of Serbia adjoining Hungary. Having lost autonomy as Slobodan Milosevic gained power, the Hungarians started the 1990s in a very weak position. Once war broke out in Croatia, the draft hit this population hard, perhaps even harder than the rest of Serbia. As Serbia's forces engaged in ethnic cleansing in Croatia and then Bosnia, there was much concern that the Hungarians could be next.

One might expect that the plight of Vojvodina's Hungarians would mobilize Hungary, but it has precisely the opposite effect.[8] Because of their record of violence, the Serbs posed a credible threat against the Hungarian minority (Schöpflin 2000, 392). Indeed, Hungarians in Vojvodina have generally asked the Hungarian government to avoid antagonizing Serbia (Oltay 1992b, 29).[9] Their demand has been the return of autonomy to Vojvodina, an appeal that reaches beyond Hungarians given Vojvodina's multiethnic composition.

Wary Kin, Hungary Out of Sync

The Hungarians abroad do not seem to play the same role as the Armenians, Croats, and Serbs outside of their mother states. The Hungarians are cautious, having significant doubts about Hungary's role. Most of the groups representing Hungarians in the neighboring countries have not pushed for reunion, but rather some reform of the states in which they reside. They are not irredentist, despite the fears stated or exaggerated by various governments in the region. Indeed, the Hungarians abroad have been circumspect about Hungary's activities on their behalf. They have come to understand that they represent an issue that is fair game in Hungary's domestic politics, and they feel used as a result.[10] Of course, within each community, there is competition, with the various groups appealing to Budapest for support in their battles (Schöpflin 2000, chapter 24).

Most strikingly, Hungary's most aggressive foreign policy stances have occurred when the kin abroad faced the most favorable conditions. Hungary passed the Status Law after Milosevic lost power in Serbia, while Hungarians were in the governing coalition in Slovakia and a relatively marginalized Meciar, and while the kin were in informal alliance with the ruling party in Romania. Likewise, the dual citizenship referendum took place at a time where the Hungarians abroad were facing the best political climate of the post–Cold War period. Indeed, these efforts seem to be most counterproductive, for they endanger the Hungarians' progress over the past decade.

Before explaining this paradox by focusing on Hungary's sense of nationalism and the dynamics of its domestic politics, we review a series of events in Hungary's foreign relations. The variations in efforts over time and across the different administrations reflect much ambivalence about the kin abroad and their priority in Hungary's politics.

Involvement Short of Irredentism

Hungary has not engaged in violence, and its citizens and policymakers argue that violent efforts to unite the territories lost in the Treaty of Trianon are unimaginable. However, their neighbors do seem capable of imagining it, and any effort on the part of Hungary to encourage greater autonomy for their kin is met with accusations about Hungary's darker intentions.[11] This has led to much tension, delaying successful negotiations of bilateral basic treaties and causing some concern within the European Union (EU) and North Atlantic Treaty Organization (NATO) about the stability of the new applicants for membership.

Five aspects of Hungary's foreign policy demonstrate both its assertiveness and restraint.[12] First, the first prime minister of newly democratic Hungary, Jozsef Antall, said that he was the prime minister of fifteen million Hungarians, even though Hungary's population is around ten million, thus clearly referring to the Hungarians abroad. Second, during the transition to democracy, Hungary created and funded and maintained a government agency, the Office of Hungarians Abroad. Third, Hungary engaged in negotiations of varying difficulty with its neighbors to develop bilateral treaties that would recognize the existing borders but hopefully give greater protections to the Hungarian minorities. Fourth, Hungary developed a new law—the Status Law—that would give Hungarians outside of Hungary particular benefits. Fifth, in the fall of 2004, Hungary held a referendum on giving dual citizenship to the kin abroad. Each of these events raised tensions with the neighbors, but provided relatively little in the way of material gains for Hungary or for the Hungarians abroad. They reached beyond what one might have expected if Hungary was maximizing its security or economic interests, but these efforts were much less challenging or significant than its more irredentist neighbors in the former Yugoslavia. Ultimately, each of these efforts revealed tensions within Hungarian foreign policy, which, in turn, have produced stress in its relations with the neighboring countries, particularly Romania and Slovakia.

Before discussing the specific events, it is important to note that all of Hungary's postcommunist governments have had three priorities: the Hungarian minorities outside of Hungary, integration into Euro-Atlantic institutions (EU and NATO), and good neighborly relations.[13] However, they have differed on the relative priority of each, and this is important since these three goals are not entirely compatible. Pursuit of integration required good relations with the neighbors, but asserting Hungary's role as protector of the Hungarian minorities hurts relations with the neighbors. This has raised critical tradeoffs over time, generally finessed in ways that reduce the international criticism, providing evidence for those arguing that international constraints matter the most.

Importantly, not all Hungarian minorities gain Hungary's attention; the focus has largely been on those in Romania and in Slovakia. Hungary seems to have been less concerned about Hungarians in the Ukraine and Serbia (Vojvodina). Ukraine has generally treated its Hungarian population well (Stroschein 1996), and despite Serbia's various problems, the Hungarians in Vojvodina have been treated better than one might have expected, making them less visible in Hungary's politics. Only recently has Hungary given Vojvodina's Hungarians attention similar to those in Romania and Slovakia.[14] The latter have been more salient in large part because anti-Hungarian parties have played important roles in the governments of Romania and Slovakia, and both countries passed legislation that restricts Hungarian education and language use. A series of events put Hungary on the edge between irredentism and apathy.

Antall's Fifteen-Million Constituency?

"In the legal sense, on the basis of Hungarian constitutional law, I wish to be the premier of all Hungarian citizens, of this country with a population of ten million, while in spirit, in feeling I wish to be the premier of 15 million Hungarians."[15] This statement came at a time when Hungary was trying to reassure its neighbors that it was not going to revise the borders as established by Trianon. Antall's quote got more attention than the more accommodating noises made by other officials. This statement was not an aberration, as the Antall administration had emphasized the border issue repeatedly: "We never said that the minority question was the only factor in interstate relations, but we find it impossible to have good relations with a country that mistreats its Hungarian minority."[16] Antall even indicated that revisions of Yugoslavia's boundaries would impact Serbia's possession of Vojvodina since Serbia was not an independent state when the original boundary was negotiated (Kardos 1995). His minister of defense, Lajos Fur, went so far as to say that Hungarian agencies "should do everything in their power, using all legal and diplomatic means, to end the threat to the minorities and to guarantee their survival."[17]

Every promise to respect the current boundaries was hedged—that Hungary would not forcibly change them. While this might sound reassuring to most, the neighbors perceived this as an effort to open the door to negotiated boundary changes, as permitted by the Helsinki Final Act. An official at Slovakia's Foreign Ministry indicated that the speech was "a signal aimed at undermining the borders defined in the Trianon Peace Treaty of 4 June 1920" (Nas 1996, 153).

Why cause increased tensions over some rhetoric? One reason may be that Antall had ties to the diaspora community. Zsolt Szekeres helped to organize the prime minister's office when he first came to power.[18] Then, he went on to help found the Hungarian-American Coalition, which he continues to serve as its treasurer. This community has consistently had a stronger concern about the Hungarians in the neighboring states than the average Hungarian.[19] A second reason is that the Hungarian communities abroad, particularly in Romania, faced a high degree of threat and uncertainty during the transition toward democracy.[20] Third, as the first postcommunist leader, Antall had to reach out to a variety of communities, and being strong on this issue was something that could appeal more broadly than other, more divisive issues. Further, Antall's party, the Hungarian Democratic Forum (MDF), a center-right coalition, included a nationalist wing. These individuals, led by Istvan Csurka, were eventually expelled from the party and the governing coalition after the bilateral treaty with the Ukraine was signed, but they may have had an impact before then (Tóka 2004).

The various statements, along with the use of national symbols, were attempts, in the end, to create support for a somewhat nationalist party. The 1994 election indicated that such a nationalist course was less important to the Hungarian people than other issues of more immediate concern (Schöpflin 2000, 372; Shafir 2004). Indeed, in one 1994 survey, 59 percent of Hungarians agreed with that "the public debate over the destiny of Hungarians is aimed at diverting the public's attention from discussion of more pertinent issues" (Csepeli and Örkény 1996, 271). The key is that Hungarian voters, except a small number on the far right, care about the Hungarians in the neighboring countries, but not enough to expend a considerable effort. Still, it is worth noting that the successors to Antall and the MDF, Viktor Orban and the Fidesz Party, made similar statements about the larger Hungarian nation after they came to power in 1998.

Office of Hungarians Abroad

One of the most surprising omissions in the study of Hungary's foreign policy is the Office of Hungarians Abroad. Originally part of a larger organization aimed at minorities within Hungary and Hungarians abroad, it was split off shortly after the election that brought Antall to power.[21] It was supposed to be small and discreet, but it grew over time, getting more funds and increasing its responsibilities. Its officials saw its role mostly as keeping contact with the Hungarians abroad,[22] but this contact was more than mere record keeping. They met regularly with Hungarian elites, particularly politicians, in the neighboring countries, trying to coordinate their efforts. This was controversial as the neighboring governments naturally resented this intrusion. In addition, some of the Hungarians abroad saw this as unwarranted meddling—that the political competition between Hungary's parties gets played out in other countries. That is, the center-right parties support Hungarian politicians with similar outlooks in Romania, Slovakia, and elsewhere, whereas the Socialists support left-leaning Hungarian parties in the nearby countries.

The office's officials also sat on the intergovernmental consultative committees created by the various bilateral treaties. Further, they had additional responsibilities to observe implementation of the Status Law. This was a relatively unique organization—a government body responsible for relations with and the treatment of coethnics in other countries.[23] It was not the Office of Irredentism, but one could easily see how neighboring countries might have been concerned about violations of sovereignty.

Quite revealing, its location within the bureaucracy changed, depending on which party is in power. Under the MDF and the Fidesz governments, the office was housed within the Ministry of Foreign Affairs. Under the Socialists, it was in the prime minister's office. This is more than symbolic as Fidesz defined its foreign policy priorities with a greater focus on the minority issue, while the Socialists did not want this office to be as visible in making foreign policy (Waterbury 2006). Thus, the changing organizational structure demonstrates that the two wings of Hungarian politics have different priorities, helping to explain shifts in Hungarian foreign policy.

Thus, the Office of Hungarians Abroad was important because its evolution demonstrates a course of action in between doing nothing and engaging in irredentism.[24] It served as a substitute for more assertive efforts, demonstrating to the domestic audience that the government cares about the kin abroad; it also tried to help the kin abroad so that their condition would not become a salient issue in domestic politics.

Bilateral Treaties

Hungary has negotiated a series of bilateral basic treaties with its neighbors, promising not to revise the boundaries, and has generally sought assurances of good treatment of the Hungarian minorities in return. These efforts have been quite controversial both inside and beyond Hungary; opposition parties in Hungary have criticized each treaty, and Romania and Slovakia have failed to live up to their promises. These agreements are particularly important inasmuch as they seem to have been driven by NATO and EU admissions requirements.

The first agreement, with Ukraine, was signed shortly after it became independent and long before NATO and EU membership criteria were established. Indeed, Ukraine was very interested in signing a deal so that its independence could be solidified. The Ukrainian government sought a treaty to cement the territorial status quo, and Hungary wanted a provision that referred to compliance with European norms of minority rights. As Ukrainians were much more focused on the large Russian minority than on the Hungarian minority, they were willing to make a deal. Further, the Hungarians in the Ukraine faced little conflict, so they supported the agreement (Nas 1996, 126). The treaty, ratified by Hungary in June 1992, gave Hungary most of what it desired but not autonomy. Ukraine was facing a crisis over the Crimea and over Russian demands, so autonomy was problematic. Istvan Csurka and a few members of the ruling party were strongly opposed to the renunciation of territorial claims, leading to a political crisis and eventually their expulsion from the incumbent MDF party and the creation of the Hungarian Justice and Life Party (MIEP) party, which now represents the far right wing of the Hungarian political spectrum.[25]

The negotiations with Slovakia and Romania took several more years, and were hardly a smooth process. Hungary wanted Slovakia to give significant autonomy to the Hungary minority as a condition for a bilateral treaty, which would include another affirmation of the territorial status quo. Slovakia considered autonomy to be the first step toward secession and then irredentism. This stalemate was worsened significantly, as Slovakia's prime minister, Vladimir Meciar, had a record of Slovak nationalism, and aimed against the Hungarian minority. Further, he depended upon an even more nationalist coalition partner. The treaty was signed on March 19, 1995, despite a disagreement over the interpretation of a key clause regarding Slovakia's obligations to its Hungarian minority. Specifically, the Hungarians wanted a reference to the Council of Europe's Recommendation 1201 included. The key article in this recommendation states, "In the regions where they are in a majority the persons belonging to a national minority shall have the right to have at their disposal appropriate local or autonomous authorities or to have a special status, matching the specific historical and territorial situation and in accordance with the domestic legislation of the state."[26]

Immediately after signing the treaty, Meciar announced that individual rights were more important and legally superior to collective rights including autonomy, essentially renouncing the clause referring to 1201. To say the least, this complicated the ratification process in Hungary.

This treaty, negotiated by the Socialist government, was rejected by most of the opposition, including Fidesz. Its chairman and subsequent prime minister, Viktor Orban, said, "The Hungarian government has capitulated" (Ambrosio 2001, 129). The opponents argued, correctly as it turned out, that it would not be implemented sincerely. The Socialist government compensated for the criticism by holding a "Hungarian Minority Summit" in Budapest during the last stages of negotiations with the Romanians. At this summit, the Hungarian foreign minister signed on to a document that called for autonomy for the minorities to "to mitigate opposition from the diaspora and the domestic right wing to the Hungarian-Romanian Basic Treaty."[27]

In 1996, Hungary and Romania finally concluded their bilateral treaty, facing pressure from members of NATO, particularly the United States, and the EU. As Slovakia followed its treaty by passing language laws vehemently opposed by Hungarians, a deal with Romania became harder, as fears of reneging increased. Still, a deal was signed, since Romania wanted a Hungarian pledge to respect the borders (Shafir 1996). The language in the treaty was ambiguous enough that Romanian officials could claim that they did not give away much while Hungarian leaders could claim that they gained protection of minorities. Leaders on both sides defended the treaty as necessary for integration efforts.[28]

These agreements satisfied the outside actors, and Hungary was in the first set of successful applicants to both NATO and the European Union. The treaties reinforced Hungary's commitment to the existing boundaries. However, the neighbors found the process troublesome, and have continued to suspect Hungary of lingering irredentist intentions. Nor did the agreements provide significant protections for the Hungarian minorities, as Nas (1996) discusses at length. In both Slovakia and Romania, laws passed after the treaties were signed, made it harder for Hungarians to use and be educated in Hungarian. Apparently, politicians needed to prove their nationalist credentials after compromising with Hungary, even though the treaties did not give away much. It is true that treatment of Hungarians in Romania has improved since 1996, despite the initial spurt of unfriendly laws. However, this probably has more to do with the requirements of coalition formation and the weight of the Hungarian minority party than promises made in the treaties.[29]

Thus, the treaties are somewhat puzzling—Hungary gave up its leverage, gaining little, and its leaders faced much criticism for the effort. Each treaty passed with overwhelming majorities in the Hungarian parliament, despite much critical rhetoric. What did Hungarians want? This is the key question, again. They seemed to want to help their kin, but not to endanger other priorities. The Status Law is another example of this combination of impulses, leading to much ado about nothing, or at least not much progress.

Status Law

The Law on Hungarians Living in Neighboring Countries, known to many as the Status Law, or the Benefits Law as Hungarians call it, has been quite controversial.[30] It originally gave Hungarians outside of Hungary benefits to which other nationalities were not to be entitled. The Orban government (led by the Fidesz Party) proposed the law, and it was passed in June 1999 by a 92 percent majority. The law was to give educational and cultural opportunities to Hungarians where they currently reside, as well as special access when they visit Hungary. This was especially important once Hungary made it inside the EU and would be separated from its kin by the Schengen borders.[31] Local ethnic Hungarian organizations in Slovakia, Romania, Ukraine, and former Yugoslav republics were supposed to have the responsibility of deciding whether applicants were genuinely Hungarian.[32]

Despite the large majority in favor, the law engendered some opposition domestically. The Alliance of Free Democrats was opposed, arguing that it would both encourage more immigration and upset the neighbors. The Socialists supported passage because they did not want to be accused of being poor nationalists[33] and because they supported the idea of fostering links with kin abroad. Then, they distanced themselves from the law, saying that more should be done to encourage the Hungarians abroad to stay where they are (Kingston 2001).

The law faced even greater criticism from outside; all of the relevant neighbors as well as the European Union criticized the law.[34] Romania, Slovakia, Ukraine, and the Federal Republic of Yugoslavia (Serbia and Montenegro) saw the law as violations of their sovereignty, since it would give Hungary a formal responsibility in their internal affairs and empower local groups to determine who met the law's criteria. They also objected to some of the original language about a "unified Hungarian nation" as possibly signaling renewed irredentism (Ieda 2004, 17). Romania threatened to cancel its bilateral treaty with Hungary. The European Union's Venice Commission reviewed the legislation and considered portions of it to be in violation of EU standards regarding discrimination.[35] Ultimately, Hungary changed the law so that the local Hungarian bodies could not have a role in determining who is or is not Hungarian.[36] Furthermore, to satisfy Romania's complaints, the law was modified to allow non-Hungarian Romanians to take advantage, an alteration that created controversy, with the Socialists arguing that it would lead to a flood of Romanians entering Hungary. The critique played well in the subsequent election campaign.[37]

These changes did not satisfy the EU or the neighbors, so the new Socialist government reformed the law in advance of a Council of Europe meeting in June 2003. The changes included:

- changing the phrase from "Hungarian" national to "persons with Hungarian heritage";
- increasing the categories of people who could apply—to include those studying Hungarian (even those of non-Hungarian descent);

- making Hungary's consulates, rather than local centers, responsible;
- weakening the connections between the ID card and benefits.

Others have criticized the law for not doing enough. It falls short of dual citizenship, which was initially considered but dropped, in part because it seemed politically unwise to give votes to people who did not have to pay taxes. Others indicate that it does not do enough to preserve the Hungarian identities of those outside of Hungary.[38]

Hungarian officials and experts explain the law as driven by two interests: the desire for the Fidesz party to focus on nationalist issues; and the general preference on the part of Hungarian citizens to keep Hungarians in the near abroad where they are.[39] First, despite its initial opposition to nationalist causes, Fidesz rose to power, in part by taking votes away from other parties on the right, including the nationalist Smallholders party. By introducing this legislation, Fidesz was trying to cement its credentials to an important part of its constituency (Kingston 2001). In addition, in part, Fidesz may have been trying to ride the rising wave of opposition to globalization, which might include European-imposed nationality policies.[40]

Second, a variety of officials cited a brain drain occurring—that Hungarian intellectuals, politicians, priests, and other leaders in Slovakia and Romania (and perhaps elsewhere to a lesser extent) were emigrating to Hungary.[41] This is bad for two reasons. One, it would leave the Hungarian communities in the neighbors leaderless, and, therefore, more likely to be radicalized.[42] This would only cause more problems for the Hungarians, for Hungary, and for incumbent politicians in Hungary. Two, Hungarian citizens would prefer less immigration, not more, even by Hungarians (Csepeli and Örkény 1996, 267–270). Hungary has supported Hungarian language institutions of higher education in Romania so that ethnic Hungarians would "stay put."[43] Apparently, the law has worked, as polls have indicated that one quarter of the Hungarians abroad wanted to immigrate to Hungary before the Status Law, but afterward only twelve percent still want to immigrate.[44] Thus, the Status Law could be considered an "Immigration Prevention Act."[45]

The Status Law, like other initiatives, did not have a huge material impact, but did seem to be enough both to appeal to the Hungarians abroad and to anger the neighbors. Indeed, more than one analyst considers it to have shaped the Hungarian sense of nation—centered on ethnicity as opposed to citizenship (Bárdi 2003, 137). It again showed that the Fidesz party was more interested in one pillar of Hungarian foreign policy—the condition of the kin abroad—than in good neighborly relations, while the Socialists were more focused on integration. This pattern reoccurred recently during a referendum over dual citizenship.

Dual Citizenship: A Referendum

On December 5, 2004, Hungary held a referendum to consider dual citizenship for Hungarians outside of the country. The question was:

> Do you think parliament should pass a law allowing Hungarian citizenship with preferential naturalization to be granted to those, at their request, who claim to have Hungarian nationality, do not live in Hungary and are not Hungarian citizens, and who prove their Hungarian nationality by means of a "Hungarian Identity Card" issued pursuant to article 19 of Act LXII/2001 or in another way to be determined by the law which is to be passed?

This was highly controversial both within Hungary and outside of it, and the timing was particularly problematic as it occurred during Romania's elections. References during the campaign to a "unitary Hungarian nation" did little to assuage the neighbors about Hungary's nonirredentist intentions. This form of dual citizenship is distinct from that practiced by immigrant states, giving rights to those abroad while allowing them to continue to enjoy the citizenship rights of the country in which they reside, as opposed to easing naturalization processes (Iordachi 2004).[46] Thus, if approved, it might have meant that as many as 3.5 million Hungarians outside of the country could become citizens of Hungary without changing residency.

To be clear, the petition for this referendum was not organized by the government, but by the World Federation of Hungarians.[47] This nongovernmental organization gained the necessary signatures (200,000) to have a referendum. While the majority of voters (51.6 percent) supported dual citizenship, they fell short of the necessary 25 percent of registered voters, so the referendum failed.

The referendum is interesting and relevant here because of its timing and the positions played by the competing parties. First, this effort took place shortly after Hungary was admitted to the European Union. While the EU ultimately ruled that Hungary's referendum was not in violation of EU regulations, it hardly seems coincidental that major players in Hungary are advocating energetically for more assertive steps now that Hungary is inside the EU. One of the major limitations of conditionality is that countries will be less restrained once they are members of the desired institution.

Second, the two major parties took opposite stands on this issue, with the Fidesz party predictably supporting the referendum and the Socialists, the incumbents, opposing it. This makes sense for a few reasons. If enacted, the new dual citizens were likely to vote Fidesz,[48] giving Orban's party a significant advantage in future elections. Whether it passed or failed, it gave Fidesz the opportunity to prove that it was the more nationalist party. While this was rather obvious, this event still gave Orban and Fidesz a chance to criticize the government and the Socialist Party. One notable example of Orban's rhetoric at this time is:

> The invitations to the December 5th wedding were sent 84 years ago. *Recreating a 15 million-strong nation from a country of 10 million is a historic deed.* Fifty years from now, this decision will be spelled out in capital letters in the history books, and our descendants will know *what kind of Hungarians* we were.[49]

Indeed, this statement renders the "Hungarians do not imagine irredentism" line moot, as Orban is clearly referring to a Hungary that is larger than its current boundaries.

This proposal put the Socialists into an awkward position, because dual citizenship would have weakened them in future elections against Fidesz as well as antagonizing the neighbors, yet opposing the referendum made them appear to be less caring about the kin abroad. As in the case of the Office of Hungarian Abroad and the Status Law, the Socialists were clearly less enthusiastic about the nationalism project than Fidesz. Because the new dual citizens were more likely to be Fidesz voters, the Socialists ultimately and successfully led the opposition to the referendum, calling for a boycott, so that the results would not count.

Most interestingly, the Socialists could not argue that the referendum was bad for their party because that would appear too cynical—to emphasize the pursuit of office at the expense of the kin. Instead, Prime Minister Ferenc

Gyurcsany, leader of the Socialists, argued that dual citizenship would increase the flow of Hungarians from other countries into Hungary, dramatically increasing the costs of social welfare programs.[50] Either apathy reigned or this argument was strong enough to keep enough voters home so that the referendum failed to reach the necessary level of participation.

Just as the Status Law seemed to be an Immigration Prevention Act that lost popularity once it threatened to increase Romanian immigration, the dual-citizenship referendum lost popularity as the Socialists articulated its possible impact on immigration. This is quite suggestive. Perhaps irredentism in its most forceful forms is less desirable because it is not only likely to cause Hungary to incur significant international costs, but also would increase the flow of Hungarians from abroad, something that Hungarians within Hungary have consistently sought to avoid. "Hungarians from all points on the political spectrum agree that the state should not promote the resettlement of ethnic Hungarians in Hungary" (Brubaker 1998, 1055).

Finally, the desire among Hungarians in Hungary to maintain their own influence may have also played a role in their opposition. If passed, the referendum and its subsequent implementation would mean that millions of Hungarians abroad would be able to vote in Hungary's elections. The addition of so many nonresident voters would potentially weaken the influence of Hungarians within the country, giving votes to those who do not pay taxes (Csergo and Goldgeier 2001) and potentially altering the party system (Kovács 2005).

These five instances—Antall's rhetoric, the OHMA, the Bilateral Treaties, the Status Law, and the dual-citizenship referendum—demonstrate that Hungary cares about the kin abroad, but that this interest varies among Hungary's parties and competes with other foreign policy priorities. As a result, Hungary seems to push enough to upset the neighbors but not enough to change significantly the lives of the Hungarians abroad. Indeed, Hungarian politicians of nearly all stripes seem to be balancing on a razor's edge—to do enough to satisfy the domestic audience but not enough to anger them for misplaced priorities. Hungary is notable for having pushed the envelope but yet refraining from irredentism. Before applying our theory to this case, we consider the conventional wisdom—that Hungary moderated its foreign policy in response to international pressures, and particularly owing to its desire to join the European Union and the North Atlantic Treaty Organization.[51]

The International Community Made Me Do It

To be clear, the international community, particularly NATO and the EU, have played a tremendous role in Hungary's thinking. There is no doubt that Hungary's decisions are shaped with the reactions of NATO and the EU in mind.[52] Hungarian leaders definitely felt pressured to sign bilateral treaties with its neighbors, particularly Romania and Slovakia. Likewise, Hungary went to great lengths to revise the Status Law once it was required by the Venice Commission. However, it is Hungary's eagerness to join these institutions that needs some explaining, particularly because Hungary seems most willing to defy institutions once it is a member. Our claim here is that the causal argument has been reversed—it is not that the international community pressures Hungary, but that Hungarian elites have seen international institutions as tools to further Hungarian interests, including handling their kin problems. For instance, Hungary supported the creation of the High Commissioner for National Minorities (Oltay 1992b, 32), seeing it as an instrument for improving the kin's condition in the neighbors. Below, we consider the timing of Hungarian interest in these institutions, and then examine how these institutions fit into Hungary's strategies for handling its kin problem.

To understand the relationship between regional institutions and Hungary, it is important to note that Hungary's interest in NATO, EU, and other organizations significantly preceded the decisions to enlarge these institutions. Hungary first declared interest in joining NATO in 1990, at a time when the Warsaw Pact and the Soviet Union still existed (Valki 1999), causing more than a few ripples in Europe. At this time and for a while afterward, NATO did not foresee expansion to Eastern Europe, agreeing that enlargement was possible only in 1994 and announcing criteria and membership processes in 1995. Similarly, Hungary was the first East European country to apply to the European Union for association status in 1991 and then membership in 1994 (Böröcz 2000). Hungarian leaders, despite varying in enthusiasm, all saw the regional institutions as critical to Hungary's future. Interestingly, enthusiasm for these institutions has varied among the parties, with Fidesz less interested although still committed than the Socialists (Dauderstädt and Joerissen 2004). Interest in these institutions came before enlargement was seen as likely, and this needs to be explained, not just assumed.

While these institutions provide members with many benefits, Hungarian elites saw NATO, the EU, and others as means to a particular end—improving the condition of the kin in neighboring countries. Indeed, even before membership was likely, Hungary sought to use existing international organizations to manage the problem of minorities abroad (Oltay 1992a). Rather than a constraint on Hungary, NATO (and, by extension, the EU) was seen as an "opportunity to assert national interests" not unlike Greece's efforts with regard to Macedonia (Carpenter and Kislitsyn 1997, 10).

Hungary has sought several strategies to use these institutions to help the Hungarians in the neighboring countries. First, while forced by NATO and the EU to sign bilateral treaties with the neighbors, Hungary realized that these neighbors were also under the same pressure, so much effort was given to including minority protection clauses in these agreements. Slovakia and Romania eventually signed these treaties with such clauses, though they were ultimately watered down and then substantially ignored. Second, during the process of writing the European Union's new constitution, Hungary tried hard to insert clauses that would guarantee collective minority rights.[53] Ultimately, Hungary failed in this effort, largely owing to the resistance of the major powers in Europe, which have their own minority problems. Still, Hungarian politicians have used to try to handle the kin issue through these institutions. Third, because Hungary attained membership in both institutions before Romania, it gained some leverage, although not much, over whether Romania could join. An early example of this strategy was Hungary's abstaining from the vote to admit Romania to the Council of Europe (Oltay 1992a, 19). As early as 1996, Viktor Orbán, leader of Fidesz, advocated the tying of Hungary's support of the accession of neighbors to the condition of Hungarians abroad (Bardai 2003, 132). Later, Hungarian politicians had hoped to use their relative advantage within NATO to negotiate acceptance of the Status Law (Ieda 2004, 39–40).

Hungary has been reluctant to use this weapon because membership of the kin's host countries is seen as a net good. Indeed, one of the principal benefits of NATO and EU expansion, in Hungarian eyes, is that the condition of the Hungarians in the neighboring countries will improve.[54] There is the sense that joint membership in the EU would mean greater constraints upon public policy, and thus less discrimination, in the neighboring countries.[55] As more policy is driven by decision makers in Brussels, Strasbourg, and Luxembourg,[56] Hungarians across Eastern Europe will receive fairer treatment, according to this belief.[57] Hungarians also view mutual prosperity arising from integration as likely to improve the circumstances of the Hungarians abroad, since it reduces the appeal of anti-Hungarian nationalists.

Joint membership would also mean the free flow of peoples, so that travel to see relatives would no longer be an issue.[58] In fact, Hungarians believe that pressures for Hungarians abroad to immigrate would decline. As borders become less relevant, there is less need to move.

The point of this section is not to say that conditionality does not matter, but rather to help to explain why Hungarians opted for membership in the first place, thus giving the various conditions some bite. Rather than a force or an imperative pushing Hungarian foreign policy, membership in NATO and the EU is seen as a tool to advance Hungary's foreign policy priorities, including the improvement of the kin's situations in and outside of these institutions. This has ramifications not only for the relevance of international institutions but also for how and when they are relevant.

Xenophobia and the Limits of Hungarian Foreign Policy

For any study of irredentism, Hungary is an interesting case because there is a strong interest in the condition of the kin abroad and because there is still a lingering grievance about the Treaty of Trianon as an injustice. In one poll, 84 percent of Hungarians viewed the Treaty of Trianon as a bad decision (Csepeli 1997, 194). In another, 68 percent of Hungarians surveyed indicated that there were parts of neighboring countries that they felt belonged to Hungary, highest in Eastern Europe (Miklenberg 2002, 345). Given this widespread sentiment, it is significant that Hungarian politicians have taken positions that are simultaneously less than aggressive but more than apathetic and that seem to suffice to satisfy the domestic audience but antagonize the neighbors. We can make sense of these contradictions by first examining the content of modern Hungarian nationalism, then by considering the dynamics of party politics since the end of the Cold War.

Understanding the Meaning of "Hungarian"

As we discussed in chapter 1, identity marks who is us and who is them. While there are many dimensions of this distinction, two are most important here. The nationalist identity, or the content of the nationalism, determines who is the us and who is the them; and the degree of tolerance of the other. Determining what is meant by Hungarian is not just an academic question, but was the focus of much discussion, particularly during the passage of the Status Law.

For Hungarians inside of Hungary, those outside of the country now are identified as simultaneously us and them. They are kin and they matter, but they are not completely us. "The minority Hungarians are indeed Hungarian, but not in the same way as those in Hungary. . . . Their definition of what it means to be Hungarian will be subtly or not so subtly different from Hungary's" (Schöpflin 2004, 103). This attitude seems to be the product of a distinct break between Hungarians that endured post-1956 Hungary and those that did not.[59] Those who did not endure the post 1956-uprising repression in Hungry are not viewed as being identical in salience as Hungarians who did. Survey evidence supports this: Hungarians in Hungary tend to define birth in Hungary as the key condition for defining who is Hungarian (Behr et al. 2002).[60] Thus, the borders between Hungary and its neighbors, and the shared experience of those within Hungary after 1956, have modified what is meant by Hungarian.[61] Hungarian identity is not just about language, but sharing a common experience. Those who did not have the same experience do not count as much.

There is a second key dimension in Hungarian identity—its exclusivity. Indeed, in one study of Hungarian nationalism, a key component was "national closedness" (Todosijevic 2001). Where Hungary was once a dominant part of a multiethnic empire, it is now perhaps the most homogeneous country in Eastern Europe. Rather than tolerate diversity, Hungarians seem to value their homogeneity.[62] Indeed, Csepeli and Örkény (2000, 377) assert that the basis of Hungarian identity is more of alienation than of pride, leading to fears of extinction and, thus, intolerance of others. Surveys consistently show strongly negative attitudes toward immigrants, even those of Hungarian descent.[63] To be clear, attitudes are distinct—while there is ambivalence about immigrants of Hungarian descent, there is strong opposition to the possibility of non-Hungarian immigrants (Behr et al. 2002, 295; Szántay and Velladics 1995). Figure 4.2 illustrates these two dimensions of Hungarian identity.

Equation A illustrates that Hungarians in Hungary $[H_H]$ prefer themselves to all others, and then prefer Hungarians outside of Hungary $[H_O]$ to Romanians $[R]$. Romanians are clearly not Hungarians—they are the "them" that Hungarians use to help define who is "us." However, this preference ordering does not contain any sense of the relative intensity of feelings about each of these groups. So, if on a scale of ten to negative ten, one could easily

A: $H_H > H_O > R$

B: $|H_H| > |R| > |H_O|$

FIGURE 4.2.   Hungary, Its Kin, and Its Neighbors

imagine that Hungary's Hungarians consider themselves a ten. They feel kinship but not complete identification with the kin, so one could imagine the Hungarians outside as receiving a six or perhaps a seven.[64] Hungarians in Hungary would probably rank Romanians with a highly negative number, such as -8 or -9, because of their history of conflict and as the representation of the "them" or "the other." In polls, Hungarians report highly unfavorable attitudes Romanians, only topped by their views toward Roma (Nelson 1998, 315). If one considers the magnitude of the attitudes—how strongly do the Hungarians feel—toward kin and non-kin in the neighboring states, as equation B illustrates with the ranking of absolute values, then Hungarians prioritize themselves first, the non-kin second, and then their kin abroad third. This has profound implications for any potential irredentism.

Any effort to change international boundaries would increase the non-Hungarian population of Hungary (barring ethnic cleansing to the point of genocide), and this is anathema. One of the more consistent opinions voiced during interviews was that irredentism was unthinkable for the changes it would make to Hungary's demographic balance. Trying to regain Transylvania would lead to the inclusion of 2.5 to 6 million Romanians in Hungary.[65] Even Hungarians in Romania are aware of the consequences: "To kill Hungary, give it Transylvania."[66] This opinion is not just a product of a few interviews,[67] for the Socialists were able to capitalize politically on the possibility that changes in the Status Law would increase the number of Romanians visiting or moving to Hungary. Even members of the diaspora who seek more assertive Hungarian foreign policies acknowledge that irredentism is not in the cards, since it would create a large minority within Hungary: "Not a real estate problem."[68] As a result, "Nearly all politicians realize that they will lose support if they pursue irredentism."[69]

Obviously, Hungarians do not have identical preferences. The different parties seem to be composed of individuals with varying priorities. The two most significant parties for much of the period were Fidesz and the Socialists.

Hungarian Politics

The behavior of the two leading parties indicates that there is a basic ambivalence in Hungary about competing priorities—good neighborly relations, the Hungarian diaspora, and integration into European institutions.[70] Any effort to help the diaspora risks good neighborly relations, and, that, in turn, would raise alarms about membership until, of course, Hungary became a member of both NATO and the EU. Over the course of the past fifteen years, the conservative parties, the MDF and now Fidesz, have consistently valued the Hungarians in the neighboring countries more than the Socialists do. The center-right parties have launched a series of policies aimed at helping the kin, and perhaps even "'the reunification of the nation,'" in the words of one Fidesz official.[71] The Socialists have consistently reminded Hungarians of the costs that these policies will impose on those within the country. As of late, the Socialists have had the winning argument, as represented by both the 2002 election and the 2004 referendum.[72]

Fidesz[73] started out as a non- or antinationalist liberal party. Over time, it moved across the center and to the right, seeking to replace the MDF (Haraszti 1998; Kiss 2002; Waterbury 2006). It is now the biggest party on the right, governing from 1998 to 2002. Three key dynamics help to explain Fidesz's strategies and policies over the past decade: the requirements of office seeking; constituencies that are less enthusiastic about economic integration; and personal ties.

First, moving from left to right over time, Fidesz has sought to become the representative of conservative voters. Indeed, its early history may have pushed Fidesz to be more nationalist than it would have otherwise needed to be. Its origins raised doubts about the sincerity of its nationalism—it was actually anti-nationalist with the party walking out of Parliament during a session on the Treaty of Trianon (Kiss 2002). So, Fidesz needed to compensate and become more assertive as it sought votes from the right side of the spectrum (Toka 2004).[74] While conservative voters care about many issues, one of the salient topics has been the condition of the Hungarians abroad. In assessing its stand on the Status Law, Kingston asserts, "Fidesz's motivation is clear. By urging passage of the law it is clearly targeting, on one hand, the disillusioned electorate from the camp of the disintegrated Independent Smallholders' Party (FKGP), and, on the other hand, the less radical elements of the ultra-right Hungarian Justice and Life Party (MIEP)." In this, Fidesz has been successful, gaining more votes in 2002 (41.1 percent), than it did in 1998 (29.5

percent), at the expense of the other ones. The Independent Smallholders received 13.1 percent in 1998 and .75 percent in 2002. MIEP went from 5.5 percent and fourteen seats in parliament in 1998 to 4.4 percent and zero seats. Shafir (2004, 3) summarizes the role of nationalism in Fidesz's party-building strategy "in terms of sheer political opportunism."

Second, Fidesz has been less enthusiastic about integration than the other parties. One explanation for this is that key constituencies included small business owners and Hungarians outside of Budapest. Small businesses are at significant risk in an integrated economy, fearing foreign multinational corporations. Likewise, Fidesz was also able to take advantage of the split between Budapest and the provinces, appealing to those who feared foreign capital and values (Shafir 2004). In addition, when in government, Fidesz relied on a coalition with the Smallholders Party, which is largely agrarian and hostile to foreign capital. The importance of this constituency became apparent as Fidesz turned against globalization during the last campaign, despite also relying on those who prefer integration.[75]

Third, of the major parties, Fidesz has the closest ties to the Hungarians abroad. Its elites have a direct interest in the condition of the kin, not only because they travel to these areas more than other parties,[76] but also because they have relationships with people who are from there.[77] "The party apparatus of Fidesz involved the greatest number of persons coming or descending form beyond the borders or having personal relations with Hungarians living beyond the borders" (Bárdi 2003). Thus, there are quite direct interests in the kin abroad, since they are actually kin.

Ironies abound when it comes to Fidesz. Starting out as one of the most antinationalist parties, it is clearly the most nationalist mainstream party, as it legislated the Status Law and supported the dual-citizenship referendum. It rose to power in the ashes of the MDF party, which was, in part, done in by its focus on the Hungarians abroad, only to lose an election in 2002 in part because of the implications of the Status Law. Perhaps most ironically, despite being a nationalist party or perhaps because of it, Fidesz has actually ceded some of the xenophobia vote to the Socialists.

The Socialists: Better Xenophobes Than the Nationalists

To be clear, the priority of the Socialist Party is not xenophobia but rather the economy. As the former Communist Party, the Socialists faced much suspicion. They were able to reform themselves in large part by pushing for a reformed, modernized, integrated economy. Focusing on becoming part of the European Union has made the Socialists appear to be a modern party that appealed beyond the traditional working class audience to those benefiting from the new capitalist economy. While some former communist parties tried to delay reform and used nationalism as a substitute, the Hungarian Socialists became proreform and antinationalist (Bozóki 2002, 90).[78] Ultimately, three factors shaped how the Socialists reacted to the dynamics of political competition in the aftermath of communism: the nature of their new constituency, rivalry with the right wing, and opportunities to create wedges between Fidesz and the median Hungarian voter.

First, as the Socialists changed their identity, they developed a broader view of who their audience was. They expanded beyond the urban working classes to other city-dwellers—particularly middle-class and young voters. As a result of the difficulties of the first few years after communism under the conservative MDF, the Socialists were able to appeal on the basis of expertise—that they had experience in running the economy—and thus expanded their appeal to technocrats (O'Neil 1998).[79] The Socialists defined themselves as pragmatists, particularly when compared with the Antall government. The 1994 election proved the Socialists correct in their strategy—that their supporters had more at stake in European integration than in the kin in the neighboring countries (Shafir 2004; Csepeli and Örkény 1996, 271).

Second, the Socialists considered themselves to be the bulwark against the radical right. This was not only consistent ideologically, but also made strategic sense as concentration of the left under the Socialists would be the best defense against the right (Bozóki 2002, 100). Just as the Fidesz took advantage of the fractionalized conservative vote, the Socialists sought to concentrate the left side of the spectrum, and the best way to do that was to oppose MDF and, later, Fidesz. This meant trying to deny the right-wing parties the gains from nationalist positions—always identifying their costs, even as the Socialists voted for the Status Law.

This leads to the third dynamic driving Socialist behavior—the opportunity to use xenophobia to undermine Fidesz's nationalist appeals. The Status Law and Dual Referendum debates both revealed a willingness on the part of the Socialists to play to baser fears among Hungarians. Once the Status Law was reformed according to EU demands, it raised the possibility that more Romanians might immigrate. The Socialists used this prospect in the 2002 election, helping to turn the polls.[80] Similarly, during the dual-citizenship referendum campaign, the Socialists not only sought a boycott but also argued that the referendum was problematic precisely because it would lead to more immigration. This produced a key irony in Hungarian politics, with the left stressing, essentially, xenophobia to counter the nationalist appeal of the right.[81]

The differences between Fidesz and the Socialist Party illustrate the complicated dimensions of national identity. Fidesz (and the MDF before it) cares more about those sharing ethnic ties—about the "us" that is outside the border. The Socialists focus on the tolerance of the "other" or lack thereof. In the Hungarian case, these two aspects of nationalism push in opposite directions, and neither party can ignore either aspect. Thus, both parties are, ultimately, ambivalent. They both care about the kin and seek to prevent immigration, but Fidesz emphasizes the kin and the Socialists stress the costs of these policies in the form of immigration.

Assessing the Arguments

Before concluding, we need to examine the various arguments presented earlier in the book and see how they apply to the case of Hungary. Some have already been addressed extensively, while others need to be discussed briefly here.

This case provides confirming evidence for several arguments but raises questions about others. Hungary did not aggress across international boundaries, giving some support to the idea that boundary norms might constrain states. Likewise, Hungary's history of failed irredentism, cited in some interviews, also may have deterred aggressive efforts in the 1990s. Two other arguments we seek to challenge find less support here—the impact of international institutions and the role of relative power. We discussed extensively how Hungary's interests in NATO and the European Union preceded their interest in expansion and how Hungary's assertiveness increased as membership approached.

We have not discussed the role of relative power until now. Was Hungary deterred by its own weakness? Perhaps, but the problem is that the conventional measurements of power indicate that while Hungary was consistently weaker than Romania in the 1990s, it was also stronger than Slovakia, especially early on.[82] While Hungary's relative power compared to Serbia varied between somewhat stronger and somewhat weaker, Hungary could have

TABLE 4.1   Hypotheses and Hungary

	Hypothesis	
1:	Interstate boundaries limit irredentism	Confirmed: No aggression across international boundaries
2:	Admissions processes limit irredentism	Mixed: Moderation both before and after admissions processes developed; increasing assertiveness as and after membership is granted
3:	States will be deterred by stronger targets	Mixed: Hungary was weaker than Romania but stronger than Slovakia
4:	History of irredentism	Confirmed: World War II was negative experience
5:	Tolerance of homogeneity/ xenophobia	Confirmed: Constituents were intolerant of diversity
6:	Economics/irredentist interests	Confirmed: Variation in support for kin covaried with parties with differing interests in international integration, and general interest in integration constrained foreign policy
7a:	Actively irredentist kin	Confirmed: No kin were actively irredentist
7b:	Danger	Mixed: Kin faced significant discrimination in Romania and Slovakia and some danger in Serbia and early in Romania
7c:	Kin in positions of power	Confirmed: Kin largely absent from power, but did receive more support when a party with greater connections was in power

taken advantage of Serbia's poor strategic situation but did not.[83] Serbia was bogged down early on in Croatia, then Bosnia, and then Kosovo, and quite isolated throughout the decade due to its activities in all three, so Hungary could have acted aggressively then. Instead, Hungary became most interested and active in the plight of the Hungarians in Vojvodina after the Kosovo war, when Serbia's forces were more concentrated. Thus, Hungary's behavior does not correlate with the opportunities and constraints presented by the regional balance of power.

Some aspects of the kin abroad seem to matter more consistently in this case than others. Danger is not one of them, as the kin facing the greatest risks—those in Serbia—received the least attention, counter to what we might have expected. Moreover, some of the most serious efforts made by Hungary on behalf of the kin abroad were precisely at the times when they faced the lowest risks—the late 1990s and early 2000s when Hungary parties in Romania and Slovakia held significant political power. The hypothesis concerning the kin's activity is supported; the lack of serious irredentist movements abroad might have made it harder for Hungary to engage in irredentism, since there was no one seeking rescue. The relationship between country and kin here is somewhat tense, inasmuch as there was much attention and influence exerted from Budapest, but not always to the liking of the co-ethnics in the neighboring states. In some important ways, the kin abroad are seen as an object of Hungary's politics, similar but not identical to the role played by the Serbs outside of Serbia. The kin had relatively little influence in Hungary, although Fidesz seems to be better connected.

Finally, the key claims developed in chapter 1 receive support here, for Hungary's varying efforts to address their kin can be explained by the interaction between economic interests and identity. The parties varied in how much they cared about integrating into the European and international economies, and they varied in which aspects of Hungarian nationalism they emphasized the most. Fidesz and its predecessors stressed ethnic Hungarian unity, while the Socialists focused on the consequences of various policies that might lead to more immigration, underscoring the xenophobia that exists within Hungarian nationalism.

Conclusion: Ambivalent Assertiveness

"Hungary will do as much as it can get away with; or as much until it costs."[84] So what explains this paradox—assertive yet cautious foreign policies, varying over time, and often failing to accomplish the goals yet expending a fair amount of political capital? The answers have much to do with the complexity of Hungarian nationalism and how they play out in the political system.

Hungarians in Hungary clearly care about the kin in the neighboring countries, but do not identify with them as completely as they identify with those within Hungary. The strong attitudes against immigration, even by Hungarians from abroad, are quite striking, particularly as the population of Hungary itself declines. Irredentism is not desirable because of two dimensions of Hungarian xenophobia: Hungarians certainly do not want to include Romanians and Slovaks in Hungary, and they are not so attached to their kin abroad as to consider possible remedies to the first issue. That is, to say that xenophobic attitudes toward the Romanians would deter irredentism is to beg the question of why Hungary would not simply clean the gained territory of non-Hungarians. While there are many issues involved in this, a critical one is simply that the Hungarians do not care enough about their kin to engage in such policies.

Thus, irredentism is off the table, but Hungary's politicians cannot ignore the kin's situation without facing criticism. However, elites must also be wary not to pay too much attention to the kin or else they may lose their positions, as we saw in 1994. Fidesz, with its balance of conservative voters, must address these issues more directly, but risks losing votes and elections when its efforts go too far from the median Hungarian voter. Likewise, the Socialists can take a softer line, since their supporters are not quite as passionate about the kin abroad, but must avoid being tagged as traitors to the kin. Each party faces conflicting imperatives, although the mix is somewhat different. As a result, each party must spend a significant amount of its foreign policy attention on this issue, but the emphasis and style varies between the parties because they represent different constituencies.

Consequently, Hungary focuses considerable attention toward the kin, as one of three competing foreign policy priorities, along with integration and good relations with the neighbors. The balance changes, depending more on who is in power in Budapest than on who is in power in Bratislava (Slovakia), Bucharest (Romania), and Belgrade (Serbia). International organizations do matter, but rather than shaping and constraining Hungary, they are viewed more as a tool for advancing Hungarian interests, including the improvement of the kin's condition in the neighboring territories.

Notes to Chapter 4: Pushing the Envelope

1. Among the first things one sees upon entering the House of Terror, a museum in Budapest focused on the crimes of the Nazis and Communists who governed Hungary from the 1940s until 1989, is a video map showing Hungary contracting, growing, and contracting again through the first half of the twentieth century.

2. See Deets and Stroschein (2005) for analyses of how the Hungarians are treated.

3. Bárdi (2004) reviews the conditions of the different Hungarians abroad.

4. Chapter 5 discusses Romania's domestic politics in greater detail.

5. In interviews in Romania, it was always surprising how minimal the apparent policy victories seemed to be. Again, see chapter 5.

6. This concession is not supported wholeheartedly by the entire Hungarian community.

7. Interview with László Szarka, director of the Minority Studies Institute of the Hungarian Academy of Sciences, April 18, 2002, among others.

8. For an interesting argument explaining Hungarian mobilization or its absence in Vojvodina, see Jenne (2004).

9. In interviews, Hungarian officials reported some concern about the U.S. pushing Serbia too hard. Interviews with Sára Görömbei and Mária Gyetvai Pintér, both of OHMA's Department of Strategic Analysis, June 26, 2003.

10. Interview with Tóni Niculescu.

11. See, for instance, Nas (1996, 153). However, this may be a bargaining strategy, as it puts Hungary on the defensive. Interview with Zoltán Kántor, Teleki Lászlo Institute, Centre for Central European Studies, June 24, 2003.

12. Ambrosio (2001) looks at similar set of events, but comes to a different conclusion: that international pressures matter the most.

13. The differences among Hungarian government is one of degree, not magnitude, as indicated in an interview with Kinga Dal, vice president of the Government Office for Hungarian Minorities Abroad, April 17, 2002. Deputy State Secretary of Foreign Affairs Csaba Lörincz concurred in a separate interview that day.

14. Because Serbia is unlikely to join the EU anytime soon, the eventual entry of Hungary into the Schengen zone will make it harder for Hungarians in Serbia to gain entry to Hungary; they will need visas. As a result, the Hungarians of Vojvodina have received more attention lately. This is striking, since it seems to be the case that access to Hungary may be more important for gaining salience than one's plight. Or it may be the case that Hungary's elites feel that it is safe to consider their kin in Serbia now that the threat of their repression is diminished.

15. Summer 1990; different sources give conflicting accounts of the actual day.

16. President Antall, cited in Oltay (1992b, 27).

17. Cited in ibid., 28.

18. Interview with Zsolt Szerkeres, April 18, 2002.

19. Multiple interviewees argued that the diaspora is far more concerned with the Hungarians abroad than with Hungarians residing in Hungary.

20. Again, this is discussed later in this chapter, but is also addressed in chapter 5.

21. The first state secretary, Geza Entz, was originally from Transylvania (Oltay 1992b, 26).

22. Interview with Kinga Gal.

23. However, it should be noted that, as Hungarians are quick to point out, Romania has a similar office, addressed in chapter 5.

24. The office was recently closed.

25. Csurka's party is considered to be the most extreme politically relevant party, not only Hungarian nationalist but also anti-Semitic. It advocates the recovery of the pre-Trianon territories (Milkenberg 2002). For more on Csurka, his challenge to Antall and Antall's initial tolerance, see Szayna 1993 and Bigler 1996.

26. The text of 1201 is available at http://assembly.coe.int/Documents/Adopted Text/TA93/EREC1201.HTM.

27. Nelson (1998) cites personal communications and interviews with Hungarian officials. See Szilagyi 1996.

28. As noted in the next chapter, domestic dynamics within Romania made this treaty politically possible and even attractive, as the party representing the Hungarian minority became a key actor.

29. Chapter 5 addresses the roles of the Hungarian minority party and international pressures in Romanian domestic and foreign policy.

30. For a comprehensive analysis of the Status Law, see Kantor et al. (2004). For an intellectual defense of the law, see George Schöplfin's contribution to that volume.

31. Schengen borders refer to the lines delimiting EU and non-EU space. A central component of the European Union is to have almost no borders between members, but that also requires significant barriers separating members from nonmembers. To be clear, the new entrants to the EU would not be immediately included in the Schengen zone, but eventually would be. For some discussion of this, see Ieda (2004).

32. Austria was omitted due to early EU pressure.

33. Interview with Biró Gáspár.

34. Venice Commission (2004).

35. Deets (2006) examines the Status Law controversies in Hungary and at the EU, with implications for larger debates about minority rights and the role of kin states and the international community.

36. See Deets (2006); Deets and Stroschein (2005).

37. Interview with Mária Kovács, program director of the Nationalities Studies Program at Central European University, April 15, 2002.

38. Interview with László Szarka.

39. King (2005) does not quite say this, but his take generally is that the status law was aimed at regulating immigration.

40. Interview with Kyle Scott, political counsel, United States Embassy in Hungary, April 15, 2002.

41. Interviews with Csaba Lörincz and Biró Gáspár.

42. Interview with Csaba Lörincz.

43. "Budapest Wants Ethnic Hungarians in Romania to Stay Put," RFE/RL report, February 24, 2000. On the other hand, it may be the case that Hungarians want their kin to stay where they are at so that the "reach and breadth of the Hungarian nation" would not shrink (Waterbury 2006, 498).

44. Interview with Csaba Lörincz.

45. The interview with Deputy State Secretary Csaba Lörincz was particularly instructive on this point. See also Bárdai (2004), Behr et al. (2002), and Ieda (2004).

46. Iordachi (2004) goes on to note that this form of kinship dual citizenship has been practiced by Romania since 1991, initially aimed at Moldova.

47. The organization is named Magyarok Vilagszovetsege, which has been translated into English in different ways, including World Association of Hungarians. Kovács (2005) considers the process, and the role of the World Federation, quite clearly.

48. Reported in a number of interviews. This parallels the voting patterns of the Croats outside of Croatia—to vote for the nationalist, right-wing party.

49. Italics added. Daniel McLaughlin, "Hungary Divided on Extending Citizenship," *The Irish Times*, December 6, 2004.

50. On average, the Hungarians coming in from abroad are below the average income of those already residing in Hungary.

51. Another alternative argument is that the history of failed irredentism, particularly the experience of World War II, has caused Hungarians to give up the dream of a Greater Hungary. This view has been espoused by Sebestyen L. v. Gorka, executive director of the Centre for Euroatlantic Integration and Democracy, April 16, 2002; and Deputy State Secretary of Foreign Affairs Csaba Lörincz, interview on April 17, 2002. We return to this counterargument in chapter 7.

52. Indeed, this was apparent in nearly every interview over the course of two years.

53. Interview with Sára Görömbei and Mária Gyetvai Pintér. Some individual rights were included in the EU constitution, but collective rights were omitted.

54. This was asserted in multiple interviews in Budapest in 2002 and 2003, including Kinga Dal of the OHMA. See also Csergo and Goldgeier (2002). It is important to note that Hungarians are not as infatuated with the EU as other Eastern European countries (European Commission 1996).

55. Some Hungarian elites are aware that joint membership in the EU is not a panacea, since the EU has lower minority-rights standards than those applied to applicants. Interviews with Zoltán Kántor, Sára Görömbei, and Mária Gyetvai Pintér.

56. The European Parliament conducts its business in these three cities, the European Court of Justice is in Strasbourg, and the European Commission meets in Brussels.

57. We are suspicious about the eventual impact of European institutions, since implementation will still be conducted locally (Saideman and Ayres 2007).

58. This has led to a renewed focus on Hungarians in Vojvodina, since Serbia's membership is a very distant prospect. Interviews with Sára Görömbei and Mária Gyetvai Pintér.

59. Several interviews, April 2002, including with Arpad Szurgyi, director, Hungarian Defense Programs, Center for European Security (and former U.S. defense attaché to Hungary), and with Ferenc Kalmár.

60. Differences in attitudes among adults and teenagers support this. In 1995, adult Hungarians had significantly more negative views of the Hungarians immigrants from Romania than teenage Hungarians had, suggesting that the shared experience of post-1956 Hungary shaped attitudes; Csepeli and Örkény (2000, 391).

61. See Csepeli (1997) for a thorough examination of Hungarian identity.

62. Csergo (2003) discusses this view, going on to suggest that nationalism is much more complicated than this. However, for our question, this evolution toward increasing focus on the homogeneity within Hungary's boundaries is significant.

63. Csepeli (1997, 251–252); Behr et al. (2002, 295); Brubaker (1998, 1055); Enyedi, Fábián, and Sik (2004). See also Fox (2007), who finds that the economic consequences of labor migration produce resistance to Hungarians from Romania.

64. The point here is of illustration, not exact ranking.

65. Interviews with Aprad Szurgyi, Biró Gáspár, and Kinga Gal. Indeed, despite his many other policy failures, Ceausescu seemed to have developed a successful strategy, as he changed the demographics of the border lands, increasing the numbers of Romanians in formerly Hungarian areas (Nastase 2002, 58). We do not recommend forcefully changing the composition of territories, but this dynamic tells us where irredentism might be more or less likely.

66. Interview with Tóni Niculescu, executive vice president, Department for European Immigration, Executive Presidency of the Democratic Alliance of Hungarians in Romania (UDMR), May 14, 2004.

67. To be clear, the interviewees supporting this argument included past officials working at the Office of Hungarians Abroad as well as Arpad Szurgyi, a former U.S. defense attaché of Hungarian descent.

68. Interview with Zsolt Szerkeres.

69. Interview with Biró Gáspár.

70. For thorough discussions of the parties in Hungary, see Toka (2004). For a review of their differing stands on Hungarians abroad, see Bárdi (2003).

71. Zsolt Németh, who was secretary of state for foreign affairs in the Orbán government, as cited in Bárdi 2003.

72. To be fair, other issues and dynamics matter within Hungarian politics, but the issues discussed here are certainly salient.

73. For an extensive treatment of Fidesz's use of the Hungarians abroad and the Status Law as an effort to develop the party, see Waterbury (2006).

74. Ibid.

75. Interview with Kyle Scott.

76. Interview with Zoltán Kántor.

77. In one interview where the subject preferred to remain anonymous, I was told that Fidesz (Alliance of Young Democrats), the governing party of Hungary at the time, was more focused on Hungarians abroad because of these contacts.

78. Bozóki and Ishiyama (2002) consider two paths for the successor Communist parties—reformed and transmuted, with the Hungarian Socialists in the former category and the Socialist Party of Serbia in the latter.

79. In the time since we conducted our interviews (2002–2004), the Hungarian economy has declined significantly, and the Socialists have lost their credibility on economic performance, with their leadership even admitting that they lied to the public.

80. This was reported in several interviews and in Ieda (2004 n 142); Stewart (2004, 141); and Waterbury (2006, 510).

81. In the 2007 Quebec provincial election, a three-sided race developed between the separatist Parti Quebecois, the federalist Liberal Party, and a relatively new party, Action Democratique due Quebec, which successfully used xenophobic appeals. That nationalist and xenophobes could compete against each other is not unique to Hungary.

82. Using EUGene to develop a national capabilities index from Correlates of War data, we find that Hungary was less than half as strong as Romania but 20–25 percent more powerful than Slovakia.

83. During the relevant period of the early to late 1990s, the data codes Yugoslavia, which, after 1991 and before 2005, meant Serbia and Montenegro.

84. Anonymous interview, April 2002.

5

Romania's Restraint?

Avoiding the Worst Through Domestic Scapegoating

We will be everything we once were, and even more than that.
— GREATER ROMANIA PARTY MOTTO

R OMANIA HAS FOLLOWED A PEACEFUL COURSE in its foreign policy since the "revolution" of 1989. This is especially surprising for several reasons. First, compared to other countries in the region with the exception of Yugoslavia, Romania's transition from dictatorship to democracy was the most violent. While other communist leaders stepped aside in Eastern Europe, Nicolae Ceausescu lost power only after trying to repress the rising opposition, leading to blood in the streets and eventually his own execution. Even after the National Salvation Front (NSF) took power, force, including the use of miners to repress the opposition, continued to play a role. As recently as 1999, miners approached the city, threatening to use violence. Further, members of the former secret police apparatus, the Securitate, are still considered by many to be playing a significant role in the current political system (Tismaneanu 1997).

Second, of all the borders in Europe, the line dividing Romania and Moldova may be one of the least legitimate. The separation of these two territories is a legacy of the Molotov-Ribbentrop pact that ushered in World War II. Other parts of that treaty, including the absorption of Estonia, Latvia, and Lithuania into the Soviet Union, have been reversed, but the boundary between Romania and Moldova still stands. Third, there was much discussion of reunification in 1991 as Moldova became independent from the Soviet Union, but it did not occur. Still, one recurrent theme heard during interviews with Romanian elites in May 2004 was that unification was inevitable but need not be rushed.[1] Fourth, the second most successful party in the 2000 elections, at both the presidential and parliamentary levels, was the Greater Romania Party.[2] Its name signals an interest in irredentism, as does its slogan. Its leader, Corneliu Vadim Tudor, has consistently been one of the most vocal nationalists in Romania, and he received more than 30 percent of the vote in 2000, potentially a strong indicator of popular interest in irredentism.

Together, these dynamics suggest that irredentism is and has been a possibility, yet Romania's efforts have fallen short of even Hungary's relatively moderate interventions on behalf of their kin abroad. Thus, Romania presents an interesting puzzle, particularly as its path toward Euro-Atlantic integration has been significantly bumpier than Hungary's. In this chapter, we lay out the history of the lost territory and its relationship with Romania and the current relationships between Romania, Moldova, and Moldova's Romanian population.[3] We then consider Romania's behavior since the fall of the Ceausescu government. To explain the enigma of Romanian restraint, we compare the impact of international institutions and their membership processes to two important ethnopolitical dynamics within Romania: how the populations of Moldova fit into the identity of Romanians and the requirements of nationalist politics. We conclude with a review of the various explanations and how they perform in this case.

To preview, we find that the most important dynamic driving Romanian restraint is the presence of more important targets of nationalist politics than the lost Romanians in Moldova: the Hungarian and Roma populations within the country. To be a successful nationalist requires taking positions on domestic issues and groups internally challenging Romanian identity, not on foreign policy and not on Romanian-speakers abroad.

Romanians, Bessarabia, and Moldova

Romania gained much territory[4] in the aftermath of World War I, including Transylvania and Bessarabia, in what is still called the Great Unification. The addition of Transylvania was central to the previous chapter and to Hungary's potential irredentism. Bessarabia, which largely but not entirely coincides with modern Moldova, was added to modern Romania in 1918. This territory

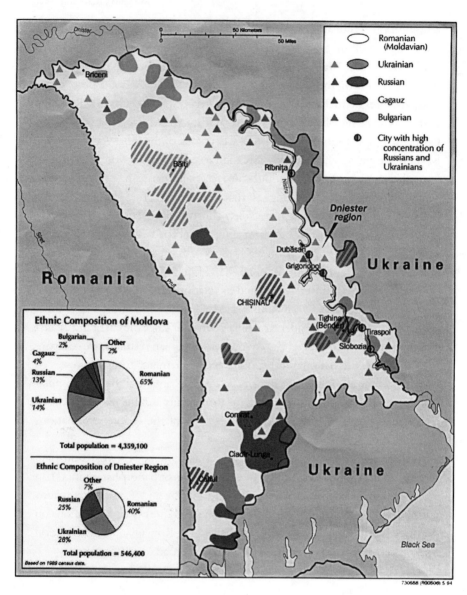

Romanian (Moldavian)
Ukrainian
Russian
Gagauz
Bulgarian
City with high concentration of Russians and Ukrainians

Dnister

Briceni

Bălți

Ribnița

Nistru

Dniester region

Dubăsari

Grigoriopol

Ukraine

Romania

Prut

CHIȘINĂU

Tighina (Bender)

Tiraspol

Slobozia

Comrat

Ciadîr-Lunga

Cahul

Ukraine

Black Sea

Ethnic Composition of Moldova

Bulgarian 2%
Other 2%
Gagauz 4%
Russian 13%
Ukrainian 14%
Romanian 65%

Total population = 4,359,100

Ethnic Composition of Dniester Region

Other 7%
Russian 25%
Romanian 40%
Ukrainian 28%

Total population = 546,400

Based on 1989 census data.

730588 (R00508) 5 94

FIGURE 5.1   Moldova's Ethnic Composition

was then administered by Romania until 1939, when Germany and the Soviet Union agreed to divide Eastern Europe, including Poland, the Baltics, and Romania—the Molotov-Ribbentrop pact. Bessarabia was then added to the Soviet Union as part of a federal unit—the Moldavian Soviet Socialist Republic, which incorporated most of Bessarabia (some portions were given to Ukraine) along with some additional territory, Transnistria (listed as Dniester region in figure 5.1)—where it remained until the disintegration of the Soviet Union in 1991.

As in the other republics of the Soviet Union, glasnost and perestroika led to an increased focus on identities and troubling examinations of the past. Throughout its time in the Soviet Union, Moldova's identity has been examined, revised, and challenged. Soviet leaders had sought to distance the territory and people from Romania, changing the script to Cyrillic. One of the first efforts by the Popular Front, the group leading the separatist effort in Moldova, aimed at changing the language again, back to a Latin script, bringing the language back to essentially Romanian at the end of August 1989.[5] As the Soviet Union was falling apart, Moldovan elites challenged the past and the status quo. One of the first steps taken included a renunciation of the Molotov-Ribbentrop pact. A second step was the assertion that Moldova was never in the Soviet Union due to its own will. This was part of the larger context of declaring independence, suggesting that this was an intermediate stage before reunion with Romania.

However, language laws and unification were only priorities for a minority of residents of Moldova. Moldovans of Romanian descent—somewhat more than 60 percent of the population—favored unification, but not overwhelmingly so. Russians, Ukrainians, Gagauz, and other minorities did not want be united with Romania.[6] Union would make them even smaller minorities in a state with a poor record of minority treatment (Kolstø 2000). As unification appeared increasingly possible, separatism within Moldova developed—even before the Soviet Union collapsed. Indeed, Crowther (1992, 248) asserts that "increased Romanian national consciousness and the issue of national reunification have been acutely destabilizing in the Moldavian political context."[7] In August 1990, the Gagauz declared their own independence, and then the Transnistrians did the same in September. This led to an outbreak of violence, with the Soviet/Russian Fourteenth Army playing a crucial role on the side of the Transnistrian rebels. Moldova's enthusiasm for unification declined. Ultimately, Mircea Snegur broke with the Popular Front in the

December 1991 presidential campaign, pushing for independence rather than unification, and won.

"The partner for reunification disappeared."[8] Irredentism became difficult for Romania, as the lost territory no longer wanted to be united. For much of the population of Moldova, they had no ties to Romania. Surveys show that only a small share of those of Romanian descent was interested in union (Crowther 1998, 153). Radical members of the Popular Front have continued their interest, but the rest have considered union not to be worth the trouble of extended conflict. The remaining population, largely Russophones in Transnistria and Bessarabia, along with the Gagauz, do not want to be part of Romania. Because the Russophones in Bessarabia are concentrated in the urban areas of Moldova, including Chisinau, the capital, a seemingly simple partition of Transnistria and Bessarabia, with the latter uniting with Romania, is still quite unpopular. Finally, Moldovan elites realized that union would lead to their irrelevancy (Crowther 1992; Kolstø 2000). Better to rule in Moldova than serve in Romania.

In 1994, this reality was recognized, as the Moldovan officials, including President Snegur, continued to consider the population as being largely Romanian and to favor the primacy of the Romanian language, but that the Republic of Moldova would remain independent. The 1994 election in Moldova was seen, in part, as a referendum on union, with the unionists losing quite badly (Crowther 1998). The consensus emerged that there would be two Romanian-speaking countries in Eastern Europe, just as there are two German-speaking countries in Central Europe—Germany and Austria (Roper 2000, 125).[9] This produced a lull in interest in unification in both countries and a period of relatively uncontested relations between the two, particularly as Moldova focused on settling the dispute with the Transnistria population (Kolstø 2000).

Tensions later escalated, coinciding with the communists coming back into power in Moldova in 2001. Romanian elites blame the new Moldovan government for its efforts to create a new Moldovan identity (or, rather to reaffirm the Soviet concept of Moldovan identity)[10]—one that asserts the distinctiveness of the Moldovan language, the history of Moldovan ties to Russia, and the denial of ties with Romania.[11] Indeed, protests in Chisinau—referred to as an identity crisis by Romanians—developed between 2001 and 2003, as a result of new language policies, including compulsory education in Russian. This has resulted in the contestation of even the two Romanian-speaking states' formulation.

This identity debate has raised Moldova's salience in Romania, as there are growing concerns that Romanian speakers in Moldova are being oppressed and that their identity is being challenged.[12] This produced an interesting irony in the region: despite the fact that Romania was first to recognize Moldova's independence, these two countries are among the last to sign a bilateral treaty.[13] Romania would like a bilateral treaty to recognize a special relationship between the two countries, whereas Moldova would prefer a simpler and more generic treaty, an ironic parallel to the Hungarian-Romanian negotiations.

The Moldovan governments have been increasingly opposed to union with Romania. At first, there seemed to be a genuine interest, which declined as conflict within Moldova increased. Over time, the status quo seemed to gain supporters, and, more recently, a government quite hostile to Romania has taken power. Vladimir Voronin, leader of Moldova's Communist Party and President of Moldova, has referred to Romania as Europe's last empire, even suggesting that Transylvania was part of this empire, due to collapse at some point.[14] Moldova has considered Romanian interest in Moldova to be unwarranted and illegitimate interference, not unlike the rhetoric that Romania has used to describe Hungary's interest in Romania's Hungarians. Since the end of the Cold War, these huge swings have shaped Romania's behavior and attitudes, but, overall, Romania has taken a far lower profile and has generally been less active in assisting its kin abroad than Hungary's efforts for the Hungarians abroad, despite some parallel efforts and institutions.

Romania: A Pale Imitation of Hungary?

While there are Romanians living in Bulgaria, Greece, Serbia, and Ukraine, the focus of this section is on Romania's relationship with Moldova, where the possibility of irredentism has been the greatest. When Moldova became independent in 1991, it seemed like a replay of 1918, where first the region became a state and then unified with Romania. Many saw independence again as a temporary stop along the road to Greater Romania. What is rather surprising is Romania's willingness to go with the flow—unification would have been nice, but once it was no longer a possibility, Romania did not pursue it. Even today, with much resentment toward the creation and enforcement of Moldavian identity to replace Romanian identification in Moldova, Romania largely sits on the sidelines, waiting for the inevitable day when unification finally occurs, rather than trying to make it happen.

At the outset of Moldovan independence, Romania expected unification. When the border was opened, citizens from both countries met along the "Bridge of Flowers," heralding a future union. President Iliescu even indicated that reunification was inevitable.[15] Romania was quick to recognize Moldova, as this was seen as the first step toward reunification. Indeed, President Iliescu was quick to point out that recognition did not mean the "renunciation of rights" due Romania as a result of the illegitimacy of the Molotov-Ribbentrop Pact. Foreign Minister Adrian Nastase suggested that reunification would follow the German model (Roper 2000, 124). Excitement quickly led to disappointment, particularly as elites in Moldova sought to emphasize a distinct identity—Moldovan rather than Romanian.

Yet, Romania's efforts toward Moldova have been a pale imitation of Hungary's efforts toward its kin abroad.[16] Romania has developed institutions and aid efforts that seem quite similar to Hungary's, and Moldova's accusations about Romania's interference are very similar to Romania's and Slovakia's criticisms of Hungary's behavior. Long before Hungary's dual-citizenship referendum, Romania passed a law on citizenship in 1991, allowing Romanians outside the country to apply. Ironically, what may have been intended as a path toward reunification may have ultimately undermined the irredentist cause by facilitating the movement of likely irredentists from Moldova to Romania (Iordachi 2004, 250).[17] Demand for Romanian citizenship became quite high in both Moldova and Ukraine, as a Romanian passport allowed access to the rest of Europe once Romanians were granted visa-free entry to the Schengen area.

Similar to the Office of Hungarians Abroad, Romania has a Department for the Romanians Living Abroad, which is situated within the Ministry of Foreign Affairs. However, it has not been as visible domestically or internationally as the Hungarian equivalent. It largely aims to help preserve Romanian culture outside of the country—providing school books, funding newspapers, and the like. It is notable that this office seems to be carrying out a mandate within the Romanian Constitution. Specifically, Article Seven states: "The State shall support the strengthening of links with the Romanians living abroad and shall act accordingly for the preservation, development and expression of their ethnic, cultural, linguistic and religious identity, under observance of the legislation of the State of which they are citizens." While the members of this office consider their efforts significant,[18] others have criticized their efforts as being inefficient and modest.[19]

More striking has been the failure of the two countries to reach a bilateral treaty. While Hungary, with a great deal of controversy and angst, was able to negotiate agreements with all of its neighbors, Romania and Moldova have failed to reach an accord. The first efforts focused on brotherhood and perhaps even integration, but these turned into drafts focusing on a special relationship. Romania wanted language referring to the illegitimacy of the Molotov-Ribbentrop pact, but eventually gave this condition up in 1997. Insistence on the treaty being drafted in Romanian prolonged the negotiations. Dual citizenship also was an issue—with Romanians favoring it.

The special relationship clause became the key bone of contention, with Moldova resisting, claiming that its minorities found it problematic.[20] The two presidents initialed a draft treaty in 2000, but Romania backed away, as it was rejected as giving too much away during an election year. Even a special relationship is now off the table as the latest Moldovan proposal is a more standard bilateral treaty and is, therefore, even more objectionable, as it gives Romania no role to play in Moldova.[21] Romania is now emphasizing the existence of two "Romanian" states and a future unity within an expanded EU.[22] Voronin's election and increased hostility, including the denial of two Romanian countries, have made progress on a bilateral treaty unlikely for the near future.

To further parallel Hungary, there has even been an effort to draft a Romanian status law, despite Romania's opposition to Hungary's legislation.[23] Just as Hungary was concerned about its kin if it were to join the European Union but its kin remained outside, Romania is now concerned about a future inside the EU but with Moldova and its Romanian population outside. Romania has considered legislation that would give it a role even after EU membership, just as Hungary did. Thus far, this legislation has not made it through the parliament, although a draft was submitted to the EU Commission for Democracy Through Law (the Venice Commission).[24]

Overall, Romania has been surprisingly patient in its actual policies even if the rhetoric gets overheated when it comes to the unification of the territory and population lost at the outset of World War II. While there is an expectation that unification will occur someday, there is very little effort to hasten the process. Romania's effort focuses on the maintenance of Romanian identity in Moldova, with significant resentment toward Moldova's attempts to create an alternative Moldavian identity. These policies are not only modest when compared to the irredentist attempts by Armenia, Croatia, and Serbia, but they are also quite underwhelming when compared to Hungary's more consistent and more brash efforts.

Explaining Restraint

Some of the explanations often used to understand Hungary's reluctance to engage in traditional irredentism may also apply to Romania while others clearly do not. Two key differences between Hungary and Romania are the legacies of past irredentist efforts and the level of democracy during the critical early post–Cold War years. As will become clear, these factors, advanced to explain Hungary's pacific foreign policies, cannot address Romania, so efforts to develop general explanations must look elsewhere. On the other hand, two other arguments may apply: Romania was loathe to violate international boundaries, and, more importantly, cared a great deal about integration into Euro-Atlantic institutions—namely, the European Union (EU) and the North Atlantic Treaty Organization (NATO). We spent more effort on the latter argument, as it is the most commonly given explanation of Romania's good behavior and because it has the most important policy implications if true.

As in the case of Hungary, these dynamics have mattered, but analysts largely assume away why politicians within Romania were able to focus on these priorities, rather than more parochial issues. By investigating the place of Moldova in Romanian identity and by focusing on the requisites for political competition, particularly the abundance of domestic targets for nationalist politicians, we can see how leaders have had greater latitude in foreign policy in general, particularly toward the lost territory of Moldova.

Democratic Restraints and Limiting Legacies

Before focusing on the more relevant accounts, we need to consider two arguments generally applied to the topic: the impact of democracy and of failed past efforts. Neither helps to explain Romania's restrained responses in the first part of the 1990s, when irredentism may have been most tempting and potentially feasible.

While some have argued that democracy does not deter irredentism (Saideman 1998), Linden (2000) argues that conditionality influenced the more democratic states of Eastern Europe. The key problem in using democracy to explain Romanian foreign policy is that neither democratic norms nor institutions were very binding in the first half of the 1990s. Romanians refer to the overthrow of Nicolae Ceausescu as a revolution, although many, particularly elites, acknowledge that it was largely a coup, where one set of elites replaced another, rather than a restructuring of society: "Many old faces remained in power while skillfully putting on new masks" (Tismaneanu 1997).[25] Ion Iliescu's National Salvation Front came to power after the coup and was legitimized by the elections of 1990 and 1992. However, neither these elections nor the regime's behavior indicated a deep belief in the rule of law and of institutionalized politics. Specifically, it is fairly clear that the regime mobilized aggrieved miners whenever they were needed to put down opposition through force. This occurred in June 1990 and September 1991 and was even attempted as late as July 1999.

Since the government could and did rely upon extraordinary means outside of the normal institutions to address dissent, it is unlikely that the mere existence of elections, of parties, and of a legislature restrained a more aggressive foreign policy. Instead, the events of the 1990s suggest that institutions really did not bind behavior, at least not until the first peaceful turnover of power in 1996. Even after that, there was a crisis in 1999 where the miners were once again bused, armed, liquored up, and sent to Bucharest. As late as 2004, there was much suspicion throughout the political system about nondemocratic means to be used to maintain the government in power.[26]

If one considers either liberal norms or representative institutions, Romania is on the very margins of European standards. It was particularly so in the early 1990s, where the behavior and attitudes of elites toward democratic contestation did not seem to be that different from those of Serbia.[27] Further, popular support for democracy may be relatively weak, if one considers how well the Greater Romania Party (with clearly authoritarian tendencies) did in the 2000 election, gaining more than 20 percent of the seats and more than 30 percent of the vote in the presidential election. It may be the case that this was a protest vote against the other parties, but it still suggests significant support for nationalist positions, authoritarian policies or both.

The second argument from the Hungarian experience is that failed efforts in the past have delegitimated irredentism in the present. It has been asserted that Hungary was chastened by its failed irredentism, but this is not a shared experience. In the twentieth century, war was generally good for Romanian unification. World War I led directly to a tremendous increase in the territory belonging to Romania, largely at Hungary's expense. Bessarabia/Moldova became independent, too, and then joined with Romania. The end of World War II led to the restoration of territory lost at its outset, with only Moldova remaining to be unified. In a series of interviews with Romanian elites, not one subject mentioned the past as presenting lessons that deterred post–Cold War irredentism.[28]

While German and Hungarian failures may have discredited irredentism, efforts elsewhere in the world (see chapters 2, 3, and 7) suggest that history does not handcuff the future. Even Germany's past failures did not stop re-unification, although that project started and ended with East Germany with no effort to bring in other German-speaking territories (namely Austria). Thus, either Hungary alone is restrained by its past, or other dynamics explain both Hungary's reticence and Romania's.

Joining the Club?

"Many of the encouraging trends in recent years . . . are directly related to the pressure exerted by the European Union and its affiliated organizations on the political elites of the new democracies" (Tismaneanu 2002, 81).[29] A deep desire to join key regional institutions is a shared feature of modern Hungarian and Romanian politics. NATO agreed in 2002 to admit Romania and formal accession occurred in April 2004, fulfilling a major foreign policy objective. The EU is a very visible presence in Bucharest, with its flag hanging on many government buildings, and the political discourse focusing on whether membership would be achieved in 2007 or after.[30] There is no doubt that achieving EU membership has been perhaps the most important foreign policy priority,[31] and that the polls show more support for EU membership in Romania than in any other country (Nastase 2002). Of course, such high popularity may indicate that the people of Romania do not really know what membership in the EU will really mean—that some groups will lose and that the benefits may not be immediately or directly felt.[32]

For our purposes, the key question is whether the desire for membership is the primary cause of Romania's lack of irredentism and its better-than-expected treatment of its minorities. Three different sets of arguments can be applied to challenge the impact of membership on Romania. First, much of what really mattered happened long before EU/NATO membership was relevant. Second, membership is based on politics more than merit, so concrete progress on checklists may be less important than argued. Further, the concessions made in order to satisfy external monitors were often "pie-crust promises"—easily made, easily broken. Third, there is something logically prior to both membership and restrained foreign policy that accounts for both: domestic political incentives.

International Constraints Before Copenhagen?

To argue that the prospect of membership constrained Romania, one would have to argue that this carrot was not only desirable but clearly visible from 1990 onward. Did Romanians care about NATO and the EU and expect that membership would be contingent on good relations with the neighbors and the minorities in the early 1990s? This is crucial, since the greatest likelihood for violence would have been the years shortly after the "revolution." Violence between Hungarians and Romanians broke out in March 1990 in Tirgu-Mureş (Socor 1990). Politicians were most desperate to stay in office and used whatever means necessary to do so, as was clearly demonstrated in the Western Balkans at this exact moment. Furthermore, this was the time when Moldova was most interested in unification.

However, NATO started the expansion process only in 1994 with the Partnership for Peace Program (PfP), with Romania involved from its creation onward. Even this may exaggerate the lure of NATO membership at the time, inasmuch as PfP was seen by many as a substitute for membership rather than the path toward admission that it eventually became for many states.[33] Still, Romania took PfP seriously, participating in nearly a thousand activities with NATO forces by 1996, contributing to NATO effort in Bosnia, and even during the Kosovo campaign (Freyberg-Inan 2002). The key here is that NATO's appeal was most significant in the latter part of the 1990s, rather than during the most dangerous period in Romania's transition.

During the first half of the 1990s, those coming to power during the revolution did not consider moderate policies as the key to EU membership. Initially, Romania tried to play on its historical links to France to get its foot in the door. Hungary was seen as an obstacle to surmount, rather than the key toward membership. Indeed, a proto-alliance emerged among those neighbors of Hungary that were slow to make the transition to democracy—

Serbia, Slovakia, and Romania.[34] Until 1993, it was not even clear that expansion was going to occur. Nor was it easy to determine what the criteria for accession would be, if expansion did happen. To be sure, the Council of Europe (CE) and the Organization for Cooperation and Security in Europe (OSCE) were already engaging these issues, but they had much less in the way of carrots and sticks to motivate countries. After the EU meeting in Copenhagen in 1993, EU admission was a possibility and standards about minority rights were set. The questions then remain: Were Romanian domestic actors acting moderately, and, if so, was this due to international pressures?

During this period, Romania developed a series of policies and created a set of institutions that reflected that a set of domestic political strategies, not international pressures, was at work. The Council for National Minorities was founded in 1993, although its significance was limited. The Department for Overseas Minorities was created in 1992–93, and this later became the Department for Romanians Overseas, which as institution, could have been the instrument for irredentist foreign policies, akin to the Office of Hungarians Abroad in Budapest.

Anti-Hungarian policies and, to a lesser extent, rhetoric, declined as 1996 approached, not because of the upcoming bilateral treaty, but largely due to the approaching election. The party representing the Hungarian minority, the Democratic Alliance for Hungarians in Romania (UDMR), was a potentially viable coalition partner, so as one diplomat in Bucharest put it, it was pragmatic politics to treat the Hungarians better.[35] This is particularly true, given the two-stage elections that Romania tends to have—where runoffs between the top two presidential candidates (as well as those at lower levels) cause politicians to play to more marginal constituencies whose favored candidates have been eliminated.[36]

Indeed, in conversations with many elites in Bucharest, the pivotal event in 1996 was not the signing of the bilateral treaty with Hungary, but the election and the subsequent inclusion of the UDMR in the governing coalition. Hungary's ambassador, István Íjgyártó, asserted that the UDMR's entry into government and its subsequent responsible membership in an otherwise irresponsible coalition had a greater impact than the bilateral treaty, despite the fact that he and other Hungarian diplomats worked on the treaty.[37] This is largely seconded by noted dissident and opinion leader Gabriel Andreescu, although he gives more credit to the international community.[38] It is notable that the Department for the Protection of National Minorities was created shortly after the 1996 elections, suggesting that the change in parties shaped outcomes in national politics, as opposed to international demands. Its subsequent fate, marginalized under the Ministry of Public Information during the Social Democratic Party (PSD) government of 2000–2004, provides additional evidence that domestic dynamics drive this issue more than external scrutiny (CEDIME 2001; Oprescu 2002).

The Limits of Conditionality: Who Really Cares About the Conditions?

While Romania behaved moderately, it is not clear that external pressures drove the policies. Indeed, efforts to link external criteria to domestic reforms have generally been weaker than advertised in two senses: that the international community has not placed as much pressure as has been reputed; and implementation of externally pressured reforms has been weak at best.[39]

One American diplomat asserted in 2004 that although Romania did not make it into the first wave of EU expansions, but that it would certainly join in 2007. He argued that the United States, the EU, and the Romanian government all understand that it is a done deal—that Romania would enter in 2007 even if it, as expected, falls short of the formal requirements.[40] Even those who believe that conditionality matters assert that Romanian integration depends more on the EU's political interests as Romania is not and will not be in a position to observe EU principles and laws.[41] Indeed, Tóni Niculescu, who was responsible for the European Integration portfolio of the UDMR, asserted that European companies are happy to have an unprepared Romania in the EU, since it would give them greater latitude to operate.[42]

This is supported by the NATO expansion experience. Members of the U.S. bureaucracy were considering expansion of NATO to include seven Eastern European countries in 2001.[43] Officers of the U.S. Joint Staff were responsible for assessing the readiness, particularly for the various military criteria, of Romania, Bulgaria, Slovakia, Slovenia, and the Baltic republics. It was readily apparent to all that their work was marginal to the decision-making process. Clearly, these seven countries were going to join NATO regardless of whether they met the established criteria, with one notable exception.[44] Indeed, none of the first wave of applicants—the Czech Republic, Hungary, and Poland—fully met the criteria when they were admitted, either. In the case of Romania, not all the conditions apparently applied, since it did not have a bilateral treaty with Moldova, but it was admitted nonetheless.[45] Indeed, the EU created additional procedures to allow Bulgaria and Romania to be admitted despite falling short of stated criteria.

While there have been efforts at all levels to define admissions standards, to complete paperwork about progress made toward these criteria, and to track reforms, the decisions in the end are political ones—whether members, for domestic or international reasons, want particular countries to join or not. The recent admission of Cyprus to the EU, despite its failure to resolve the conflict, is more evidence of this dynamic, as will be Turkey's continuing struggle.

It is difficult to determine who cares less about the conditions for membership—the outside actors who ultimately focus on political criteria or the governments being conditioned as they often develop superficial policies to satisfy the relevant institutions while only modestly changing their own behavior. One consistent thread through most interviews was that Romania failed to implement or fund many of the promises made to outsiders. Indeed, one observer said about the bilateral treaty with Hungary in 1996: "It worked, it was harmless,"[46] indicating that the treaty satisfied external actors without sacrificing much. An official in the Ministry of Defense essentially concurred: "Even if on paper, there is no guarantee that they [treaties] will be followed."[47]

In the case of the bilateral treaty between Hungary and Romania, both sides ultimately violated the spirit, if not the letter, of the treaty. As discussed in chapter 4, Hungary's Status Law, with its extraterritoriality, violated the essence of its concession in the treaty—that it would not seek to govern Hungarians in Romania. On the Romanian side, there was much backtracking on promises of minority treatment even as the treaty was being signed and ratified (Nas 1996). For instance, there is still no publicly funded Hungarian language university despite a long history of promises, including article 15.3 of the bilateral treaty. Indeed, a UDMR deputy referred to the treaty as "inefficient, inaccessible, and ultimately ignored by both parties" (CEDIME 2001, 45). Admittedly, the treaty had enough content to anger nationalists on both sides.

The point of this section is to demonstrate that existing explanations fall short of explaining Romania's reluctance to engage in irredentism. It is certainly true that membership in the EU is an important foreign policy goal in Romania. What is less clear is how such processes could have constrained Romania before its criteria were established. Further, the pressures of accession are limited by the realities of international politics—the decision to admit new members is based on politics, not whether every item on the check-list is satisfied. Likewise, it is one thing to pass a law or make a new policy to satisfy external monitors, but it is another thing to change funding patterns and implement fully what has been promised. Indeed, in a volume stressing the impact of international norms and organizations upon Eastern European countries, the chapter on Romania essentially concludes that the EU, NATO, and other institutions largely matter because domestic actors use them cynically as tools to promote their own preferences (Freyberg-Inan 2002, 156–157).

Even if membership processes restrained Romania from engaging in nationalistic domestic and foreign policies, there is still a basic question that must be addressed—how were politicians able to focus on integration into Europe, rather than unification with Moldova? Have they had to sacrifice domestic political priorities in order to meet international standards? In other countries, other priorities were more important than satisfying the international community, so why did Romania, despite its troubled path from dictatorship to democracy, manage to avoid engaging in self-destructive foreign policies? In the next section, we focus on how a more nuanced understanding of nationalism and the dynamics of political competition created room for Romanian politicians to accommodate international pressures and resist the irredentist temptation.

The Domestic Politics of Averted Irredentism

To understand why unification has not been at the center of Romanian politics and why Romanian politicians have been able to satisfy outside observers, at least enough to get into NATO and be next in line for the EU, we need to examine the components of Romanian national identity and the dynamics of political competition. To preview, Romanians care as much (or more) about not being Hungarian and not being Roma as they care about the Romanian speakers of Moldova.[48]

A Romanian Is What?

Romanians define themselves in opposition to their immediate neighbors, particularly Hungarians, Jews, Roma, and Russians.[49] "The predominant features of Romanian nationalism are its general xenophobia (though mainly directed at Hungarians and Russians) and particularly virulent anti-Semitism" (Rohozinksa 1999).[50] Nationalisms can range from civic, where the attachment is to a government and a territory, to ethnic, where ties are with groups based on a shared sense of ancestry (Snyder 1999). Romanian nationalism has always been of the ethnic variety, despite or because of a history of heterogeneity. Even after gaining Transylvania, Moldova, and other territories that increased the number of non-Romanians in the country, the focus was on Romania as a state for Romanians (Barkey 2000). "Liberty was defined as essentially meaning collective freedom from foreign domination rather than liberty of the individual" (Gallagher 1995, 17–18). Ceausescu reinforced "the myth of the homogeneous nation" and xenophobic tendencies (Tismaneunu 1997, 412). Indeed, a consensus still exists among Romanians that Romania is and should remain a unitary national state. Article 1.1 of the 1991 Constitution states: "Romania is a sovereign, independent, *unitary* and indivisible National State."[51] Article 6 states that minorities are considered entitled to the maintenance of their identity and culture, but the rest of the Constitution indicates that the state should not devolve its responsibilities to lower levels.

The historical antagonism between Hungary and Romania and between Hungarians and Romanians still resonates, even though the two groups get along better now than perhaps ever before. The Hungarian-Romanian coalition that brought down Ceausescu was short-lived, as interethnic violence in Tirgu-Mureş in March 1990 quickly indicated.[52] That identity still plays a role in this division is quite visible when various symbolic issues become salient, such as the funding of a Hungarian language public university.[53] Concessions toward the Hungarians are always met with much resistance and narrow votes, even over relatively trivial issues, such as statues of historic Hungarian generals. Initial polls taken in the early 1990s indicated that only one in five ethnic Romanians had positive views about Hungarians (McIntosh 1995, 945). There is still some suspicion about what Hungarians want. In 1993, President Iliescu accused the Hungarians of being a "fifth column" (Mihailescu 2005). In a 2003 survey of Romanians, 57 percent believed that Hungarians would always claim Transylvania and that Hungarians have different interests than Romanians. Additionally, 78 percent of Romanians opposed giving autonomy to Hungarians where they are the majority,[54] inasmuch as Romanians strongly view Romania as a unitary national state—a single state with no decentralization for the Romanian people.

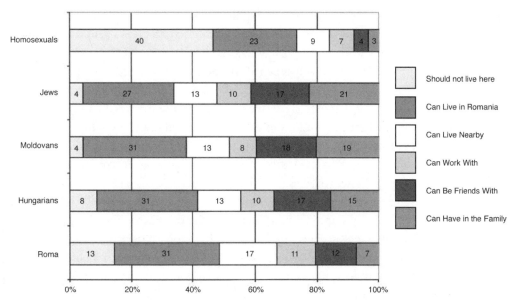

FIGURE 5.2   Romanian Views of Minorities

Similarly, a key element of being Romanian is not being Roma.[55] The stereotypes and attitudes toward the Roma are quite negative and widely
shared.[56] As figure 5.2 illustrates,[57] Roma are barely tolerated, with 13 percent
of Romanians favoring a Romania that was free of Roma, and another 31 percent tolerating their existence in the country but with no closer ties than that.
Opinion leaders consider the Roma to be the most hated community in Romania, perhaps not considering gays and lesbians to be a community in the
same sense as Roma, Hungarians and Jews.[58] Even the Hungarians consider
the Roma to be the most hated group.[59]

Interestingly, despite the decimation of the Romanian Jewish community, anti-Semitism is still a key part of Romanian identity. Historically, anti-
Semitism has been a core part of Romanian identity.[60] Romanian parties mobilized around this issue, where it came to dominate pre–World War II politics,[61] ultimately leading to Romania's participation in the Holocaust. Only
recently have Romanian elites recognized not only that Jews were killed in
Romania but also that Romanians played a part in this process, besides that
of victims. Jews are now a small minority, due to the Holocaust and subsequent emigration.[62] Still, they have been a target for nationalists, including
the Greater Romania Party.

In one of the most intriguing developments of late, Vadim Tudor, leader of the Greater Romania Party, has declared himself to be a philo-Semite (his phrase for being a friend of the Jews and antonym of anti-Semite), visited Auschwitz in 2004, and visibly retained an Israeli Jew as a key campaign consultant. While this has been part of a general effort to soften his image and the rhetoric of the party, it actually seems to testify to the ingrained nature of anti-Semitism. That is, if Tudor can be seen as a friend of the Jews, then the rest of his negative baggage will not matter since the Jews are so powerful in both Romanian and European political circles. Thus, the stereotype and suspicion about the power of Jews is driving the Greater Romania party to find other targets for its rhetoric, at least for the time being.

The remaining group that clearly serves as the other (the "them" to the Romanian "us") are Russians. This is, in part, based on a history of resistance to Russian domination (Gallagher 1995). More recently, Ceausescu, in his efforts to build and shape Romanian nationalism to legitimate his rule, focused on Russia as the threat to Romanian independence.[63] His opposition to the invasion of Czechoslovakia was more of a nationalist position than anything else (Gallagher 1995, 57). This seems to have worked, inasmuch as members of the Romanian government still harbor very suspicious views of Russia and of Russians in Moldova.[64]

These attitudes seem to be shared even by those Romanians in the conflict prevention area, as Iulian Chifu presented similar beliefs when discussing Moldova.[65] Individuals outside of the Romanian government find attitudes toward Russians to be the most strident. An American diplomat indicated that Romanians "hate Russians the most."[66] While these attitudes may have been stirred up by Ceausescu, they remain in play. Russia's relations with Moldova, the activities of the Fourteenth Army (which is still present in Moldova), and the efforts of the Communist Party in Moldova to replace Romanian identity with Moldavianism all help to reinforce existing attitudes about Russia. The result is less enthusiasm for reunification: "Welcoming the prodigal cousins back into the pan-Romanian fold, with significant numbers of Ukrainians and Russians in tow, was hardly an appealing proposition" (King 2000, 228).

Finally, Moldova and its residents play a mixed role in Romanian identity. It was only a part of Romania for a brief period between the two world wars and was seen as a backward province at best. Being sent to Moldova during this time was seen as a punishment, and the quality of government officials sent there were seen as being inferior to those in the rest of Romania.[67] "Many

Moldovans . . . remembered that the interwar years had not been any rose garden for the Moldovans" (Kolstø 2000). During most of the communist period, the regime de-emphasized the loss of Bessarabia, even as Ceausescu tried to portray his independence from Moscow. Bessarabia was left off school maps during this time (Petrescu 2004). Only in the last few years of Ceausescu's regime did he begin to play the card of lost territories out of increasing desperation. At that point his efforts lacked credibility, and the strategy did not resonate.

Individuals who come from Moldova are frequently shunned and seen as backward. "Moldavians . . . were simply too marginal and helpless to be good material for nationalist recruiters" (Gallagher 1995, 174). Moldovan students who go the universities in Bucharest live apart, the males are seen as being more violent, and they are generally outsiders.[68] Even Roma in Romania consider the visitors and immigrants from Moldova to be victims of discrimination.[69] It is quite interesting that Moldovans are considered as warmly or as coldly as Jews (figure 5.2), not a favored group by any stretch of the imagination, as discussed above. Romanians are about as tolerant or accepting of Moldovans as they are of Jews and Hungarians. Respondents could have been focusing more on the Russophones who live in Moldova, as opposed to Romanian citizens of Moldova when they answered the question, but the pattern is still suggestive. Surveys in 1991 and 1992 indicated that only about 20 percent of Romanians supported early unification with Moldova (Gallagher 1995, 187). These are not the kind of attitudes upon which irredentism is built; they are not strong enough for politicians to use to gain votes and power, nor do they build support among Moldovans for reunification (King 2000, 230).

On the other hand, Romanians see the Romanian-speakers of Moldova as Romanians. They see the Moldavian identity as invented by elites, particularly Russian ones, and they believe that the Romanians in Moldova are being denied their identity.[70] Romanians see Bessarabia as being part of Romania; they believe that unification will likely happen in time, as it should, and that Romania should help maintain the identities of Romanians outside the country.

To be a Romanian means many things, and these multiple meanings, particularly the number of "them/others" that one can oppose, provides politicians with greater latitude as they develop strategies to gain and maintain office and as they develop policies. To be a successful nationalist, a Romanian politician does not have to focus on foreign policy, but may select from a plethora of domestic targets, particularly Hungarians and Roma. Moreover, because of Romanians' ambivalence about their kin in Moldova, there have been limited incentives to engage in irredentism. This is especially true if union means incorporating a significant Russophone/Russian population. Even the recently revived compromise of giving Ukraine or Russia Transnistria while Romania receives the rest of Moldova is problematic, since the cities of Moldova are largely Russophone (see figure 5.1). Thus, xenophobia actually constrains irredentist sentiment while providing politicians with alternative strategies to gain and maintain power.

To Be a Successful Nationalist . . .

For our purposes, two related questions stand out: Is being a nationalist necessary or at least helpful for political success in Romania in the 1990s? If so, what does it take to be a successful Romanian nationalist? In short, the answers are yes, and scapegoats are aplenty. All mainstream parties have to be careful about defending the interests of Romanians against other groups, especially domestic ones, even as they try to address international and domestic pressures to accommodate minorities. These cross-pressures have forced a process that seems evolutionary. Politicians have emphasized particular minorities as a threat until the costs become too high and the strategy becomes less successful, and then they move onto another, less closely observed minority. Thus, the basic tendency has been to move from anti-Semitism and anti-Hungarian rhetoric to anti-Roma, and now more recently to anti-Arab, anti-Muslim, anti-immigrant and homophobic statements. To be clear, the older attitudes and claims are still present and are still voiced, just not as loudly. Again, the most visible nationalist, Tudor, now claims to be a philo-Semite, despite the shrill anti-Semitism of his past and of his party's newspapers—*România Mare* and *Politica*.

While the Greater Romania Party is most widely known for its nationalist positions, minorities actually fear the other parties more, as they suspect the hidden nationalists more than the ones that are in the open.[71] Most of the parties except the minority ones (UDMR, those of the Roma and smaller minorities) have a significant Romanian nationalist component in their past and current ideologies and behavior.[72] By going through the claims and actions of each party, we can easily demonstrate that Romanian nationalism has consistently played a key role in the political system. Through this analysis, we can also show that proving one's nationalist credentials requires a specific set of domestic policies, rather than foreign policies.

The first post-Ceausescu government (1990–1996) was the National Salvation Front, led by Ion Iliescu and former members of the Communist Party. The NSF later became the Social Democratic Party (PSD), returning to power in 2000 and fell just short of winning the presidential election in 2004. During its initial incarnation, the NSF was quite nationalist, as it either condoned or generated the miners' violence against Hungarians and others, and as it formed informal and then formal coalitions with the Greater Romanian Party and the Party of Romanian National Unity, the two most extremely nationalist parties. These two parties led the ministries of education, justice, and culture during this period.

Despite an initial mood of multiethnic unity, the government quickly displayed a tendency toward nationalist rhetoric and policies (Roper 2000, 69). President Iliescu was referring obliquely to "separatist trends" in Transylvania within a month of the "Revolution" (Gallagher 1995, 83). Iliescu and the NSF, rather than marginalizing the extremely nationalist group, Vatra Româneascu (Union of the Romanian Hearth), included its members in important positions (Gallagher 1995, 101–102).[73] "Anti-Hungarianism was a key resource."[74] In its campaigns and other messages, the NSF would modify its opponents' names to make them appear Hungarian rather than Romanian (Shafir 1999a). A series of laws was passed, including the 1991 Law on Local Public Administration excluding minority languages in local administration, and the 1995 Law on Education, limiting the teaching of minority languages (Csergo 2007). As the 1996 election approached, Iliescu, attacking the UDMR, accusing it of "planning the 'Yugoslavization' of Romania and the secession of Transylvania" (Shafir 1999b). He sought to tap into Romanian fears of dismemberment, which seem to be widely shared, as evidenced by the widespread hostility to autonomy.[75] When this failed, the NSF went in the other direction, signing the bilateral treaty with Hungary, to show that his party could lead Romania into Europe. This was too little, too late—the NSF lost the election to a coalition of opposition parties termed the Convention. And then, the party swung back in the other direction. While in opposition (1996–2000), the renamed PSD voted against measures that would benefit the Hungarian minority, positioning the party as a better defender of Romanian interests than the coalition in power.

The PSD returned to power in 2000, riding on the backlash against the Convention's failures—largely economic ones. Instead of creating a formal coalition with any party, they created an informal one with the UDMR. The UDMR did not get any cabinet posts, but agreed to vote with the PSD in exchange for support for particular issues. This was nearly as striking as the inclusion of the UDMR in the Convention, given the PSD's previous anti-Hungarian positions.

This switch highlights the opportunism driving both the PSD and the UDMR. The PSD record of supporting Hungarian issues is mixed, as autonomy is still taboo, but Hungarians can now access courts in their language. There is some suspicion that the PSD has been using the Greater Romania Party and Tudor—that their existence makes the PSD look moderate in comparison, both for domestic and international audiences.[76] Gallagher (1995, 78) considers Iliescu to be an opportunist, rather than a nationalist: "He did not hold rigid views on minority questions and . . . his policy approach was subordinate to the overriding demands of political survival." Ironically, Gallagher wrote this when assessing Iliescu's first term in office, when he formed coalitions with nationalists, but this quote anticipates the turn toward more moderate stances when Iliescu returned to office in 2000.

The Democratic Convention of Romania replaced the NSF. The Convention was a coalition of most of the opposition, including the Democratic Party (PD), the National Liberal Party (PNL), Christian Democrat Peasant Party of Romania (PNTCD), and UDMR.[77] The PNL's participation in the Convention was in flux in the early 1990s, alternating with periods of anti-Hungarian rhetoric (Gallagher 1995, 175). The PNTCD did not have an unblemished record either, as its members had taken anti-Semitic and anti-Hungarian stances in the early days of Romania's democracy (Gallagher 1995, 147, 159). It also had the strongest interest in Bessarabia: "Recovering Bessarabia has to be the cause of each Romanian and each party."[78]

The PNTCD was the largest party in the coalition from 1996 to 2000, but it felt most of the backlash in 2000, falling short of getting any representation in parliament. With the UDMR's participation, the coalition passed legislation and proclaimed a series of executive decrees that benefited the Hungarian minority, including the use of Hungarian in public administration where Hungarians are in sufficient numbers. The PSD and the Greater Romanian Party challenged these efforts. Once out of power, the Liberals and Democrats then opposed PSD/UDMR efforts to solidify the relevant executive decrees.[79] This reinforced the post-1996 pattern of opposition parties taking more nationalist positions than those in power. In the 2004 election, the PD

and PNL formed an alliance to compete against the PSD, successfully returning to power.

The two most significant nationalist parties have been the Party of Romanian National Unity (PUNR) and the Greater Romania Party. The former
played a greater role earlier on, and the latter has played a more significant
role since then.[80] Gheorge Funar, the mayor of Cluj, led the PUNR during its
heyday, peaking in the 1992 election with approximately 8 percent of the vote.
In addition to trying to rehabilitate the fascists of the interwar period, Funar
lauded Ceausescu repeatedly, though criticized communist leaders' overly
generous treatment of the Hungarians (Shafir 1999a, 1999b). "The one consistent note in the PUNR discourse is the existence of the alleged threat to
Romanian sovereignty over Transylvania by Hungarian groups both within
the province and across the border in Hungary" (Gallagher 1995, 201). After
Romania negotiated the bilateral treaty with Hungary, Funar accused Iliescu
of being a traitor, calling for his impeachment. This ultimately led to the
PUNR losing its place in the coalition. It was subsequently hammered in the
1996 election, with most of its supporters moving to the Greater Romania
Party.

The Greater Romania Party has gained more attention than nearly any
other party, largely because of its charismatic leader, Corneliu Vadim Tudor,
and due to its showing in the 2000 campaign.[81] Tudor did well enough to get
into the runoff with Iliescu for president, and the party became the second
largest holder of seats in the parliament. Despite its name, the party has
largely focused on events and dynamics within the country, as opposed to the
lost kin in Moldova or elsewhere. The party's message has mutated over time.
Originally, it was entirely focused on anti-Hungarian, anti-Roma, and anti-
Semitic rhetoric.[82] Over time, the Greater Romania Party has shifted its attention toward other minority groups—Arabs and Asians—as well as being
slightly more discreet in its attacks upon Jews, Roma, and Hungarians.[83]

During the 2000 campaign, Tudor sought to tap into resentment against
corruption, posing as a law-and-order candidate, promising to bring back a
more authoritarian style of government. Romanians bought into this, with
more people feeling a Tudor government would reduce corruption and improve public order.[84] Indeed, the consensus is that the Tudor's success in 2000
was due to a protest vote against the incumbents. The problem with this argument is that the protest vote could have rallied around other politicians,
but it centered on Tudor and his party. Given the history of the party and its

messages, approximately 30 percent of the electorate did not seem to mind voting for a xenophobic organization and candidate.

Finally, there is the Hungarian minority party, the UDMR. It is a single party,[85] representing a variety of ideologies. It has played a rather curious role in Romanian politics. First, its inclusion in government in 1996 was quite revolutionary, and its ability to work with the PSD after the 2000 election was almost as surprising. It is not clear whether the UDMR is successful in getting substantial gains for its constituents or settles for symbolic victories. Much energy has been focused on statues and on a publicly funded Hungarian language university, rather than on policies that might improve the lives of average Hungarians or providing lasting guarantees of Hungarian influence, such as decentralized government (or autonomy). Still, there have been some notable victories; the number of Hungarian-language schools (kindergarten through high school) has increased, and laws governing signs and language in the courts have been passed.

For our purposes, three aspects of this party are most relevant: the party's support for EU membership; its likely hostility toward unification with Moldova; and its impact on moderating anti-Hungarianism in Romania. First, while all Romanian parties, even the Greater Romania Party, voice support for EU membership, the UDMR is perhaps most clearly committed to it, and its constituents would most clearly benefit from membership. While membership would not necessarily solve the problems of minorities,[86] it would ease travel between Hungary and Romania. Second, as a minority close to the threshold of participation in parliament, the UDMR is likely to oppose any irredentist effort, as it would weaken their influence at the national level.[87]

Third, the UDMR has played a significant role in reducing the rhetoric and polices aimed against the Hungarian minority, thereby reducing the salience of Romania's Hungarians on Hungary's political agenda. Specifically, the UDMR has created incentives for other parties to moderate their behavior, since the electoral laws, combined with demography, have made the party a critical partner for the right and the left in the past two governments. Further, its performance has been quite successful, helping to change attitudes among Romanians about the Hungarians and their designs.[88]

For each party, identity has played a major role, but so has opportunism.[89] The UDMR was willing to work with any party to get into power, even the PSD with its history of anti-Hungarian rhetoric and behavior. The Democrats and Liberals were moderately supportive of Hungarian interests when they took part in the convention but opposed Hungarians once outside of government. The PSD was quite willing to play upon anti-Hungarian, anti-Roma, and anti-Semitic tendencies when it needed the support of the nationalist parties, but it was also quite willing to change its public face when the nationalists were no longer viable coalition partners. This is where the EU comes in: outside pressures might have made the Greater Romania Party a less attractive coalition partner.

What is most striking in all of this is the absence of Moldova and Romanians abroad. Each party, when it wants to play the nationalist card, focuses almost entirely on domestic groups—Hungarians, Jews (despite their small numbers), the Roma, and, increasingly, immigrants (Arabs and Asians) and homosexuals—rather than their kin abroad. It is not as if the issue does not exist—everyone is aware of the Romanians abroad, particularly in Moldova where their identity is at risk, but the issue simply does not play in Romania. During the 1992 election, efforts were taken to play the "Moldovan card," but voters did not care much (Roper 2000, 124). However, since all of the parties (except perhaps the UDMR) believe that Moldovans are really Romanians

TABLE 5.1   Hypotheses and Romania

	Hypothesis	
1:	Interstate boundaries limit irredentism	Confirmed: No aggression across international boundaries
2:	Admissions processes limit irredentism	Mixed: Moderation both before and after admissions processes developed
3:	States will be deterred by stronger targets	Disconfirmed: Romania was consistently much more powerful than Moldova
4:	History of Irredentism	Disconfirmed: World War II was a relatively positive experience
5:	Tolerance of homogeneity/ xenophobia	Confirmed: Constituents were intolerant of diversity
6:	Economics/irredentist interests	Confirmed: All parties (except perhaps the most nationalist ones) had constituents who sought integration, deterring irredentism
7a:	Actively irredentist kin	Disconfirmed: Politically active group in Moldova sought union in early 1990s, but Romania did not actively pursue
7b:	Danger	Disconfirmed: Civil war in Transnistria did not lead to efforts by Romania to rescue kin
7c:	Kin in positions of power	Confirmed: Kin largely absent from power

and that in an ideal world, the territory would be part of Romania, it is not a "wedge issue" (King 2000, 166). Even the most nationalist parties of consequence focus on other issues.[90] Indeed, one of the most interesting ironies in Romanian politics is that the Greater Romania Party is not focused on irredentism.

Xenophobia and Peace

Romania serves as an important case to compare and contrast with the others, since it shares many similarities with both the former Yugoslav republics on some dimensions and Hungary in other ways. Like Hungary, Romania's potential target for any irredentist project was on the other side of an international boundary, so we find some support for the notion that interstate boundaries may matter. Like Hungary, Romania was restrained before NATO and EU admissions processes took place. Moreover, Romania has still failed to meet important criteria (judicial reform, border treaty with Moldova), yet was admitted. So, while both countries seemed to submit to the will of the international institutions, variations in their behavior cannot be explained by outside pressures.

Romania was more like Serbia in its position relative to its target. Just as Serbia was more powerful than Croatia or Bosnia, Romania had significantly more national capabilities than Moldova, making a relatively easy target for any aggression.[91] Moreover, with Moldova crippled by its civil war with the Transnistrians, Romania could have tried to annex the rest of the country but chose not to do so.[92] Thus, concerns about international opportunities and constraints (Ambrosio 2001) do not seem to operate here.

The kin played an interesting role in this case, for there were serious irredentists in Moldova, holding political power as it became independent. While Romanians talked of reunion, the government did not act. Later, as new governments took power in Moldova and developed policies that challenged Romanian definitions of identities, Romania escalated its interest, and there were modest efforts to encourage maintaining of Romanian identity. Again, these efforts were modest. The kin faced some danger as the Transnistrians used violence to develop a semi-independent region, but this conflict was much less threatening than the potential and then realized plight of Serbs in Croatia. Still, Romania did not take strong actions to help their kin. Indeed, this fits into the broader pattern of identification—that Romanians in Moldova are marginalized in Romania's nationalism.

Romania poses a variety of interesting contradictions. First, it developed a series of institutions to address minority issues in the early 1990s when European influence was weakest but also when nationalist rhetoric was at its peak. We can explain this by focusing on an enduring tendency in post–Cold War Romanian politics: real doubts remain about the contributions of the various institutions created both before and after Euro-Atlantic pressures developed. That is, Romania seems to do a far better job of creating new institutions and drafting legislation (although efforts to pass key laws may be quite combative) than of implementing them.

Second, Romania's politics may have been more deeply nationalist than any other democracy in Eastern Europe in the 1990s outside of Yugoslavia, but its foreign policy has been perhaps the meekest. Scholars have argued that pressures to join NATO and the EU have caused Eastern European countries to put nationalist foreign policies far down the list of priorities, but these assertions raise the question of how politicians could have focused on a distant goal with vague benefits rather than on nationalist issues, which, in the short term, are easier to satisfy.

The conditionality argument raises this question: How could politicians sell their souls for Europe's approval? The case of Romania shows that the domestic politics of identity meant that there was a low price paid for friendly foreign policies and no urgency to engage in the defense of kin abroad. The Moldova/Bessarabia issue was not so central to most Romanians owing to ambivalent attitudes toward the Moldovans and because elites could prove their nationalist credentials by focusing on hated groups within the country (Jews, Roma, Hungarians, and now Asians and Arabs as well as gays and lesbians) instead. Furthermore, as in the case of Hungary's limited foreign policy, successful irredentism would mean including a hated other—Russians in this case—along with the lost kin. Consequently, Romania's foreign policy has been less assertive than Hungary's and far less aggressive than the irredentist states in the region.

In this case, the Romanian-speakers of Moldova have little influence and are widely disparaged. Romanians would like to see reunification but are willing to wait and unwilling to sacrifice. Bessarabia does resonate, but not very strongly. Politicians simply cannot run for office on this issue, and they do not need to do so. They have other nationalist tools at their disposal.

Notes to Chapter 5: Romania's Restraint

1. During a research trip to Bucharest in May 2004, we talked to government officials, party leaders, academics, personnel working within nongovernmental organizations, and members of the international community.

2. That an extreme party gets into a runoff and gets a significant number of votes is not unique to Romania. The National Front of France, led by Jean-Marie Le Pen, performed similarly well in 2002.

3. Iordachi (2002) nicely summarizes the rise and fall of Greater Romania via a review of a Romanian book by Gheorge Cojocaru on this topic.

4. There are other contested lands, including those lost to Ukraine, but the focus here is on Moldova, which has been the focal point of any irredentist effort.

5. King (2000) is the definitive effort in delineating the history and contested nature of Moldovan identities, and much of the discussion here is informed by King's work. His chapter 6 is most relevant for this discussion.

6. See Datculescu (1992, 140); King (2000, 147).

7. See also Kaufman (2001).

8. Interview with Gabriel Mico, Department for Romanians Overseas, May 11, 2004.

9. See also King (2000).

10. Ibid.

11. Iulian Chifu, director of the Centrul de Prevenire a Conflictelor si Early Warning (Conflict Prevention and Early Warning Center), was particularly emphatic about the artificiality of this Moldavian identity (interview May 4, 2004), but this sentiment was shared by all of the Romanians interviewed at this time, including government officials, academics, members of civil society, and even the students.

12. Or Romanians, as they are considered in Romania.

13. The other notable holdouts were the Baltic republics and Russia.

14. RFE/RL Newsline, Southeastern Europe, January 5, 2004.

15. RFE/RL Research Report, "Weekly Record of Events," September 6, 1991: 42.

16. Romania has supported Moldova's integration efforts, as Hungary has largely done for Romania. Both believe that their kin would be better off in Euro-Atlantic structures.

17. Ilie Ilaşcu provides an interesting link between dual citizenship and irredentism. In brief, he was a leader of irredentists within Moldova. While under arrest, he applied for and received Romanian citizenship. He was eventually elected to a seat in the Romanian Senate as a member of the Greater Romania Party, despite residing in jail in Moldova. Once freed, he moved to Romania and tried to initiate legislation that would grant all Moldovans citizenship in Romania without an application process (Iordachi 2004, 250–252).

18. Interviews with Gabriel Mico, Department for the Romanians Overseas, diplomat, Minister of Foreign Affairs, May 11, 2004 and Titus Corlşean, Secretary of State, Department for the Romanians Living Abroad, Government of Romania, May 13, 2004.

19. Interview with Dan Pavel, Chief Advisor to Gheorge (GiGi) Becali, leader of the New Generation Party (PNG), former director of the Bucharest office of Project on Ethnic Relations, May 10, 2004.

20. RFE/RL Newsline, Southeastern Europe, September 1, 1999.

21. Interview with Iulian Chiufu.

22. RFE/RL Newsline 2003. Csergo and Goldgeier (2004) place this development in a broader context, and how nationalists have tried to use the EU in their strategies.

23. These two countries are not alone: a variety of countries have developed legislation that gives benefits to kin groups outside of the homeland.

24. Because Romania's draft was written after the Venice Commission's review and criticism of Hungary's Status Law, it is largely, although not entirely, in compliance with EU standards. See Venice Commission (2004). Opinion on the Draft Law Concerning Support to Romanians Living Abroad of the Republic of Moldova.

25. For the definitive discussion of Romania's first years of "democracy," see Gallagher (1995).

26. In interviews, a variety of accusations were made. Several subjects indicated that the incumbent Social Democratic Party (the PSD is the successor to the National Salvation front) was using the Greater Romania Party as a stalking horse. Others mentioned the PSD's manipulation of the budget to force mayors throughout the country to choose either PSD membership or the loss of funds for their cities. Institutional changes limited the competition the PSD's ally, the Democratic Alliance for Hungarians in Romania (UDMR) might have faced. Finally, there is consensus that there is a continued presence of Securitate personnel at the elite levels of most parties. However, the conduct of the 2004 election contrasts sharply with Ukraine's. Despite a very tight result, in Romania, the incumbents stepped down quite quickly, once it was clear that they lost.

27. For critiques of Romania's democratic credentials in the early 1990s, see Gallagher (1995) and Tismaneaunu (1995).

28. May 2004.

29. To be clear, Tismaneanu (2002) presents a nuanced picture, illuminating many of the continuing problems in Eastern Europe, despite the "magnetism" of Europe.

30. As it turns out, the expectations were correct: Romania, along with Bulgaria, entered the EU on January 1, 2007.

31. This was indicated in most interviews conducted in May 2004.

32. This was most clearly articulated in an interview with Dan Oprescu Zenda, Senior Advisor on Roma Issues, General Secretariat of the Government of Romania, May 4, 2004. See also Freyberg-Inan (2002).

33. For several countries, such as Armenia, Azerbaijan, Georgia, and the five "Stans" of central Asia, PfP is probably the end of the line, with membership highly unlikely.

34. Interview with Oprescu.

35. Interview with Robert Gilchrist, political counselor, United States Embassy to Romania, May 6, 2004.

36. Donald Horowitz (1985, 1991a) has advocated a similar but not identical system, where voters provide their second and third preferences, so that minorities still

have weight after their candidates fall far short of the majority's. It is important to note that the system was different from that of Serbia or Croatia, where majorities were needed at all levels. This favored the nationalists more in Yugoslavia than in Romania, but this has as much to do with the distribution of preferences as with institutions.

37. Interview with István Íjgyártó, Hungary's ambassador to Romania, May 5, 2004.

38. Interview with Gabriel Andreescu, a public intellectual who has held many positions including Chair of the Centre for Human Rights, columnist for Radio Free Europe, member of several Open Society Foundation's Expert Commissions, and the Helsinki Committee, May 12, 2004.

39. Csergo 2007 contrasts external conditionality with internal conditionality (domestic dynamics), arguing that Romanian reforms have been driven by the latter, not the former.

40. Interview with Robert Gilchrist, political counselor, United States Embassy to Romania, May 6, 2004.

41. Interview with Andreescu, May 12, 2004.

42. Interview with Tóni Niculescu, executive vice president, Department for European Immigration, Democratic Alliance of Hungarians in Romania, May 14, 2004.

43. Saideman was a Council of Foreign Relations International Affairs Fellow at this time, placed in the U.S. Joint Staff's Strategic Planning and Policy Directorate (J-5), in the Central and East European Division. While his focus was on Bosnia, his colleagues were working the issue of enlargement. The views in this paragraph are a result of this experience.

44. Slovakia might have been kept out if Vladimir Meciar was elected in 2002. The EU Ambassador to Slovakia, Eric van der Linden, said as much in a speech in Slovakia's capital on June 25, 2002: "We have particularly underlined the risk that if [Mr. Meciar prevailed] that . . . would negatively influence the process for Slovakia." Radio Free Europe, June 26, 2002.

45. Admittedly, much legislation and many policies have been developed in Eastern Europe in response to membership pressures. The point here is that the power of this process has been overestimated and assumes a great deal about how domestic politics works in these countries.

46. Interview with Oprescu.

47. Anonymous interview, May 2004.

48. Indeed, Sandra Pralong argues that Transylvania and Moldova present conflicting nationalist logics, so there is a real trade-off between the two. "Romanian Nationalism: Double Problem, Double Talk," Institute on East Central Europe Working Paper, 1996.

49. For a discussion about the debate among Romanian intellectuals about the meaning of nationalism, see Haddock and Caraiani (1999).

50. See also Chirot (2005).

51. Emphasis added.

52. See Socor (1990) and Gallagher (1995, 87–90). As discussed later, new coalitions involving the Hungarian minority party developed later on, but the point here is that

the groups that worked together to overthrow the old government fell apart shortly afterward.

53. The Romanian parties seem to be playing to the public on this issue, as there is much opposition to Hungarian language education (McIntosh 1995).

54. Institutul pentru Politici Publica (2003, 38).

55. Interview with Delia Grigoria, one of the leaders of Aven Amentza, a Roma organization, May 12, 2004. See also Bran (1995).

56. Indeed, they are widely shared outside of Romania as well (Ringold, Orenstein, and Wilkens 2003).

57. Institutul pentru Politici Publica (2003, 36). The original figure contains data about other groups as well (Arabs, Chinese, blacks, lesbians, Muslims), but I extracted the most relevant ones as well as homosexuals, the focus of the most extreme views.

58. Interview with Andreescu, May 12, 2004.

59. Interview with Niculescu, May 14, 2004.

60. Barkey (2000, 510). See also Rohozinksa (1999). For a broader look at anti-Semitism's role in East European nationalisms, see Tismaneaunu (1998).

61. Gallagher (1995, chapter 1) summarizes this dynamic quite well.

62. Only ten to fifteen thousand Jews, mostly elderly, remain in Romania, down from a community of hundreds of thousands before World War II.

63. Petrescu 2004. See also Gallagher (1995, chapter 2). It is important to note that Ceausescu also tended to isolate Romanians from the world around them, so that in the aftermath, few Romanian politicians had significant ties outside the country; neither did the public at large. I am thankful to Raluca Popa for pointing this out.

64. In the interview with Gabriel Micu of the Department for Romanians Overseas, he presented a very stark portrait of the subversive role played by Russia and the Russian elites in Moldova. He asserted that the popular fronts that led the independence movements in the former Soviet Union were the product of a Machiavellian strategy by Mikhail Gorbachev that got out of hand briefly. These views are particularly problematic, not just because of his current position, but also due to past positions as a director of the Moldova unit within the Foreign Ministry and as one of the members of the delegations working on the bilateral treaties with the various neighbors.

65. Interview with Chifu.

66. Anonymous, May 2004.

67. Interview with Pavel.

68. Interview with Christian Jura, Romanian sociologist, May 13, 2004. The Romanian graduate students serving as interpreters during this research trip concurred, having witnessed these attitudes on more than a few occasions.

69. Interview with Grigori.

70. This theme was repeated through many interviews, but most clearly by Micu and Chifu.

71. Interviews with Niculescu and Grigori.

72. To be clear, ordinary usage of the word nationalism would also apply to the UDMR, just not Romanian nationalism. See Csergo (2001).

73. See also Bugajski (2000, 77).

74. Interview with Andreescu. See also Tismaneanu (1995, 1997).

75. In the IPP survey, 78 percent of Romanians oppose autonomy for Hungarians where they are the majority (Institutul pentru Politici Publica 2003, 38). Indeed, hostility to Hungarian autonomy is so intense that a key condition for UDMR participation in government has been to downplay any discussion of autonomy (Medianu 2002, 34).

76. Interview with Niculescu. Note that this parallels what Milosevic did in Serbia, using the Serbian Radical Party as a similar foil.

77. For a critical assessment of these parties, see Stan (2003).

78. Statement issued by Cluj PNTCD in February 1992, cited in Gallagher (1995, 1875).

79. Interview with Niculescu.

80. See Gallagher (1995, chapter 6) for an extensive discussion of the origins and early evolution of these two parties, along with other nationalist groups.

81. During the second stage of the presidential campaign, some surveys showed Tudor ahead of Iliescu (Freyberg-Inan 2002).

82. For examples, see Bran (1995).

83. Interview with Violeta Bau, director, Institutal pentru Politicu Publice, May 12, 2004.

84. Institutul pentru Politici Publica (2003, 52).

85. Various claims are made about whether the UDMR is a party, a movement or some other form of collectivity, but it acts like a party when it comes to elections, negotiations with the mainstream parties, and its roles in the cabinet and the parliament. For a thorough treatment of the UDMR, see Shafir (2000).

86. Niculescu, the UDMR's executive vice president for European Integration, is well aware of the limits of existing minority regulations at the EU level; interview, May 14, 2004.

87. Indeed, as Iordacjo (2004) notes, the party has frequently been divided, including over the issue of dual citizenship between "moderates" and "radicals." Indeed, the UDMR actually supported an increase in the legal threshold for gaining representation, perhaps as a way to reduce the likelihood of a split in the party (Saideman et al. 2006).

88. Many interviewees made this point, including the Hungarian Ambassador, István Íjgyártó, and Niculescu.

89. Indeed, given the generally high level of corruption in Romanian politics (Open Society 2002), it may be the case that politicians are willing to sell out on a variety of issues, including nationalist ones, to stay in government to participate in the division of spoils.

90. Smaller groups farther out on the fringe do care and make noise about reunification, but their very marginality suggests that this is not a winning strategy. The Romanian Right and the Electoral Nationalist Bloc are two of the more prominent fringe groups (Shafir 2001).

91. According to Correlates of War data, Romania consistently was eight to ten times more powerful than Moldova throughout the 1990s. Again, EUGene (Bennett and Stam 2000) was used to generate this data.

92. Russia had the ability to help the Transnistrians, but it is not clear that they could have or would have prevented Romania from recovering the territory Romania had lost at the outset of World War II.

6

Breaking Up Is Hard to Do

Russia and Its Kin in the Near Abroad

> *In Russia, the Russians must rule. In Russia, there must be only a Russian government, a Russian parliament consisting of ethnic Russians belonging to the Great Nation by blood and spirit . . . because we are all only cells in one great organism called the Nation.*
> —NIKOLAI BONDARIK, LEADER OF THE RUSSIAN PARTY, 1993

W ITH THE COLLAPSE OF COMMUNISM, RUSSIA was perhaps the most-watched place for revanchist irredentism in the 1990s. This was entirely appropriate, given both the weight of Russian history as an empire built on contiguous territorial conquest and the substantial number of Russians left outside the new boundaries of Russia. Unlike Hungary, Romania, and other Eastern European cases, these diaspora Russian populations had not had very long to adjust to their new status outside the protection of the motherland. Whereas Transylvanian Hungarians had been outside of Hungary for generations, Russians in the Baltic States, the Ukraine, and the new central Asian republics had immediate memories of being under the governance of Moscow, even if they had been outside the borders of the Russian republic.

There were also concerns about Russia's political direction, based on its twentieth-century history. Whereas many Eastern European countries had some connection with democratic practices in the nineteenth and twentieth centuries, Russia had none. Communism had ruled there longest and most restrictively, trying at least in theory to stamp out nationalism in the name of class-consciousness. Before communism, Russia was a territory that had aggressively expanded its borders to include Central Asia, the Transcaucasus, and the Far East—an expansion built largely on power, not on appeals to national identity. Although there was a lot of optimistic rhetoric about the spread of democracy in the early 1990s, there was also legitimate concern—could countries so long under communism really become democratic? In the former Yugoslavia, a failure of democracy would be disastrous but containable; in Russia, a similar failure would have far worse consequences.

Because of this past history, the Russian course of the 1990s—which included, for all intents and purposes, no significant irredentism—is perhaps the most puzzling case of all.[1] Why did Russia not go the route of Serbia? Why did Boris Yeltsin—who had shown opportunistic political tendencies in the past, and who was no stranger to using aggressive measures such as shelling his own parliament—not turn out like Milosevic? Why was there no Russian Tudjman to rally the nation to the cause of the motherland?

Domestic forces, as we will see, seemed to weigh much more heavily in this area than international ones—particularly the underlying questions of what it means to be "Russian" in post-Soviet Russia. Russia's lack of irredentism has much more to do with the lack of an agreed-upon definition of "Russianness" than with international pressures or skillful diplomacy. Perhaps alone among postcommunist cases, Russia lacked a central definition of its own dominant ethnic group and so could not engage in the kinds of destructive nationalist policies that took root in parts of Eastern Europe and the Caucasus.

Russian Policy Toward Russians in the Near Abroad

The primary axis of potential Russian irredentist behavior has been its treatment of and policies toward Russians in the "Near Abroad"—the other fourteen former Soviet republics. When the Soviet Union collapsed in 1991, some twenty-five million Russians and perhaps an additional five million Russian speakers were left outside the borders of the new Russian Federation (Tolz 1998, 1001). Policy toward this group therefore became a bellwether for larger questions about the nature of the new Russian state and its identity. In large part, this policy has been moderate, much less aggressive certainly than Serbia's in the wake of Yugoslavia's destruction, and even less assertive than Hungary's relatively mild overtures toward its nearby ethnic kin. These policies, the dependent variable of a "dog that didn't bark," need to be explained.

Policy toward Russians in other of the Commonwealth of Independent States (CIS) generally followed three tracks in the 1990s: dual citizenship, "special relations," and state-to-state relations within the CIS community (Zevelev 2001). In 1992, as the newly created Russian Federation emerged formally from the Soviet Union, the official policy of "state building," focusing on relations with the other newly sovereign states, was contrasted with substantial amounts of nationalist rhetoric about the need to remember "our compatriots in these countries" (Zevelev 2001, 134). In 1993, a newly published Russian military doctrine identified the "rights, freedoms and legal interests of citizens of the Russian Federation in foreign countries" as an "external danger" in need of defense, potentially justifying military intervention (134). There was also some significant attention in 1993 paid to the specific case of the Crimea, a dispute between Ukraine and Russia that took on irredentist dimensions. Concerns arose early, therefore, about whether Russia would adopt an irredentist policy toward Russians in neighboring countries.

Dual Citizenship: Symbolic Irredentism Abandoned

In keeping with its early nationalist rhetoric, Russia adopted a policy of seeking "dual citizenship" for Russians living in the Near Abroad. The idea was first suggested by the foreign minister, Andrei Kozyrev, in January 1994, and had the support of the relevant government agencies, including the Federal Migration Service and significant constituencies within Russia (Zevelev 2001, 135). The idea also enjoyed fairly widespread support among Russians in other CIS countries, with support over 80 percent in some places. This proposal came amidst increasing tension between Russia and the Baltic states over citizenship issues in 1993 and 1994. Latvia and Estonia in the early 1990s adopted extremely restrictive citizenship laws, making it very difficult, if not impossible, for Russians living there to gain citizenship in their states of residence.

However, neighboring states (and European and other countries outside the former USSR) viewed the proposal with some suspicion, as a possible first move toward making irredentist claims on the territories occupied by these Russian communities within their borders. Dual citizenship would create an unusual legal category, in which the Russian Federation could have a claim over the protection (physical as well as legal) of populations living on someone else's sovereign territory, in which those populations might also be citizens. The specter of divided loyalties was likewise raised, and some worried about the creation of Russian "fifth columns."

In order to enact this policy, Russia needed agreements with its neighbors on allowing dual-citizenship status. Absent a specific agreement, residents who gain citizenship in one country ordinarily give up their citizenship in another, and it was clear that many former Soviet republics preferred it that way. In fact, while dual citizenship was an official Russian policy, the Russian government was not very successful in reaching such agreements. Despite substantial rhetoric otherwise—Russian officials demanded in 1994 that any state treaty between Russia and Ukraine must include a dual-citizenship clause, for example (Barrington 1995; Wydra 2004)—by 1995, only two former Soviet republics had signed agreements with Russia with any mention of dual-citizenship arrangements: Turkmenistan and Tajikistan, countries with the smallest Russian populations living within their borders. Ukraine, Belarus, and Kazakhstan—which together contained some 75 percent of the Russian diaspora in the Near Abroad—refused to sign any such agreements, despite sometimes high-level pressure put on them to do so (Katagoshchina 2002, 44). By the late 1990s, there were perhaps 900,000 "informal" dual citizens, mostly through government inefficiency or lack of concern, but these existed outside any legal or treaty framework and thus provided Russia with very little leverage (Zevelev 2001, 141–142).[2]

"Special Relations": A Symbolic Replacement for Symbolic Irredentism

By 1995, the dual-citizenship policy was abandoned in favor of emphasizing "special relations" with Russians outside the Russian Federation. Originally, the special-relations policy was intended as a supplement to the more legally oriented dual-citizenship initiative. When the latter was phased out, special relations became the primary Russian government policy toward Russians in the Near Abroad (Zevelev 2001, 146). The groundwork was laid in 1994, when the government endorsed the concept of "compatriots," including Russian citizens living in neighboring countries, former Soviet citizens with no citizenship, and citizens of other countries who desired close ties with Russia

(142–143). Officially, the policy made no mention of Russian ethnicity at all, and it promoted integration within the host states while providing Russian-language media and cultural support.

Even this relatively modest initiative accomplished little. Despite support-ive rhetoric from Boris Yeltsin and other top officials, the bureaucracy largely marginalized the issue, and there was very little pressure to implement the policy from constituent groups within Russia or from the Russians in the Near Abroad themselves. A series of public stabs at implementation were taken from 1996 through 1998, but the programs envisioned were always un-derfunded. In 1996, Yeltsin's government created a foundation, Rossiyane, whose objective was to provide financial support for "compatriots"—but by 1998, the government money earmarked for this fund had largely disappeared, apparently due to corruption (143–149). Far from being a Trojan horse for Russian irredentist claims, the special-relations policy was at best a symbol useful either in scoring political points rhetorically or in redirecting resources for other ends.

State-to-State Ties: Realism, Not Irredentism

In the course of developing its bilateral relations with its now-sovereign neighbors, Russia had an opportunity to engage in irredentist demands, but largely chose not to do so. There was plenty of nationalist rhetoric in the early 1990s; in 1992, for example, Yeltsin threatened to tie the issue of citizenship for Russians in Estonia and Latvia to withdrawals of Russian troops still sta-tioned in the Baltic republics from Soviet days. Despite the rhetoric, the troop withdrawals occurred on schedule, and no further significant action was taken.

Outsiders might have expected the Commonwealth of Independent States—the international framework created in 1991 on the bones of the old Soviet Union—to provide a mechanism for Russia to exert its influence over its newly sovereign neighbors. In relations across the CIS, however, no joint documents have made reference to the status of Russians in other CIS states (Zevelev 2001, 149–150). The CIS did create a number of agreements on the inviolability of borders and peace and stability, essentially ruling out seces-sionism and irredentism entirely. Newly signed agreements also respected the rights of minorities in CIS states, though these tended to be weak and to go unratified, even within Russia. Failure to ratify such agreements in the Russian Duma could be taken for an example of symbolic ethnic politics—some nationalist politicians held that Russians in the Near Abroad were not "minorities" in other states, but part of the divided Russian homeland, a symbolic stand obviously not in line with the Yeltsin government's policies (Zevelev 2001, 151). But such arguments had little practical effect on Russian foreign policy.

In fact, the creation of the CIS and its activities in the 1990s suggest an emphasis on practical and economic rather than nationalist forces, emblematic of the puzzle of Russia's "missing nationalism" after the collapse of the Soviet Union. The initial CIS agreement came on the heels of a declaration, on December 8, 1991, from the leaders of Ukraine, Belarus, and Russia. Fearing an ethnically based Slavic union that would leave them out in the cold economically, Central Asian states met first by themselves (on December 13) and then with the rest of the former USSR (on December 21), choosing a framework dictated largely by economic self-interest over a new, ethnically defined Eurasia (Gleason 2001). The CIS went on to spawn dozens, even hundreds, of agreements among members, most of which were concerned with economic relations and transborder issues of common interest. As with Eastern Europe, moreover, there was a pronounced tendency for the countries involved to interpret these agreements in light of their own interests. To the extent that Russia put substantial resources on the line in the CIS arena, it did so primarily in Tajikistan, where there were very few ethnic Russians but much concern for rising Islamist movements, an issue driving much of the security cooperation across Central Asia in the 1990s (Gleason 2001). In this context, though Russia could have chosen to pursue irredentist claims or policies aimed toward Russian populations in its neighbors, it instead allowed those concerns to take a back seat to issues of economics and transregional security.

Crimean Dispute: Irredentist Opportunity Lost

The one area in which Russia *did* appear to engage in making irredentist demands, at least initially, was the Crimea. In 1954, the Soviet regime had transferred formal control of the Crimean peninsula from the Russian republic to Ukraine, although the area was (and remains) largely populated with Russians (who make up about 70 percent of its three million inhabitants). Immediately after the creation of the Commonwealth of Independent States (CIS) on December 8, 1991, the governments of Russia and Ukraine began a struggle over control of the Soviet Black Sea Fleet, which was based on the Crimea. Part of this struggle included requests from the Russian parliament to open the question of whether the original 1954 transfer was constitutional. This set off political bickering within the Russian government, with parliament pushing the harder line while Foreign Minister Andrei Kozyrev of the executive branch preached caution (Friedman 1992). The crisis was further exacerbated by the Crimeans themselves, who in a January 1991 referendum voted for the restoration of Crimea's status as an Autonomous Republic and in September demanded independence. In the context of similar moves by Nagorno-Karabakh in Azerbaijan (see chapter 3), this move could reasonably be interpreted as a bid for reunion with Mother Russia.

The Ukrainian government responded by reasserting its right to the territory. Russians in the Crimea began to organize and demand to be part of Russia, fearful of Ukrainian attempts to regulate language and other aspects of their lives (Seward 1992). The situation appeared to be headed toward a crisis in late spring 1992, with the Ukrainian government vowing to take measures to stop any loss of its territory. But in a retreat from its earlier, more aggressive position, the Russian parliament in May declared that, while it considered the original transfer of the territory to have been illegal, there should be negotiations that would respect the interests of all parties in a settlement (Iams 1992). Russian demands continued to center not on the Crimea as a whole, but on claims to Sevastopol, where the Black Sea Fleet was based. This call for dialogue opened the door to an agreement that summer granting the territory more autonomy within Ukraine, while respecting the 1954 transfer and the boundaries it created. With the subsequent transfer of the Black Sea Fleet to Russia in 1993 in exchange for compensation and cancellation of much of Ukraine's debt to Russia, the Russian government renounced its claims to the territory, and the issue was closed with respect to formal reunification.[3] It appears in hindsight that, for Russia, the driving issue of the crisis was the strategic nature of Sevastopol and the disposition of the Black Sea Fleet, rather than the reunification of Crimean Russians with Russia (Wydra 2004).

The overall picture of Russian irredentism in the 1990s is therefore one of nationalist opportunities not taken and irredentist claims not pursued. Though Russia had ample opportunity to make claims, on a variety of grounds, against a number of its new neighbors for territory occupied by Russians, it chose not to do so in nearly all cases. Even half-measures that might imply irredentism, such as the Dual Citizenship initiative, were abandoned in favor of good relations and repeated statements of respect for borders. Where Russia did choose to exert its muscle—in the Tajik civil war, in Chechnya, and to a lesser extent in Moldova and Georgia—it did so with little regard to ethnic Russians in the Near Abroad.[4] In places where a nationalist-minded foreign policy would seem to demand a significant response—particularly in the Baltic states, with sizeable and embattled Russian minorities—the Russian government did surprisingly little. Russia did certainly exert substantial influence over many former Soviet states, but its pattern of doing so had much less to do with either the number or treatment of diaspora Russians and more to do with economic interests and practical Russian domestic politics. Given the parallels between the Soviet Union and Yugoslavia, whose collapse engendered a great deal of violent irredentism, we must ask why Russia chose to avoid irredentism in favor of more moderate policies on ethnic kin issues.

International Pressures on Russian Ethnic Kin Policy

As the Soviet Union collapsed and Eastern Europe was set free from Moscow's domination, there was a growing realization in the West that pent-up nationalisms could well erupt into violent irredentism. A number of Western international organizations, including the EU, NATO, and the OSCE, tried to create incentives for avoiding disruptive and destabilizing behavior. The very desire of the former communist countries to join these institutions and integrate themselves with the West (and thereby get access to Western capital, technology, and markets) suggested, for some, a logic that would lead these states to behave themselves and put the interests of their states over the nationalist desire to reunite with ethnic kin.[5]

For Russia, however, these external forces were not sufficient to explain the lack of irredentist effort in the face of the opportunities of the 1990s. Russia's interaction with Western organizations came primarily in its complex relationship with the "big two," NATO and the EU. This interaction included Russia's joining in NATO's Partnership for Peace initiative and the Council of Europe, as well as ongoing negotiations about the expansion of NATO and, to a certain extent, the EU as well. Russia also interacted with the OSCE, which it already had a relationship with, over a variety of security issues, including its involvement in the Caucasus and in Chechnya. All of these demonstrate the relative weakness of external pressures on Russia's foreign policy. One external circumstance *did* play a restraining role—the lack of organization among the Russian diaspora itself. But even in this case, Russia failed to take steps to try to unite diaspora Russians, suggesting that this was not a definitive restraining factor. Overall, Russian behavior has been much more a function of domestic dynamics than of international organizations and the pressures and influence they bring to bear (Mendelson 2002).

NATO, the EU, and Russia: Insufficient Incentives

As the fear of irredentism grew with the Balkan wars and the uncertainty caused by the collapse of the Soviet Union, Western European countries sought to use the desire of their Eastern European counterparts to join various European organizations such as the EU and NATO as a lever to regulate their behavior and discourage irredentist activity.

In the case of Russia, these pressures were ineffective, in large part because they were irrelevant. Russia did not seek entry into the EU and sought only a managed connection with NATO. In 1992, the Russian government did begin talks with the European Community on a free-trade agreement and "partnership accord." The agreement was held up for a year, largely on trade issues though with some concerns expressed about human rights, and was completed in late 1993 (Shargorodsky 1993). No particular attempt seems to have been made to use this process as a means of affecting Russia's nationalism policies, and indeed the agreement was concluded before the issue of dual citizenship—the first significant potential Russian irredentist tool—came up.

As with the European Union, Russia never made a claim to desire membership in NATO. Indeed, Russia's relations with NATO were dominated throughout the early 1990s by the former's concerns about NATO expansion into former Warsaw Pact countries, which they feared could ignite a "new division in Europe" (Jacobson 1994). Russia signed on to NATO's Partnership for Peace initiative in mid-1994, but relations remained focused on NATO expansion, which Russia continued to resist. As with the Russia-EU relationship, no significant pressure with respect to nationalism issues was attempted, and relations continued to focus throughout the 1990s on expansion and military issues, particularly Russia's relations with Iran (Schweid 1995). Concerns were raised that rapid NATO expansion could drive Russia away from liberal internationalism and toward a more Eurasia-focused nationalism (the appointment of Yevgenii Primakov to replace Andrei Kozyrev as foreign minister in 1996 was thought to signal such a shift), but those concerns did not stop NATO from continuing its efforts to integrate much of Eastern Europe rapidly (Lynch 2002).

The one pan-European organization to which Russia did apply was the Council of Europe. Its entrance was initially delayed over concerns regarding its progress toward democracy and the rule of law (Council of Europe Ministers 1994), and talks were suspended for part of 1995 regarding Russia's actions in Chechnya. Russia was eventually admitted, despite its Chechnya policies, in early 1996. Being a largely political and diplomatic body set up to promote human rights, democracy and the rule of law, Council of Europe membership gave Russia a certain amount of political clout in the West, but it lacked the tangible benefits that membership in the European Union and NATO entailed.

The lack of Russian irredentism is, therefore, not a function of pressure applied by Western organizations. Unlike many of the smaller Eastern European countries, Russia had little desire to join most Western-dominated European institutions as a full member, preferring instead to negotiate bilateral relationship agreements with them. Most of these agreements were in place by 1994, removing the negotiations surrounding these ties as a potential influence on Russian policy thereafter.

The Russian Diaspora: Unfavorable International Conditions

Previous studies (Saideman and Ayres 2000) have suggested that irredentism is more likely when the targeted ethnic kin group is politically mobilized. It is easier for an irredentist state to make a claim on behalf of its ethnic kin if those kin can be seen to desire such intervention and are engaged in behavior showing their interest in being reincorporated into the homeland. While this is not an absolute requirement, it helps quite a bit; a mobilized diaspora provides both a partner to work with within the host state and a measure of international legitimacy, as the irredentist state can claim simply to want "the will of the people."

In the case of the Russian diaspora in the Near Abroad, this condition was for the most part lacking. This is true in part because Russians in the Near Abroad are an extraordinarily diverse population. References to the twenty-five million Russians living outside Russia proper create the illusion that there exists a reasonably homogenous population just beyond Russia's borders that could be mobilized, if only leaders would try. This not only overstates the extent to which Russians share a common understanding of what it means to be Russian but also glosses over the diversity of historical circumstances that brought these populations into the republics in the first place.

Many Russians living in the Near Abroad have been there for generations, sometimes even centuries, and share historical and cultural ties to those lands. In the Baltic States, where some of the most significant Russian minorities reside, much of the Russian population settled there in the 1940s, and significant numbers trace their roots back to the late nineteenth and early twentieth centuries (Iwaskiw 1995). Similarly, the Russian populations in Belarus and Moldova arrived in large numbers immediately after World War II as part of the Soviet rebuilding effort (Fedor 1995, 30–31, 117–120). Given the demographic trends in former Soviet republics, which are skewed toward the young, most Russians in the Near Abroad were born and raised in those places, and have no direct personal experience with Russia itself. This has led to a situation in which, while acknowledging some common titular "Russianness," Russians in bordering countries may well have more in common with their immediate neighbors than they do with Russians across the border in the Russian Federation (Service 2003, 43–59).

Given this historical diversity, it is unsurprising that the Russian population outside Russia has provided very little pull for an irredentist foreign policy. With the exception of the Russians in the Crimea, Russians in neighboring states made very few attempts to mobilize or take collective political action. Ethnographic studies in the 1990s suggested that "Russians in the borderland states display a weak sense of communal identity or willingness to engage in a politics of collective action, even when they have been marginalized by the new regimes in power" (Smith 1999: 501).[6] Surveys conducted across a range of Near Abroad states in 1995–96 found that only 10 percent—25 percent identified themselves as primarily Russian, as opposed to Soviet or as citizens of their home republics (Poppe and Hagendoorn 2001). Some of this may have been geographic—Russians in non-Russian republics tended to concentrate themselves overwhelmingly in cities, and especially in capital cities, where they tended to be far from the borders of the new Russia and relatively entrenched in their communities (Katagoshchina 2002). Much was also due to these Russians' historical ties to the areas in which they lived. In short, Russians in the Near Abroad in the 1990s did not seem to consider themselves as kin in need of the protection of the Russian state.

This has been true even where those populations have been most heavily disadvantaged by being Russian—in Estonia and Latvia, the only two post-Soviet states that did not automatically grant citizenship to all residents living within their borders. As the Soviet Union was collapsing, thousands of Russians supported independence for Latvia and Estonia, both in demonstrations and by voting (Bremmer 1994). After independence, however, surveys of the Russians in these countries indicated that they felt their situation to be unjust and discriminatory, largely because of the citizenship problem. But they took no action in the public arena. From 1993 to 1999, only one Russian demonstration of any significant size took place in the Baltic States: roughly a thousand mostly elderly Russians demonstrated in Riga in 1998, primarily over economic issues (Smith 1999, 519). Relatively few opted to "return" to Russia (fewer than 100,000 Russians emigrated to Russia from Estonia and Latvia in 1991–97), and few attempted to protect themselves by applying for Russian extraterritorial citizenship (fewer than 200,000 in Estonia and Latvia by the end of the 1990s). Most Russians in the Near Abroad seemed committed to a strategy of political integration with their host states (Smith 1999, 517–518).[7]

In some cases, the background of Russian political power appears to have been enough to curb the worst excesses against ethnic Russians. In Uzbekistan, an extremely repressive language policy put in place in the early 1990s was modified in light of "the role of Russia as a strategic partner of Uzbekistan" (Katagoshchina 2002, 32). Part of this apathy on the part of diaspora Russians was undoubtedly fed by the sense that the Russian Federation was not going to stick its neck out very far for their interests. Still, the fact that this lack of mobilization goes back to the early 1990s suggests that, even had there been greater irredentist desire within Russia, it would have had a difficult time in the face of disinterest on the part of the kin who are supposed to be "saved."

Russian Domestic Circumstances

The picture of international pressures on Russian irredentist policy is thus mixed at best, with the primary international check on potential irredentism coming from the diaspora Russians themselves. Even this need not have presented an insurmountable obstacle; some combination of dual citizenship and a well-funded and well-articulated "special relationship" policy could have encouraged Russians abroad to reidentify themselves as Russians and to mobilize as such. The lack of even these efforts, therefore, must be explained with reference to the internal political dynamics of the Russian Federation. Potential domestic dynamics include the ethnic diversity of the Russian Federation itself, economic conditions over time, domestic power politics, and the politics of Russian identity.

Domestic Structure of Russia: Diversity and Glass Houses

One factor potentially encouraging caution in Russian nationalism policy in the 1990s was its ethnic diversity. The Russian Republic within its old Soviet boundaries contained sixteen out of twenty of the "autonomous republics" set up under the Soviet system to accommodate ethnic minorities, and another fifteen of eighteen "autonomous regions" and "autonomous districts." In all, a total of 27 percent of Russian territory within its new, Federation borders was tied up in regions specifically oriented toward non-Russians (Colton and Legvold 1992, 21–32). Some of these, notably Chechnya and Tatarstan, had a history of resistance to (as well as collaboration with) Russian rule going back centuries. It could be argued, therefore, that Russia was reluctant to pursue irredentism toward its own ethnic kin for fear of sparking separatist sentiments within its own boundaries.

Several factors argue against this conclusion. With regard to Chechnya, Russia's most significant separatist problem, the issue was never one of trying to *prevent* secessionism: Chechen independence efforts began in 1991, before the new Russian Federation had a chance to decide on its own policies. The cause-and-effect train therefore runs backward here—separatism had already broken out with regards to Chechnya. Subsequently, Russian leaders did use the presence of Russians in Chechnya as a justification for retaining the territory (that is, for resisting separatism)—but the strategic location of key oil infrastructure facilities leading to the Caspian Sea, and the fact that Russia never seriously considered splitting off the northern parts of Chechnya where Russians were concentrated, suggest that Russian ethnic nationalism was never a serious driving factor.[8] Heavy-handed tactics in Chechnya had the potential not only to inflame Chechen nationalism—which they did—but to spark separatist sentiments elsewhere. Yet Russia's pursuit of its self-defined economic and strategic interests suggests that the Russian government was perfectly willing to run such risks, or did not take them seriously. Finally, the power differential between Russia and its neighbors makes the mutual vulnerability issue highly asymmetric: Russia is so much larger than its surrounding neighbors, and than any one of its smaller internal regions, as to preclude any significant counterirredentism on someone else's part. Russia's relationship with Georgia (for example) is far different from Somalia's relationship with Ethiopia, and should be expected to reflect the power imbalance between the two.

Economic Conditions: Motivation Versus Capacity

Economic conditions can also be seen as a force driving irredentist foreign policy. Diversionary theories in foreign policy have a long lineage, trading on the logic that governments will engage in aggression to distract their populations from difficulties at home, including economic problems (Morgan and Bickers 1992; DeRouen 1995; Heldt 1999). This is primarily a motivational theory: it presumes that leaders are given a motivation to engage in aggressive foreign policy by domestic difficulties. As an emerging democracy in the early 1990s (Mansfield and Snyder 2005), Russia would seem to be a good candidate for this theory; emerging institutions are generally believed to possess less legitimacy, and leaders therefore need to rally the people more than might be the case in more established systems. Economic difficulty can be a double-edged sword, however. A country with financial problems may have the motive but lack the means to engage in aggression, since actual aggression costs money that the state may not have. Finally, there is the countervailing dimension of economic interests—whether the powers that be gain or lose from increased connections to the world economy. It thus makes sense to see if Russia's economic fortunes in the 1990s bore any connection to nationalist policies.

While many observers talk of the Russian economic crisis of 1998 (Ahrend 2004), the Russian economy was to a large extent in a tailspin throughout the 1990s, with recovery beginning only in 1999 (Popov 2000; for an alternative view, see Shleifer and Treisman 2004). From 1991 to 1998, Russian GDP dropped by 39 percent, according to official figures (and as much as 45 percent by some estimates; see Proskournina 2002). Energy consumption decreased by nearly 20 percent over the same period, the ruble lost 99 percent of its value against the dollar by decade's end (Shleifer and Treisman 2004), and investment in 1999 was four times lower than it had been in 1989, insufficient even to compensate for the loss of capital stock in the economy (Popov 2000). Inflation soared, especially in the early 1990s, with price increases over 2000 percent in 1992 and 1,000 percent in 1993 (Curtis 1996). Added to the macroeconomic numbers was the instability and confusion brought about by the privatization process, in which Russians who had lived their lives under a state-run economy needed to adjust to an entirely new economic system.

Overall, Russia's economic conditions were dreadful throughout the 1990s, particularly for large portions of the population suffering from the dislocation of suddenly shifting from planned to market economics. Such conditions might well be expected to generate incentives for Russian leaders to divert attention to problems abroad; but in the 1990s, Russian policy toward Russians in the Near Abroad was by and large not used in this manner. Indeed, there were some indications that the logic ran the other way; some Russian officials saw the dual-citizenship initiative as a means of preventing Russians in neighboring states from moving back to Russia and contributing further to Russia's economic woes (Zevelev 2001, 133).[9] In this sense, Russia's dual-citizenship plan was similar to Hungary's Status Law: a measure designed more to keep ethnic kin outside the country than to incorporate them into it (see chapter 4).

If the motive was unrealized, was this because of resource constraints? Did a bad economy restrain rather than fuel Russian irredentism? To the extent that Russia had economic resources in the 1990s, these were mostly a function of the price of oil, as the Russian economy was heavily dependent on exports of oil and other resources. In the mid-1990s, Russia ranked third in the world in oil production, after only Saudi Arabia and the United States, making oil the main source of foreign exchange for the Russian government (Curtis 1996). Oil prices in the 1990s fluctuated in both directions: after a spike in 1991 (a function of the Persian Gulf War), prices declined through 1994, rose again through 1996, plummeted to a twenty-five-year low in 1998, and then began a steep increase. These price fluctuations do correlate with Russia's aggression in Chechnya (which began when oil revenues started rising in 1994, stopped in 1996, and resumed again when oil prices jumped in 1999), which is not surprising given Chechnya's location at the nexus of much of Russia's oil infrastructure. But they do not seem to have any relation to Russia's dual-citizenship initiative or other aspects of its nationalism policies. Indeed, dual citizenship was dropped at around the same time (1995) that oil prices were beginning to climb. Had there been a stronger incentive toward aggressive irredentism held back by resource constraints, we ought to have expected a shift in the other direction at that point. It appears, then, that Russia's economic conditions provided a potential motive, and at some points some available means, which were not matched by irredentist policies.

Some of this may be attributable to the nature of the new Russian economy. Russia's rapid economic privatization put a substantial amount of its wealth and productive resources—shrinking though they were—in the hands of a relatively small number of powerful businessmen (often referred to as "oligarchs"; see Hoffman 2002). While the connections between this group and the Kremlin were complex, it is clear that these businessmen had a fairly substantial say in Russian policy—that they were certainly part of the politically relevant "selectorate." The interests of this group were largely in economic openness, because only through connections to the world economy could it export oil and gain access to Western financial sources and institutions. Rather than provide a source of discontent for isolationist nationalist politicians like Zhirinovsky, therefore, the structure of the Russian economy in the 1990s mitigated against aggressive military actions against neighboring countries, particularly countries like Ukraine that served as gateways to Europe through which goods and capital could pass.

Building Domestic Political Power

As the previous discussion suggests, political calculations based on who has access to power can affect foreign policy judgments. Many have argued that electoral cycles and other major political events can influence governments to engage in foreign policy actions, including more aggressive behavior (Putnam 1988; Hagan 1994; Smith 1996). Given Russia's circumstances—a transition from Communist Party rule to elected institutions unknown in Russia's history—there was certainly the potential for politicians to play the "ethnic card" in trying to garner votes. There are enough cases of aggression in these kinds of circumstances to have considered it a very real possibility for Russia in the 1990s. But the fact that Russian nationalism has been more about imperialism than ethnicity made ethnically based political appeals less effective than they were in other parts of the former communist world.

There were certainly plenty of opportunities for ethnic political dynamics. Soon after becoming an independent country in 1992, the Russian Federation suffered a severe political crisis in the fall of 1993, followed almost immediately by the first Russian parliamentary elections in December. Elections were again held for the Duma (Russia's lower house of parliament) in December 1995; these were dominated by Gennady Zyuganov and the Communist Party of the Russian Federation, which took a harder line toward the Near Abroad than did Yeltsin. The President faced a reelection cycle the following summer, with Zyuganov as his closest competitor in a runoff election in July. Further governmental crises in 1998 and 1999 led up to an attempt in the Duma to impeach Yeltsin in May 1999. The subsequent government shakeup brought Vladimir Putin into the government; he went on to win the next presidential election in March 2000.

A closer look at Russian elections in the 1990s reveals a complex interaction between emerging political structures and nationalism as a political force—or a political tool. A great many political parties were created in the 1990s as multiparty elections became the norm, but many of these parties had few if any actual constituents, and many others did little to advance the interests of their constituencies, focusing instead largely on getting elected or reelected (Mendelson 2002, 45). The use of nationalism as a political tool was often contradictory. Zhirinovsky, the most prominent Russian nationalist politician whose Liberal Democratic Party did surprisingly well in the December 1993 elections, attacked non-Russian minorities and threatened neighboring republics who treated Russians badly. But his central political platform in 1993 was the reconstruction of the Russian Empire, which would bring millions of non-Russians back under Moscow's rule. Many of the LDP's positions were territorial or economic rather than ethnic—returning Alaska or Finland to Russian control would serve no obvious ethnic Russian purpose. Much of Zhirinovsky's support came from the military, which was substantially weakened by the collapse of the USSR—support based on self-interest rather than ethnicity (Cooperman 1993). The LDP did well in 1993, capturing nearly 25 percent of the vote, but by the 1995 elections saw its share slip to less than half that.

In the 1995 Duma elections, Zyuganov's Communist Party—which had a "nationalist" flavor because of its demands for a return to the USSR—attempted to ally itself with Alexander Lebed's Congress of Russian Communities, but political tensions and mistrust remained high between them. Running on a platform heavily laced with arguments about external threats to Russia but primarily focused on economic conditions, the Communists again did well, taking over 20 percent of the vote. Though nationalism played a role here, the continued Russian economic malaise appears to have stoked most of the anti-Yeltsin voting, into which both Communists and nationalists were able to tap.

Perhaps most notable, in terms of Russia's institutional development as a democracy, is the extent to which these putative nationalist "victories" in Duma elections failed to translate into significant policies toward Russians abroad, or even inside Russia itself. This had mostly to do with the nature of the Russian constitution, which vested substantial amounts of power in the presidency. Zyuganov lost the 1996 election to Yeltsin, despite widespread appeals to Russian nationalists. Yeltsin may have been able to undercut those appeals by bringing Alexander Lebed, who had run on a nationalist platform, into his administration.[10] The precise nature of Zyuganov's nationalism is also an issue: while he clearly did reach out to Russians as Russians, he also campaigned to non-Russian peoples on an "Eurasianist" platform, which did not really resonate with Russian irredentism (Clover 1999). In any case, in that election, nationalist (especially irredentist) issues appeared to take a back seat to other concerns. Although Yeltsin signed an agreement on "reintegration" with Belarus in March ahead of the voting, it did little to affect his poll numbers, and some surveys indicated that only one in eight voters put reintegration on their list of top five priorities for the new president (Treisman 1996, 66). With the Russian economy taking a beating, it appears that economic issues took precedence over nationalist ones, with one analysis of Yeltsin's victory giving credit to a Russian version of Tammany Hall social spending (Treisman 1996).

In 2000, the ultranationalist Zhirinovsky did very poorly against Putin, while Putin's campaign was run primarily on issues of economics, corruption, and crime (Isachenkov 2000). Even Putin's use of the Chechen conflict was in non-Russian terms, emphasizing issues of crime and terrorism rather than casting the conflict as a Russian/non-Russian issue (Isachenkov 2000; Charleton 1999). Putin finished with over 52 percent of the vote, avoiding a runoff election against a field of ten other candidates. While appeals to ethnic Russian politics played a role in various Duma elections, therefore, this never translated into power where it counted: the presidency.

Though one can observe the use of nationalism (as a broad category, including ethnic nationalism) as an electoral tool throughout the 1990s—there were certainly plenty of political opportunities which various pronationalist alliances led by the Communist Party tried to exploit—there seems to have been little impact on government policy toward ethnic Russians, which remained largely in the hands of the president. The coincidence of the Crimea dispute with Russia's early political crises could have created an opportunity for Yeltsin to rally Russians around the flag rather than falling into factions, as happened by 1993; yet he made no attempt to do so. Though dual citizenship and, later, "Special Relations" had strong support in the Duma, Yeltsin did little to implement these ideas, instead allowing them to die off quietly. At the point when Yeltsin faced a serious electoral challenge—in 1995 and 1996—though his rhetoric was frequently nationalistic (in the sense of appealing to "Russians" or the "Russian nation" in at least an implicitly ethnic way), he made no attempt to engage in more aggressive policies toward the diaspora Russian issue.

To the extent that Russia's turbulent political dynamics had any impact on its policies toward Russians in the Near Abroad in the 1990s, the effect seems to have been mostly rhetorical—tough talk designed for domestic consumption and the winning of parliamentary elections but unmatched by any serious action on the part of the government (Zevelev 2001, 155). The conclusion is that, while some level of symbolic nationalism was necessary for power in Russia, real nationalism—that is, policies that expended resources in advancing the interests of ethnic Russians beyond Russia's new borders—was not. Yeltsin, and Putin after him, were able to get and hold power by being rhetorically nationalist, championing ethnic nationalist causes, while not actually doing anything about them (Phillips 1997). This, combined with the lack of a coherent vision for what Russian nationalists wanted, led to a domestic political system in which actual nationalist actions that might threaten the power and welfare of the state—like aggressive irredentism—were not necessary to gain and remain in power.

Content of National Identity: What Does It Mean to Be "Russian"?

This lack of a coherent "nationalist" platform in Russia needs careful examination. The electoral picture of the 1990s suggests that there was a consistent minority of the population—perhaps 20–30 percent—that would respond to nationalist appeals invoking Russians as an ethnic group, though even within this minority there may have been little agreement on the boundaries of that group. But given the conditions of economic and political uncertainly, we might have expected this number to be much higher, particularly if a politician had made the effort to mobilize Russians on ethnic political grounds. Some politicians *did* make that effort, but failed to garner more than a quarter or so of the vote, despite what appear to be favorable economic and political conditions. If these conditions do not explain the lack of Russian irredentism, then, what of the substance of nationalism itself?

Given that Russian history for centuries had been tied up in the possession of an empire of one sort or another, it is hardly surprising that the question of "what does it mean to be Russian?" should loom so large in the wake of the Soviet collapse.[11] Indeed, the field seemed in the early 1990s wide open to redefining the extent and boundaries of the Russian people, and there was substantial debate over the various meanings of "Russian" (Laitin 1998, 312–314). This was true in part because Russia was, in terms of nationalism, something of an historical blank slate. The Communist Party had spent seventy years trying to deny nationalism altogether (with some exceptions during World War II), while the tsarist period previously had largely not relied on notions of a "Russian nation" to sustain its rule (Laitin 1998, 300–302). So an opportunity existed for politicians to present new and novel definitions of "Russian," to see which would fly politically. Some of these new definitions could support or even demand irredentism; others would have no room for it. These definitional questions are key for our account, because irredentism only makes sense under certain definitions of who counts as a Russian (Szporluk 1992, 99–100).

Tolz (1998, 995–996) argues that five definitions of the Russian nation were put forth in the 1990s:

1. Empire: Russians are defined as an "imperial people," and "Russian" is synonymous with the possession of an empire more or less coterminous with the old USSR.
2. Eastern Slavs: Russians, Ukrainians, and Belarusians are part of the same nation, bound together by ethno-cultural similarities and a common past.
3. Language: Russians are defined as the community of Russian speakers, regardless of their ethnic heritage; language is the "main marker of national identity."
4. Race: Russians are those with specific blood ties to the nation.
5. Citizenship: Russians are all citizens of the Russian Federation, regardless of ethnic or cultural background.

Each of these views was championed by some leaders and parties in the 1990s, and none gained a clear and definitive hold over the Russian body politic.[12] Different choices, of course, have different consequences on Russia's policy toward Russians in the Near Abroad, and on the prospects for Russian irredentism.

Given that the last choice, identifying the Russian nation as coterminous with the borders of the Russian Federation, leaves no room for irredentism, the most obviously irredentist of these identity choices is the "Russia as empire" option. This also had the advantage of the weight of Russian history; both before and during the Soviet period, Russians were encouraged to think of the entire empire as their "homeland," rather than the "Russian Republic" portion of it (Szporluk 1992, 95; Smith 1999, 506). For centuries, Russians (however defined) had not had a state to themselves; they had existed at the center of a vast, multiethnic empire that always included non-Russians. This view of Russianness was adopted by both communists and self-proclaimed Russian nationalists in the early 1990s, who came together to form political alliances like the National Salvation Front and the People's Alliance (Tolz 1998, 997–998).

As time passed, however, this view was increasingly discredited as it became clear that a return to empire was unlikely.[13] Moreover, Yeltsin, by quickly and firmly recognizing the sovereignty of the other republics during his own rise to power in the early 1990s, had clearly put himself out of that camp (Szporluk 1992, 95). The grandest form of Russian irredentism, therefore, had already been ruled out. By rejecting the notion of rebuilding the empire, Russia lost its claim on the totality of its former territories. This version of Russian nationalism was, however, notable in Russian elections throughout the 1990s: alliances between Communists and nationalists were common but became increasingly uneasy, and when such alliances were tested at the highest level—presidential elections—they always failed. Ultimately, broad Russian nationalism based on restoring the empire was a victim of its own history— many Russians did not like conditions in the 1990s, but not enough were willing to embrace the solution of returning to the past of the USSR. This kind of Russian nationalism was therefore saddled with ideological baggage—Soviet Communism—which other movements (like Milosevic's demand for a Greater Serbia) were not.

The remaining question, therefore, was of the more traditional irredentist sort—what to do with the twenty-five million Russians living outside the borders of the newly created Russian Federation? Three other alternatives—

Russians as Eastern Slavs, Russians as Russian-speakers, and Russians by blood—held the possibility of some form of irredentism toward this group. Of those advocating the first of these positions, the most prominent was Alexander Solzhenitsyn, though his was primarily an academic, not a political, role. More significant were politicians like the leader of the Russian Public Union, Sergei Baburin, and (by 1994) many members of the National Salvation Front, who adopted unity with Ukraine and Belarus as a more attainable goal (Tolz 1998, 999–1000). For this group, the troubles of Russians in the Baltic States, or issues of pan-CIS dual citizenship, were not significant issues. A variation on this theme was carried in early post-Soviet relations between Belarus and Russia. Elements of the Belarusian government prior to 1993 appeared eager for a Russian nationalist victory, hoping that this would lead to reunification of the Belarus republic with Russia (Kozlovich 1993), though this was by no means a consensus view ("Belarus Opposition" 1993). But Zhirinovsky, whose LDP won nearly 25 percent of the vote, confused the issue by both refusing to recognize Belarus as a sovereign country (hinting at reunion) and calling for a cutoff of Russian aid to all former Soviet republics. In 1995, Zyuganov's Communist party pressed for renewed union with republics—but he singled out Ukraine, Belarus, and Kazakhstan as the most likely targets, moving the definition beyond Eastern Slavs (Smith 1995). On the whole, visions of Russian national unity with their brethren to the west never played a significant role in Russian electoral politics.

Those focusing on Russians as holding a common language or blood ties would obviously be much more inclined to support irredentist-looking policies. These views have focused not only on defining the in- and out-groups, but also on the importance of the territory in which they reside (Tolz 1998, 1001). This is precisely the sort of aggressive nationalism most feared in the West as likely to cause instability. However, the rhetoric and actions of the groups advocating these views—especially those who tie Russianness to race, like N. N. Lysenko's National Republican Party of Russia and A. P. Barkashov's Russian National Unity party—have tended to focus more on Russian survival vis-à-vis non-Russian peoples *within* the Russian Federation, in particular Central Asians and Muslims in the North Caucasus (Tolz 1998, 1004). The concern is not so much to reincorporate Russians living in Central Asian republics—there are relatively few—but to expel non-Russians back to those areas. There has long been a strain of Russian nationalism concerned much more with purity within the heart of Russia than with the outer boundaries of the empire; even during the Soviet era, underground Russian nationalist groups focused their attention on anti-Semitism and similar issues of Russian purity (Laitin 1998, 314). This racial view parallels Romanian nationalism: ethnically aggressive toward minorities at home, but much less concerned about kin abroad. This form of Russian nationalism was much more inward-looking and xenophobic than outward-looking and expansionist.

Nationalism based on race also had more traction than that based on language, because within Russia itself the Russian language was largely uncontested and was used not only among Russians but also as the common language for intergroup communication (Laitin 1998, 310). Russian nationalists within Russia tended to consider Russian-speaking migrants and refugees from the Near Abroad as unwanted foreigners, rather than coethnic kin to be welcomed home (Laitin 1998, 315). The Russian language was therefore, within Russia, a poor marker of who was and who was not Russian—a key difference between Russians living inside and outside Russia.

Across the range of possible Russian nationalisms, therefore, there has been relatively little support generated for a more aggressive Russian policy stance toward Russians in the Near Abroad. Some Russian nationalism was very clearly xenophobic toward non-Russians inside Russia, and thus would have opposed taking on other territories containing still more non-Russians. Other forms of Russian nationalism had only a weak identification with potential kin outside Russia. The result of this complex combination of different nationalisms mirrors the "hostile disinterest" suggested in table 1.1, though this was the result not of one coherent worldview but a combination of several. While the debate over Russian identity will likely continue into the future, and while some of these choices are distasteful to Western multiculturalists, the content of Russian nationalism has not supported irredentist policies very strongly, and seems unlikely to do so in the near future. In the absence of a widely shared definition of Russianness that would support irredentism, it is clearer why Russian policy on this question was as moderate as it was.

Identity and Restraint

Russian irredentism in the 1990s—or, more accurately, its absence—presents a significant puzzle. Given the presence of so many forces which have generated irredentism elsewhere—ethnic kin in nearby states with borders of questionable legitimacy, a lack of significant international institutional pressures, economic and political systems which would seem to reward nationalism and diversionary politics—why did Russia do nothing to pursue Russians and their territories in the Near Abroad? Even in the one clearest-cut case, the Crimea, where Russians were a substantial local majority and where the border's recent history went back only as far as the 1950s, Russia essentially backed away without a fight. Under circumstances where many expected a Russian voice to be heard, it was silent. This leads to an interesting and different pattern with regard to our hypotheses.

TABLE 6.1   Hypotheses and Russia

	Hypothesis	
1:	Interstate boundaries limit irredentism	Mixed: No aggression across international boundaries, but no aggression across formerly intrastate boundaries
2:	Admissions processes limit irredentism	Russia did not seek entry into EU, and only a partnership with NATO; attempts to limit other forms of Russian aggression were unsuccessful, but were not based on conditionality
3:	States will be deterred by stronger targets	Disconfirmed: Russia was consistently much more powerful than any potential irredentist target
4:	History of irredentism	Disconfirmed: Russia has no history of failed irredentism
5:	Tolerance of homogeneity/ xenophobia	Confirmed: Russian nationalism was xenophobic, but lacked a coherent connection to kin abroad
6:	Economics/irredentist interests	Confirmed: The interests of those in power in Russia favored international economic integration, and were less interested in irredentism
7a:	Actively irredentist kin	Mixed: Most Russians in the Near Abroad did not organize or indicate a desire to be rejoined to Mother Russia; exception in the case of Crimea Russians, who expressed a desire to be rejoined
7b:	Danger	Disconfirmed: Some Russian kin in the Near Abroad suffered substantial discrimination
7c:	Kin in positions of power	Confirmed: Kin largely absent from power

It is tempting to compare Russia with Serbia, because each occupied a similar position as the dominant ethnic republic within a larger, nominally nonethnic, communist empire. Certainly the legal and power situations were similar: both Serbia and Russia were presented with relatively new international boundaries created out of formerly intrastate republican boundaries, whose sovereignty had existed on paper if not in reality. Both represented in some sense the center of their respective multinational communist states, with one key difference—Russia's power relative to the other Soviet republics was vastly greater than Serbia's relative to its new neighbors. Yet Serbia chose the path of aggressive irredentism, while Russia did not.

Unlike countries in Eastern Europe, Russia stood at a greater distance from the major international organizations of the West and had a very different relationship to them. While the fall of communism in the Eastern Bloc countries raised the possibility that they might be allowed to join heretofore Western organizations—primarily the European Union and NATO—no one on either side considered that Russia might be a desirable new member of either. Russia and the Western organizations instead tried to negotiate new relationships with each other, based partly on cooperation (as in NATO's Partnership for Peace plan, though this later became a road to membership for Eastern European countries) but partly on attempted influence as well. NATO and the EU could not use the conditionality of membership to influence Russian policy, but they could attempt to use other avenues. In the few instances where they did so with regard to Russia's policies toward the Near Abroad—Tajikistan, the Caucasus, and Chechnya, all areas in which many in the West saw the possibility of resurgent Russian revanchism—they largely failed to influence Russia's choices of military aggression. Should Russia have pursued aggressive irredentism, it surely must have believed that the EU and NATO would be no obstacle.

The economics of Russia in the 1990s caused some observers to fear resurgent Russian nationalism; more than one compared the impoverished post-Soviet Russia with Germany in the 1930s (Kozhemyako 1999; Vaknin 2003). But our view of the influence of economics provides a better story. While transitioning to a form of democracy, Russian politics in the 1990s was not equally accessible to all of her citizens. Privatization created a new class of extremely wealthy capitalists, at least some of whom had influence over Kremlin policies at various times, and all of whom stood to gain rather than lose from increasing Russian connections to the global economy. Russia is another illustration, therefore, of how economic interests and politics are intertwined and must be considered together; it was the wealthy oligarchs rather than impoverished Russian masses who held more sway, and created a force inconsistent with aggressive irredentism.

To be sure, the twenty-five million "Russians" in the Near Abroad did little to help their own cause. Some did organize against locally oppressive conditions, but seldom did they reach out to the motherland for help or assistance. Those who felt the strongest ties to Mother Russia voted with their feet and simply went back—where their fellow Russians often treated them as foreigners. In only one instance, the Crimea, did a population mobilize itself, define itself as Russian (against the dominant Ukrainian), and ask for territorial reunion with the motherland (a condition they had lost only decades before). Yet even then, Russia backed away, preferring a deal with Ukraine on other issues to the lure of reunited territory for which, among Russians in Russia, there seemed little desire.

As the Crimea incident illustrates, the greater part of our explanation for Russia's lack of irredentism lies in its history and identity. Russia certainly had no historical experiences that would prevent aggression against its smaller neighbors; indeed, the previous several centuries of Russian history had been dominated largely by successful conquest of those neighbors, suggesting that it could be done again. But this history as an imperial rather than a national power had also left Russia peculiarly bereft of a central national identity apart from the state—and with the collapse of the Soviet Union, the old state was gone. In the ensuing debate, many different Russian nationalisms were tried and tested in the arena of Russian politics. Those that could have supported irredentism—or those, like Solzhenitsyn's, which demanded it—failed to gain traction and win enough supporters. In the absence of a shared identity with their ethnic kin abroad, Russians could not agree on a policy of irredentism, and so few politicians tried to gain power by appealing for it. Those who did fared poorly. Successful nationalist politicians did much better working with symbols (for example, the Russian Orthodox Church) and intergroup fears (for example, of the Jews or Muslims) within Russia, rather than discussing the plight of the Russians on the "wrong" side of the border.

More than any other factor, the lack of Russian irredentism seems to be tied to the difficulty of answering the question, "What does it mean to be a Russian?" The complex history of Russia and its relations with its neighbors, both during the tsarist empire and the Soviet Union, created complicated relationships between Russians and other ethnic groups, which in some cases blurred the distinctions between them (as between Russians and Ukrainians) and in other cases had forged unusual or unique relationships. Because the Russian empire was never, for the Russians, about "being Russian" (though for non-Russians, it was about being non-Russian), there was no easy set of categories of Russian versus others to fall into when the Soviet Union collapsed. It was easier in the 1990s for Russian leaders to identify the outsiders (particularly Chechens) than to define who is inside the "nation."

Ultimately, this is what made the Russian and Serbian experiences so different, and what led to different outcomes. In Serbia, though the union was for the most part dominated by Serbs, that domination had serious competitors in other ethnic groups (particularly Croats, as well as Slovenes and others). Serbs could never be completely sure of their place in the system, and thus ethnic competition at various levels was commonplace. In both the Russian empire and the Soviet Union, the dominance of Russians was never questioned, or even open to question. With clearer relationships came less need to compete—to set Russians against Ukrainians, or Caucasians, or central Asians. Thus the odd asymmetry of the Soviet Union's collapse: while the minority ethnicities had no difficulty finding *their* ethnic voices against the backdrop of Russian domination, Russians never returned the favor. Without a clear-cut answer to the question of what it means to be Russian, support for foreign policies predicated on "being Russian" never materialized. Ultimately, the call of "Russia for the Russians" foundered on the inability of Russians in the 1990s to agree on an answer to that call.

Notes to Chapter 6: Breaking Up Is Hard to Do

1. Van Houten (1998) seeks to answer this question as well, focusing on Russia's power as a deterrent against violations of the rights of Russians in the Near Abroad.

2. As a small example, Russian officials in Simferopol, capital of the Crimea, granted Russian passports for a brief time in 1995. Although the practice stopped, the Russian Foreign Ministry would never confirm the number of Crimeans effectively granted Russian citizenship this way (Wydra 2004).

3. It is interesting to note that, as a matter of policy, the Russian government gave up any irredentist claims, but some political parties within Crimea continued to push for reunification with Russia—a call that subsequently went unheeded in Russia (ibid.).

4. Moldova would appear to be the exception here, since the issue does involve an ethnic Russian population against a majority population more related to Romanians. Moldova, however, is not contiguous with Russia, and it is therefore difficult to read Transnistrian separatism as potentially irredentist, which is our primary concern. Further, it is also unclear how much influence Moscow had over Russians in Moldova.

5. See chapter 1 for a discussion of conditionality and relevant citations.

6. See also Smith and Wilson (1997); Poppe and Hagendoorn (2001); and Zevelev (2001).

7. In cases where there appear to have been larger migrations—perhaps a million or more Russians left Central Asian republics in the 1990s (Katagoshchina 2002, 36, 38)—it should be noted that these migrations also do not foster the cause of irredentism, since they tend to weaken any future claim that Russia might have to the lands they came from.

8. This argument is also undermined by the fact that many ethnic Russians living in Grozny became victims of the war, both as casualties in the Russian bombing and as refugees who fled their homes.

9. Abdulakh Mikitaev, chief of the Citizenship Directorate of the Presidential Administration and chairman of the Presidential Commission on Citizenship, said of the policy: "One of the major tasks of state policy, in my view, is the prevention of a mass exodus of people from the states of the former Union." Interview in *Rossiyskaya federatsiya* 22–24 (November–December 1994): 55; quoted in Zevelev (2001, 133).

10. There is some question as to how much impact the Lebed appointment really had on Yeltsin's victory; see Treisman (1996, 65) for an alternative view.

11. Yeltsin himself, after his 1996 election victory over Zyuganov, put together a team of advisors to try to come up with a new "national idea" for Russia—an effort which met with a great deal of confusion but, apparently, little success ("A Mission Statement for Russia," *Economist*, August 16, 1997).

12. As an indication of the general lack of consensus on these issues, in political rhetoric expressing concern about Russians outside the Russian Federation leaders have used a wide variety of different terms (*russkie, rossiyane, russkoyazychnye, sootechestvenniki, sograzhdane*) in describing the group under concern. That none of these terms has a common, shared meaning is further evidence of the continued murkiness surrounding these basic questions of defining the nation (Tolz 1998, 1020).

13. It is interesting to note that, by Western assumptions, an alliance between communists and nationalists seemed very unlikely on ideological grounds. Westerners assumed that Russians held the same view of communism that we did: an artificial implant, imposed by force, and good riddance after 1991. In fact, alliance with empire-seeking nationalists helped keep communists relevant in Russian politics through the 1990s.

7

War and Peace in Eastern Europe, the Former Soviet Union, and Beyond

It was the best of times, it was the worst of times. . . .
—CHARLES DICKENS

W E HAVE SEEN BOTH WAR AND PEACE IN THE aftermath of communism in Eastern Europe and the former Soviet Union. We have found that domestic politics, particularly the content of nationalisms, has helped to explain the puzzle of why some countries engage in war despite the likelihood of losing (or the costs of winning) while others refrain. One could argue that these dynamics are unique to Eastern Europe and the former Soviet Union due to the perils of transition, their level of development, or the pressures of the European Union. There is nothing in our approach that limits its applicability to just one region. Politicians everywhere need support to gain positions of power and remain there. Being a successful nationalist requires an understanding of the content of the particular identities in play—the relevant "us," the "others" that matter most.

To demonstrate that our approach can apply to other parts of the world, past and present, we review a series of hot spots around the globe, applying the various arguments to see which ones perform better against this broader canvas. To preview, we find that countries often ignore international pressures, despite the perils they face, engaging in acts that are quite destructive to the country, but are in the best political interests of the key actors in the society. Milosevic, Tudjman, and Kocharian are not alone, as this chapter illustrates quite clearly.

We start by addressing a couple of additional arguments, focusing on regime type and vulnerability to ethnic strife, that also have been applied to this and similar topics. Then we examine cases both in Europe and beyond. Specifically, we examine briefly the threat of a Greater Albania, the troubles of Northern Ireland, and the dueling efforts of Greece and Turkey. We then move beyond Europe to consider Pakistan's efforts to gain Kashmir, despite its weakness relative to India. In each section, we briefly examine the irredentist effort and apply the arguments we surveyed in chapter 1.

Alternative Explanations

We have already addressed, in chapter 1, a series of theories that had been applied to the question at hand—under what conditions will countries try to retrieve "lost kin." Until now, we have omitted two alternative accounts focusing on democracy and democratization and on vulnerability to ethnic conflict. We consider them briefly here.

Democracy versus Democratization

In chapter 1, we cite Linden (2000) as part of the larger conditionality school. Equally important, he argues that the Euro-Atlantic institutions found fertile soil for their efforts with the new democracies of Eastern Europe. This is part of a larger school in international relations theory that emphasizes the pacifying impact of democracy.[1] Linden asserts that Hungary was able to build a positive relationship with Romania because of the changes in their political systems, with democratic norms and institutional constraints limiting what leaders could promise and do. Thus, we might expect democratic regimes not to engage in significant efforts to retrieve lost kin, particularly when those kin reside in other democracies.

However, Jack Snyder and Edward Mansfield have argued that whereas democracy might inhibit violence, democratization is likely to encourage war.[2] Participation with weak institutions and leadership with poorly established

norms might actually make violence more likely. Rather than point to the examples of Hungary and Romania, Snyder and Mansfield would look to Armenia, Croatia, and Serbia as exemplifying the dynamics that they see as crucial.

The point here is not to provide a definitive test of the impacts of regime
type and changes in regime upon irredentism, but to consider whether these
arguments account for the variation in our cases presented in earlier chapters
and our mini-cases that we present below. We are ultimately agnostic about
regime type, since we see political competition taking place in most regimes,
wherein the effects of political change depend on the interests and identities
of those gaining and losing influence.

Vulnerability: An Overrated Restraint

One of the purposes of this book is to determine the dynamics that might restrain interstate violence, particularly in the form of irredentism. It has long
been averred that countries that are vulnerable to ethnic strife and irredentism would refrain for fear of a backlash, and this has helped to build and reinforce international norms that prohibit such behavior.[3] Somalia was always
seen as the exception that proved the rule—the one homogeneous country in
Africa that could afford to engage in aggression. Yet, we know now and
should have known before that Somalia was actually quite fragile and that its
irredentist program was not universally lauded within the country (Saideman
1998).

In previous work, we have systematically attempted to debunk this argument as it applies to the international relations of secession.[4] The question remains as to whether the conventional wisdom applies to irredentism. If correct, we should expect that states with irredentist minorities should be
unlikely to engage in aggressive foreign policies to retrieve "lost kin." As the
header of this section suggests, we doubt that fear of retaliation inhibits leaders from engaging in aggressive foreign policies.

Irredentist Hot-Spots

To assess further the hypotheses in chapter 1 and the arguments just presented
here, we consider some additional cases briefly. These should help to determine whether the dynamics we find in our cases are unique to postcommu-

nist transformations, to the 1990s, or to a certain level of economic development. While the first case, Albania, most closely resembles the countries studied in the earlier chapters, the subsequent cases help to demonstrate the scope of our approach and the limits of the other explanations.

Avoiding a Greater Albania

Albania's refraining from irredentism might be one of the most significant nonevents of the 1990s in the Balkans (Pettifer 2001). From the fall of communism in Albania to the present day, its position has been to help the kin in Kosovo but not to change existing boundaries by force (Kola 2003). The puzzle is that Albania extended itself farther than nearly any other country to help its kin—Kosovo's Albanians—but has not pushed for altering borders. It is very interesting that Albania's leadership defined its role as equivalent to that of Hungary's: to protect the rights of Albanians outside of Albania (Judah 2001, 8). Before and especially during the war in Kosovo in 1999, Albania served as a base not only for the Kosovo Liberation Army (KLA) but also for the NATO war effort.[5] In all of the discussion of Kosovo's final status—since the postwar UN resolutions left the future in doubt—Albania has not promoted the possibility of a Greater Albania, despite what some of the neighbors had expected.

There are Albanians seeking to unite Albania with Kosovo and portions of Macedonia and Serbia. The Albanian National Army (ANA) is avowedly irredentist. However, it has gained little support from Albanians anywhere, with the Albanian state even arresting some of its leaders (Imholz 1999; Judah 2001). The KLA and the National Liberation Army (NLA) gained success only when they focused on the more concrete, local issues at the expense of pan-Albanianism (Vickers 2004).[6] The Albanian Academy of Science developed an avowedly pan-Albanian platform in 1998 in a bid to increase its relevance but ultimately had to renounce it. Arben Imami, head of a moderate party, stated that unification was a goal before the 2001 election, producing such a backlash that his own party disowned the statement (IGC 2004). The Party for National Unity, which has, as the name implies, an irredentist agenda, gets few votes. Despite some initial rhetoric, Albania's first democratically elected leader, Sali Berisha "did little to advance this cause [of Greater Albania]" (Austin 2004, 244). Subsequent leading parties have also made clear that they are not interested in an irredentist project.

Why is Albanian irredentism of such limited popularity? First, "any impression of a widespread desire for a common state of a 'greater-Albania' would be false" (Naegle 2005, 32).[7] Identification by Albanians with those in other countries is relatively modest because they have not lived together in the same country. Albania's citizens do not have a sense of shared experiences with those Albanians living in the former Yugoslavia, while they do share languages and some customs. Referring to the absence of a Greater Albania project, Kola (2003, 394) asserts that ties between Albanians in Albania and those in Kosovo are quite weak, with two separate sets of identities: "It was still, markedly a question of 'us and them.'" Consequently, Albanians care about those who are like themselves; they want to give assistance and improve their ability to connect with them, but not more than that. Indeed, Prime Minister Fatos Nanon has argued that the free movement of peoples is a way to "avert pressure from ideas associated with greater Albania."[8] Second, Albania is divided between two clans, the Tosks and the Ghegs, with the former currently running the country. Kosovars are mainly Ghegs, so a successful union would undermine those in power and strengthen their opponents.[9] "Many Albanian politicians fear that in any such union power would shift from Tirana to Pristina" (ICG 2004, 12). As a result, most of the intellectuals and other elites making strident claims for unification are from Kosovo, either directly or indirectly.

The international explanations are of mixed utility in accounting for Albania's behavior. Albania has seemed quite willing to live within its own borders, signifying respect for international boundaries. Of course, support for this norm contradicts Albania's willingness to violate another norm—that of sovereignty—given its support of Albanian insurgents seeking to secede from Serbia in 1998–99. Likewise, Albania has been quite eager to join NATO and the EU, and was quite willing to give the United States and NATO pretty much whatever they desired in 1999, despite the very distant prospects for membership. Thus, one could assert that Albania has followed an acquiescent foreign policy to meet the demands of regional powers (Bumci 2003; Kola 2003).

The other arguments are of much less use. Because Albania has not paid a steep cost for past behavior, unlike Hungary, it cannot be said to be deterred today by bad memories. While Albania fell victim to violence in World War II, it was not part of an effort to alter borders, but rather part of Mussolini's efforts to create a new Roman Empire. As a result, we cannot credibly explain Albanian restraint by focusing on the past. Similarly, we cannot consider Albania bound by its own vulnerability to separatism to explain why it did not seek a Greater Albania. Greece still has claims upon Albanian territory, so this might suggest that Albania would support existing boundaries in the Balkans and efforts to restrict separatism. The problem, again, is that Albania quite enthusiastically supported Serbia's disintegration, despite its own separatist challenges. Finally, because Albania's experience with democracy is new and the institutions are weak at best, we cannot say that the form of regime matters all that much in limiting Albanian assertiveness.

The best explanations of Albanian restraint focus on the imperatives of domestic politics and the limits of Albanian identity. Incorporating the Kosovar Albanians would dilute the power of those already residing in Albania, and the Albanians across the border are not seen as fellow citizens in waiting, but somewhat distant kin deserving better treatment. It is not the respect for the boundary between them that restrains Albania's irredentism, but rather that the boundary has created two different kinds of Albanians.

Ireland: Declining Enthusiasm for a Singular Island-State

One of the most visible ethnic conflicts in the Western world happens to be an irredentist one. The Irish Republican Army fought for many years to unify Northern Ireland with the country to the south. Yet, it has not often been thought of as a case of irredentism because of Ireland's waning enthusiasm. The purpose here is not to detail the long history of the "troubles," but to see if the various arguments in this book apply to a case of irredentism in the Western, developed world. Specifically, what role does Northern Ireland play in Irish nationalism? What must Irish politicians do to be successful regarding Northern Ireland? Whatever the answers, support for a "Greater Ireland" has been overestimated.

The origins of the Northern Ireland conflict, in the separation of the Republic of Ireland from Britain in 1923, are generally familiar because they rest on the same visible dimensions as "the troubles" of the last few decades. Nationalists, or Republicans, whose primary political identity rested with Ireland rather than the British Empire, struggled with Unionists, who gave their primary political loyalty to Parliament in London. Then as more recently, the primary marker for this divide was religion, with the Nationalist cause dominant among Catholics and the Unionist cause primary among the Protestant population. Less well appreciated has been the existence of divisions, even from the civil war period in the early 1920s, among Nationalists over both tactics and the future of the Irish Republic. While violence played a role, the support of the larger Irish population appears to have been for democratic means of change, a political trend that put the Irish Republican Army (IRA) in the political minority among supporters of Irish Nationalism (Garvin 1996). Indeed, the IRA—which was at the forefront of violent efforts to unite the island—was outlawed in the Irish Free State in the 1930s (Elliott and Flackes 1999).

Ireland's irredentism first took official form in the Irish Constitution of 1937, which explicitly laid claim to the entire island, including the six counties of Ulster previously separated by British law for their own government (Elliott and Flackes 1999). This was a peculiar form of irredentism, however, because the claim was made by Ireland against territory controlled by a state (Britain) with which it otherwise had substantial cooperative arrangements (Mansergh 1991). Moreover, the government of Ireland proceeded to do very little to back up this claim. Conflicts arose over cross-border tariffs, but this was the natural consequence of creating an artificial border rather than an Irish attempt to squeeze Northern Ireland economically (Mansergh 1991, 305). Indeed, for the three decades until the start of "the troubles," the primary concern between Ireland and Great Britain was not control over the territory of Northern Ireland so much as the status of Ireland itself, and its sovereignty within (or without) the British Commonwealth. The IRA limped along in rebellion in both south and north, receiving little help and no part in an official Irish policy of irredentism (Bell 1993, 26). Even after violence resumed in 1967, the Republic of Ireland continued to lend no more than sympathy to the IRA cause in the north.

Perhaps the best example of this weak irredentism is the relationship between the Republic of Ireland and the IRA. The latter was the only organization consistently committed to taking action to bring about unification, and as such supporting it would be the obvious choice for any irredentist Irish government. Yet even as the Irish Free State was created in 1922–23, the hardcore nationalists of the IRA considered its establishment "an act of unforgivable treachery to the nationalist cause," largely because it did not unify the island or create the kind of republic the nationalists envisioned (Garvin 1996, 30). Initially sympathetic to (and based on some of the same people as) the Fianna Fail political movement, the IRA had a falling out with the former when Fianna Fail achieved electoral dominance in 1932 and adopted the existing political structures as the primary means of change, leaving the IRA alone to continue violent revolution (Ranelagh 1983, 223–224). When the revolution turned to extralegal violence against targets within the Free State, the Fianna Fail government led by de Valera had no choice but to crack down, outlawing the organization in 1936 (Ranelagh 1983, 228). Further crackdowns followed in the late 1960s and early 1970s as violence erupted in the north. In 1970, individual members of the Fianna Fail–led government were accused of providing support for the IRA; in response, Taoiseach (that is, prime minister) Jack Lynch fired them, and they were brought up on charges that exposed the (rather limited) operation (Ranelagh 1983, 261). Both Fianna Fail and its main rival party, Fine Gael, cooperated with the British against the IRA, during their respective turns in power. Although this cooperation never alleviated Unionist fears in the north, the Irish government clearly gave little if any support for the IRA's brand of irredentism, or indeed any sort that did not include voluntary accession by the Ulster population.

Following decades of renewed violence (but little irredentist effort on the Republic of Ireland's part), articles 2 and 3 of Ireland's Constitution were amended as a result of the Anglo-Irish Agreement of 1998. The previous text referred to Ireland as a single "national territory," whereas the new text removed this language, and replaced it with the following:

> It is the firm will of the Irish Nation, in harmony and friendship, *to unite all the people who share the territory of the island of Ireland*, in all the diversity of their identities and traditions, recognising that a *united Ireland shall be brought about only by peaceful means* with the consent of a majority of the people, democratically expressed, in both jurisdictions in the island.[10]

It is interesting that this revision is seen as softening the irredentist claims. Still, this language was the result of bargaining between Britain and Ireland, and could have been quite contentious at home, as it essentially forgoes union in the short or medium terms. The significant concession in the new language was not about territory, since the principle of territorial unity is still upheld, but about identity, replacing the old, Catholic-based Irish nationalism with the reference to the "people who share the territory . . . in all the diversity of their identities and traditions." It is probably too soon to tell whether this reflects a real change among the people or simply a political compromise, but the end result was essentially to uphold a status quo that the Republic of Ireland had been living with for decades.

Despite the irredentist language in the 1937 constitution, the support of Ireland's citizens for unification has been surprisingly weak over the twentieth century. Even in the 1970s and 1980s, surveys showed that the Irish supported unity in principle but not in practice.[11] In one poll, more than half (51.3 percent) indicated that they would not be "prepared to pay heavier taxes to run a united Ireland" (Cox 1985, 35). Why? Perhaps it is because the Catholics of Ireland do not identify so closely with those in the north—that both sides in Northern Ireland (Catholic and Protestant) are seen as "extreme and unreasonable" (Cox 1985, 38). Electoral behavior follows from these views, as unificationist candidates tend to do poorly. Cox notes that living separately since partition has "created two quite different experiences *within* the Irish Catholic/nationalist group. In particular the northern conflict has sprung from and given rise to a distinctively northern Irish experience" (Cox 1985, 43). This impact of separate lives is akin to the effect of boundaries in Eastern Europe, as Hungarians and Romanians identify with the kin on the other side, but not as strongly as before or as expected.

There is also the effect of identity definitions. As we have seen in other parts of the world, irredentists often eschew seeking territory that would bring too many "others" into the fold. The IRA's goal from the beginning was not only a united Ireland, but a united *Catholic* Ireland, with Catholicism standing as the primary (though not only) marker of who constitutes "real Irish" (Bell 1993, 24). As "the troubles" progressed and violence became a recurrent part of politics, identities were hardened, illustrated by Protestants killing Catholic acquaintances in cold blood and vice versa (Taylor 1999, 5–6). Over time, extremist rhetoric and violence have led Protestants and Catholics on the island "not only [to think] of themselves as either Protestants or Catholics but also [to think] *as* Protestants or *as* Catholics" (McAllister 2000, 843; emphasis in the original). For Irish Nationalists so conceived, therefore, union with the six northern counties would involve either driving the Protestants back to England (an unlikely occurrence) or the adoption of an essentially foreign population.

The lack of irredentism on the part of the Republic of Ireland therefore makes sense from both pragmatist and nationalist points of view. For pragmatists, the separate existences of north and south in Ireland developed separate interests, particularly economic interests that would not be served by diverting resources into a costly and probably futile conflict over Ulster. Thus in Ireland a "new middle class appeared. . . . The old ways did not seem as important. . . . Everyone still voted for the same party, but the quarrels of the old soldiers seemed increasingly irrelevant" (Bell 1993, 35). Ireland's long road of political and economic development in the twentieth century took it farther and farther away from an interest in conflict with Britain. Nationalism, in its original form as a strident Catholic Irish identity, likewise ceased to support an irredentist policy in the traditional sense, because to unify with Ulster without first driving out the Protestants would be to bring far too many of "them" into the state.

Alternative Approaches to the Puzzle of Ireland

The alternative arguments largely fall short when trying to account for Ireland's weak support for a Greater Ireland and for its willingness to negotiate and accommodate. As before, we take a quick tour of the competing approaches to determine if they can help account for Ireland's policies toward Northern Ireland.

First, the variations in foreign policy do not correlate with changes in boundaries or boundary norms. Until 1998, the Irish constitution did not recognize the legitimacy of the boundary between Northern Ireland and Ireland, yet the support given to separatist groups in Northern Ireland was quite modest. Indeed, as detailed above, several Irish governments were quite hostile to the Provisional IRA, the military force most willing to fight and die for unification. An approach focused on the power of international norms should have problems with this case since the boundary was not seen as legitimate, but the behavior was quite moderate.

Second, the EU mattered and had an influence in the 1998 Anglo-Irish accord, but it was not conditionality as we think of it. Ireland's accession in 1972 was not tied to resolution of the crisis, which was accelerating then. Instead, the influx of Regional Funds and other subsidies from the European Union has helped to facilitate the emergence of the Celtic Tiger—the new Irish economy. These funds had a significant impact on the rapid growth and transformation of Ireland's economic structure, altering the basis of interests and the identity of the Irish. While Great Britain has sought agreements with Ireland to manage the conflict, its ability to pressure Ireland has declined over time, owing to the latter's economic growth and because both are members of the EU.

Third, the legacy of violence might explain some of the Irish inhibitions. The conflicts in the early part of the twentieth century were quite violent, perhaps deterring future efforts by those in the south to engage in violence. The problem, of course, is that violence in the north was not deterred by this history. Rather, as the northern conflict turned violent (in ways that, for the most part, did not reach the south), pragmatic Irish citizens grew less attached to the idea of drawing such violence inside their own borders. As Taoiseach Liam Cosgrave put it in 1974, "unity or close association with a people so deeply imbued with violence and its effects is not what they [the people of Ireland] want. Violence . . . is killing the desire for unity" (Coogan 1996, 186). Northern violence remained because the issues there were unavoidable and immediate; for the southern part of the island, insulated from the fighting, a desire to avoid violence does help explain Irish reluctance to enter the fray, but this has more to do with contemporary perceptions than with the historical legacy of the early-twentieth-century war with Britain.

Fourth, the vulnerability argument does not apply here. Ireland is not vulnerable to secession as it is quite homogeneous. The only risk would be that a successful unification might lead to separatism in the north, but in terms of potential separatism in the preunion south, there is none.

Fifth, relative power correlates poorly with changes in Ireland's stances. Over the course of time, Ireland's power gained relative to that of Great Britain, both because of the Celtic Tiger phenomenon and the latter's decline. Yet, Ireland became more, rather than less, cooperative, modifying its constitution.

Finally, considering democracy's role here is somewhat difficult. Clearly, as an established democracy, Ireland's regime type cannot explain recent changes that make it less irredentist. However, one could argue that Ireland's enduring reluctance to support violent changes in the boundaries are based on its democratic norms. That is, its focus has been on negotiations with Great Britain, rather than arming separatist groups in Northern Ireland. Still, it is only quite recently—1998—that Ireland formally agreed that Northern Ireland was not a part of Ireland and that a peaceful demonstration of majority support within the north for unification is necessary for any future change. Thus, democracy might explain the general peaceful tendency, but not the variations in Ireland's policies.

Ireland has been less assertive than one might have expected. There has been an active, violent effort by some in Northern Ireland to match reality to the rhetoric of the pre-1998 constitution, yet Irish policy has largely been hostile to the IRA. Ireland's politicians have not been punished for abandoning their brethren; in fact, there has been widespread support across political parties for the idea of unity coupled with the practicality of not wanting to fight and die for it. Over time, this practicality has, for the Republic of Ireland, come to override the distinctions between Catholic and Protestant, especially as (for the Irish in the Republic), those distinctions are less important in the face of their own state's success.

Greece: The Rise and Fall of *Enosis* Politics

Cyprus has been home to both Greeks and Turks for hundreds of years. The population balance has generally favored the Greek Cypriot side, which has tended to create the perception on Cyprus and in Greece that Cyprus is part of the Hellenistic world. Greek demands for *enosis* (union) with Cyprus date back to Greece's independence from Ottoman rule in 1830. Over most of this history, however, the impetus has come primarily from the Greek population on Cyprus (Dodd 1999, 3–5). Despite these sentiments, there was little action on the part of independent Greece in the nineteenth and early twentieth centuries. The Ottoman Empire continued to hold onto Cyprus until its end in World War I, after which the island was taken over by Britain.

Britain held the island until the 1950s, by which time anticolonialist sentiments among both Greek and Turkish Cypriots were making control increasingly difficult. In Greece itself, Cyprus became a political issue in the struggle between leftist and center-right parties. In the 1958 elections, despite eight years of center-right electoral victories in Greece, a leftist party (serving as a front for Greek Communists) became the main opposition party with 25 percent of popular vote, largely by exploiting disaffection over the Cyprus issue in Greece (Clogg 1992, 151). This led to Greek support for independence for Cyprus, culminating in negotiated agreements in 1959 and 1960 between Britain, Greece and Turkey that created an independent Republic of Cyprus. The constitution of Cyprus divided power between the two communities, giving the minority Turkish Cypriots (then roughly 20 percent of the population) enough access to veto discriminatory moves against them. Greece, along with Turkey and Britain, signed the treaties as a guarantor of the independence of Cyprus, which seemed to put the issue of *enosis* to rest.

The constitution proved to be an unstable document, however, and by 1964 serious intercommunal violence and unrest had broken out on the island. By April, Turkey was threatening to invoke its powers as Treaty Guarantor to launch an invasion of the island, ostensibly to protect the Turkish Cypriot population. In response, Greece quietly sent ten thousand of its troops to the island to deter that invasion (Joseph 1997, 44). In the continuing intercommunal violence, Greek forces operated alongside Greek Cypriots in anti-Turkish military operations. This military support in the intra-Cyprus fight, however, did not signal a clear Greek intention to pursue *enosis*; rather, the involvement by Greece seems to have been more in support of Greek Cypriots against Turkish Cypriots and Turkey, and thus supportive of Greek supremacy in an independent Cyprus, not irredentism. Indeed, both the Greek government and President Makarios of Cyprus explicitly rejected *enosis* as policy following the crisis of 1963–64, although pro-*enosis* sentiment continued in both Greece and on Cyprus in the general populations (Joseph 1997, 45–47).

In 1967, a military coup in Greece brought to power a new military government, ending electoral democracy in Greece. The new military government differed with Cypriot President Makarios over the issue of *enosis*; Makarios continued to champion Cypriot independence as the only feasible option, but the Greek Colonels wanted to pursue the union option (Solsten 1993, 217). Greek military officers serving in the Cyprus National Guard began a campaign to subvert the Makarios government, and the underground paramilitary group EOKA (which in the 1950s had been created to fight British rule) was recreated. EOKA-B, as it was known, engaged in pro-*enosis* clandestine and terrorist operations starting in 1969, supported by the Greek military government in Athens (Solsten 1993, 218).

The military junta proved to be unpopular in Greece itself, however, despite its appeals to nationalist causes, and by 1973 was having serious difficulties in maintaining control. In November of 1973, the regime was overthrown by its more hard-line military officer members, led by Dimitrios Ioannidis, former head of the secret police. Ioannidis took an even stronger pro-*enosis* position toward Cyprus, hoping to rally support from Greeks with appeals to nationalist causes (Solsten 1995, 73). The Greek government stepped up pressure on President Makarios to follow the *enosis* line. In response, in early July 1974, Makarios demanded that Greece withdraw all of its military officers from Cyprus. Ioannidis responded by initiating a coup by those officers and EOKA-B against the Makarios government; it was widely assumed that if such a government took power in Cyprus, it would immediately take steps to pursue union with Greece (Solsten 1995, 274–275). Fearing this sudden irredentist grab, Turkey launched an invasion on July 20 under the auspices of the treaties, citing its rights as a guarantor of the independence of Cyprus. In the aftermath of the invasion, Cyprus was divided into Greek and Turkish zones (the latter being the northern third of the island, under Turkish military occupation). Makarios was returned to power as the president of a now divided Cyprus, and Ioannidis was quickly overthrown in Greece and replaced with a civilian caretaker government by the end of July. The overthrow of military rule in Greece put an end to Greek irredentist policies. Although the island remains de facto partitioned, subsequent Greek governments have rejected *enosis* as policy toward Cyprus.

Like other irredentist attempts, Greece's policy in the late 1960s and early 1970s carried significant costs for the sponsoring state. Perhaps the most dramatic of these was the loss of power of the sponsoring governments. The failed coup on Cyprus in 1974, clearly incited by the Ioannides government, led more or less directly to the downfall of that government and its replacement by a civilian one. Even before the 1974 crisis, the military junta had lacked legitimacy with the Greek population, a situation which repeated appeals to *enosis* had failed to address. It was that lack of legitimacy that led to the Ioannides hard-line coup of 1973, and thence to the desperate attempt at forceful irredentism. That the attempt failed is not especially relevant to the fall of the Ioannides regime; he was, in fact, removed from power even as the Turkish forces were invading, and was thus pushed out before anyone knew what the final outcome might be.

The irredentist crisis also did significant, but very short-lived, damage to Greek relations with both the United States and Europe. Both the United States and its European allies were distressed with the military government in Athens and strongly disapproved of the drive for *enosis*, which the United States felt could destabilize the region and offer an invitation for Soviet intervention in what had been a Western stronghold. However, once a civilian government led by Konstantine Karamanlis replaced Ioannides's regime, relations with the Western powers returned more or less immediately to their normal and positive state. As in the domestic realm, the military junta had been disliked (although tolerated for Cold War reasons) by the Western powers, but had little legitimacy. Its replacement by a respectable civilian government solved most of those problems, and in the end Greece's relations with its most important allies suffered no significant damage at all—once the irredentist policy was abandoned.

Greece's brief irredentist period appears, as with the cases earlier in the book, to be based largely on its own internal political dynamics. In this case, irredentism was driven by a colossal political miscalculation—that appeals to irredentist nationalism would mobilize political support. This mistake was in turn driven by the peculiar circumstance of an undemocratic Greek government that, lacking legitimacy, needed some way of mobilizing support, or at least distracting opposition. Beyond a cultural and historical affinity, however, there was little support among the Greek population for irredentist adventurism. When the government, in the late 1960s, tried relatively low-cost irredentism, the political consequences were low. But as soon as the policy threatened to impose genuinely severe costs on Greece—including the strong possibility of a war with Turkey—any rhetorical support immediately evaporated and the government responsible was swept from power. Greece thus provides an example of a nonirredentist state whose government, in political trouble, turned to irredentism to try to solve its problems, only to discover that the domestic political ground would not sustain it. "Good nationalism" in Greece did not include spilling blood or spending money on *enosis* with Cyprus—a political fact that the junta governments discovered too late.

Turkey: Countering *Enosis* with *Taksim*

Since Turkish independence in 1923, Turkey's approach to Cyprus and its Turkish Cypriot population has largely been in reaction to Greece's calls for union with the island. Fearing that such a union would put the island's Turkish minority at risk, Turkey's response to *enosis* has been *taksim*—separation of the two communities, with self-determination of Turkish Cypriots on an equal basis with Greek Cypriots. This approach has generated a different form of irredentism than the Greek; whereas Greece has sought to incorporate the entire island as a territory, Turkey has pushed for a separate, independent, homogenous entity for its ethnic kin, either with an eye toward creating de facto ruling connections or paving the way for future integration. From a Greek perspective, therefore, Turkey's calls for *taksim* on Cyprus look little different from Serbia's calls for a "Republica Srbska" in eastern Bosnia or Armenia's support for Karabakh independence—irredentism cloaked in the language of self-determination.

After the independence of Cyprus in 1960, however, the government of Turkey did little to pursue separation of the Cypriot communities. In the 1960s, Turkey's official involvement in Cyprus tended to be in support for the existing 1960 constitution, which recognized Turkish Cypriot political rights but did not call for any real degree of communal separation. It was not until Greece moved to force *enosis*, therefore, that Turkey took direct action in support of a separate Turkish Cypriot entity.

Throughout the 1960s, as intercommunal violence flared and Greek interest in *enosis* clashed with Cyprus President Makarios's intentions to maintain an independent island (albeit one dominated by Greek Cypriots), Turkey threatened to intervene to defend its ethnic kin. It was kept from doing so by diplomatic pressure, particularly from the United States, which feared a war between NATO members Greece and Turkey—pressure that created substantial domestic difficulties for successive Turkish governments (Adamson 2001). The Turkish government was spurred to action, however, by the Greek-sponsored coup against Makarios in July 1974. Fearing that a successful coup, coupled with a highly nationalistic Ioannidis government in Greece, would lead to a Greek takeover and absorption of the island, Turkey invaded northern Cyprus with thirty thousand troops. A UN-sponsored cease-fire led to talks in mid-August between all parties (Solsten 1993, 43). These talks broke down, however, over Turkish and Turkish Cypriot demands for a bizonal federation that would include separate Turkish enclaves (Turkey's policy of *taksim*). With the diplomatic process at a standstill, Turkish forces pushed past their initial beachhead to extend their control over the northern third of the island. This second invasion phase generated substantial flight across the battle lines, as Greek Cypriots fled south and Turkish Cypriots were airlifted to the north. When the offensive stopped, Turkey again suggested that the resulting division be enshrined in a new constitution for Cyprus as a bizonal federal state with two autonomous regions.

While this proposal has been consistently rejected by Greece and Greek Cypriots, the 1974 invasion created a de facto partition on the ground. The population is almost completely divided, with very few Turkish Cypriots living in the south and no Greek Cypriots in the north (Solsten 1993, 221). Turkish government forces have continued to maintain a significant presence in the northern region, and the Turkish Cypriot leadership has pressed Turkey's policy of *taksim*, declaring a "Turkish Federated State of Cyprus" in 1975, and an independent "Turkish Republic of Northern Cyprus" (TRNC) in 1983. Thus, while these declarations have carried no legal weight (no country save Turkey has recognized the TRNC), Turkey's goal of *taksim* has been largely achieved on the ground—an outcome similar to Armenia's effective control of Karabakh. It was widely perceived through the 1990s that the government in Ankara called the important shots for the TRNC's government, as Turkish troops continued to maintain a presence in northern Cyprus. Moreover, a substantial number of settlers have been sent from Turkey to the island, which complicates the possibility of a future settlement. However, the TRNC has also developed a political system and a politics of its own, with parties both supportive and opposed to settlers and continued partition (Solsten 1983, 45). Official Turkish policy continues to support self-determination for Turks on Cyprus; absent a direct, 1974-style crisis, it is difficult to tell to what degree irredentism remains a motive in Turkish policy toward Cyprus.

Like Greece, Turkey has suffered relatively little over its policies toward Cyprus, although like Armenia its partial success has continued to cause some problems for it since the fighting stopped. These costs, and Turkey's willingness to bear them (or not), are indicative of the political forces in Turkey behind its Cyprus policy.

The 1974 intervention in Cyprus briefly helped the Turkish government of the time, but it did not have any significant long-term impact on Turkish domestic politics. The government of 1974 was led by Bülent Ecevit, head of Atatürk's Republican People's Party (CHP), in coalition with Necmettin Erbekan's Islamist National Salvation Party (NSP). During 1974, Turkey's party system was struggling to come up with a stable coalition, and was thus wracked with a certain amount of instability. During the 1974 crisis itself, all political parties across the spectrum agreed on the necessity of Turkish intervention, and there was widespread public outcry for the use of force to protect Turkish Cypriots (Adamson 2001, 286–289). The invasion's success provided an immediate political boost for the ruling government, and kept it from becoming a political liability over the long term for the CHP, but eventually Cyprus was overshadowed by other political issues in Turkey, and no successful political party or politician since has attempted to use the issue as a sole means to power (Metz 1996, 49–55). It appears that there was a strong consensus among Turks that defending their Turkish Cypriot brethren was a good thing to a point, but that active pursuit of a more aggressive policy was not important. Hence, Ecevit suffered no significant domestic political costs from his championing of Turkish Cypriot rights, although one could argue that had he failed to intervene aggressively (as previous Turkish governments had done in response to U.S. pressure), his government may well have collapsed.

The 1974 invasion also contributed significantly to an already tense Greek-Turkish relationship, which was simultaneously struggling over issues of sovereignty and oil in the Aegean Sea. In the absence of Cyprus and Turkish "separatist" irredentism, however, one would have expected this relationship to be a fairly tense one in any case. There was also some brief damage to the Turkish-U.S. relationship stemming from the invasion. In February 1975, Congress imposed an arms embargo on Turkey, claiming that U.S.-supplied equipment had been illegally used in the invasion. Turkey threatened to cut off U.S. access to military bases and installations, and later in 1975 withdrew from its 1969 defense cooperation treaty with the United States. By 1978, however, President Carter convinced Congress to lift the embargo, and Turkey restored its military cooperation ties. The United States then resumed providing both military aid (some $250 million in 1980) and economic assistance ($200 million in 1980), and worked with the OECD to help Turkey out of a financial crisis in the late 1970s (Metz 1996, 56). There were, therefore, some short-term international costs to Turkey's invasion, but they did not last beyond a few years. This reinforces our view of Turkish domestic politics: there was enough support for quasi-irredentism to justify some short-term foreign policy sacrifices, but not for a sustained set of costs over the long haul.

Some have suggested that Turkey's continued occupation of northern Cyprus has created a barrier to Turkey's desires to join the EU and integrate itself further with Europe. As the EU looks to expand, Turkey has been on a much slower track than many of the Eastern European countries, or even than Cyprus, despite the latter's continuing division. But the continued presence of Turkish troops in northern Cyprus, and any perceptions that Turkey is maintaining the island's division intentionally, do not figure substantively into the EU's assessment of Turkish accession to the organization (European Commission 2001, 60–62). Thus, while improvement in Turkey's relations with the EU remains slow, this seems to be due largely to a raft of issues unrelated to Cyprus (economic problems, human rights and treatment of Kurds, and larger cultural questions about whether a Muslim country can join the overwhelmingly Christian EU) and not a cost imposed by Turkey's support for a separate Turkish Cypriot entity. If in the future the Turkish body politic is faced with a clear choice—abandon Cyprus or give up any hope of joining the EU—that would provide a more direct test of Turkey's willingness to continue support of its Cypriot kin. Until then, the current policy appears to fit the circumstances tolerably well.

Turkey's policy of quasi-irredentism—support for the self-determination of its ethnic kin, rather than seeking outright union—appears, like most of our cases, to be a function of Turkey's internal dynamics. At a particular time and in the face of a particular crisis, Turkish politics united behind the *taksim* policy, and there has been enough residual support since then to maintain a presence in Northern Cyprus sufficient to protect that initial investment. Beyond this, however, there have been no attempts by Turkish governments to advance an irredentist agenda, and no Turkish politicians attempting to climb to power by doing so. External pressure (from the United States and, later, the EU) has been concerned primarily with other issues—preventing war with Greece (for the US) and domestic reforms in other areas (for the EU), suggesting that Turkey's relative restraint toward Cyprus is not due to outside forces keeping Turkish irredentism in check. As with Greece, Turkey's policy toward Cyprus has been primarily a domestic affair, the primary difference being Turkish leaders' failure to repeat the mistakes of Greece's governments in the early 1970s. Absent a major change in Turkish national mood, further irredentism toward Cyprus is unlikely.

Alternative Approaches to Competing Irredentisms in Cyprus

Greece and Turkey present intertwined irredentisms, cases that have fed off of each other and which, to some extent, existed in direct opposition to each other. The counterarguments we have been examining throughout the book thus deserve examination with both cases simultaneously, to see whether any provide explanatory power that our emphasis on domestic political dynamics does not. As with our other cases, we find that international forces do not explain behavior very well, and we are left with the point that keeps returning: the dominance of domestic political dynamics, of identity and struggles for power.

In 1960, Cyprus became a sovereign, independent country, fully (and especially) recognized by both Greece and Turkey, who were signatories to the treaty that brought Cyprus into being. While that treaty gave both parties the right to intervene under certain circumstances, in order to guarantee the security of Cypriot populations, it laid no groundwork for territorial claims by the states of Greece or Turkey. Moreover, because it is an island, the boundaries of Cyprus are crystal-clear. Greece's irredentist grab in the early 1970s, and Turkey's continued insistence since 1974 of an intrastate border that does not otherwise exist, suggests that respect for international but not intrastate borders does very little to explain either Greek or Turkish behavior toward Cyprus.

The Cyprus case likewise presents a significant and direct test of the EU conditionality argument, and of the influence of Western international organizations. Greece joined the EU in 1981, despite having made an overt grab for Cyprus less than a decade before—an indication of broader European recognition that there was no ongoing desire for *enosis*. The Greek government in Cyprus was allowed to join the EU in 2004, leaving the Turkish northern portion behind, despite the failure to reach an agreement on practical reunification. Turkey has not been allowed to join the EU—at least, not yet—but of all the reasons for slowing Turkey's application (or rejecting it), Turkey's Cyprus policy is never on the radar screen. Indeed, if the EU were genuinely interested in using conditionality to put an end to Turkey's *taksim* brand of irredentism as well as any possibility of a resurgence of *enosis* desire by Greece, it largely lost its influence over "the Cyprus problem" when it admitted the island as a member state in 2004, without resolving the division. For both Turkey and Greece, the "lure of Europe" was not enough to moderate their behavior in 1974 (despite the membership of both countries in NATO), and Europe has made precious little attempt since then to use that lure as a tool to resolve the problem.

Relative power and deterrence are problematic here, as the balance is quite skewed in favor of Turkey. Throughout this entire period, Turkey is roughly three times more capable than Greece, according to Correlates of War data. So, relative advantage might explain Turkey's willingness to act aggressively, but the counter to this argument is that Greece, while at a disadvantage, was the one which initiated the crisis in 1974 by pursuing the most aggressive irredentist policy. The balance of power might help to explain both Greece's reluctance since the early 1970s to engage in aggressive efforts and the failure of its efforts, but it cannot account for the irredentist moment that produced the crisis.

Finally, in terms of history and its shaping of identity, Cyprus resembles Northern Ireland in some respects. Being an island, the experiences of its inhabitants could not help but differ from those of their kin on the respective mainlands. It was Cypriots who bore the brunt of violence—first during the anticolonialist struggles of the 1950s, and then during the intercommunal strife of the 1960s and 1970s. While this history of violence has tended to harden Cypriot identities vis-à-vis each other (similar to Catholics and Protestants in Northern Ireland), that hardening has not spilled over into Greeks and Turks in the homelands. In the early 1970s, therefore, there was no experience of failed irredentism to induce caution on the part of the Greek population; yet even without such an experience, mainland Greeks rejected the spilling of blood (especially theirs) for the *enosis* project. The function of history over time has rather been as it has in Ireland—to divide the experiences of Cypriots from their mainland kin, such that the latter (like Irish in the Republic) no longer see themselves as synonymous with their Cypriot kin, nor are they willing to do much to reunite what is essentially a foreign, if affiliated, people.

Pakistan and Kashmir: Doomed to Repetition?

In the late 1980s and 1990s, Pakistan replaced Somalia as the state most likely to upset international peace and security through its efforts to unify "lost territories," namely Kashmir. The stakes in South Asia dwarfed those in the Horn of Africa, as the conflicting territorial claims over Kashmir became enmeshed in a nuclear standoff between India and Pakistan. While there are many issues between two countries,[12] the continuing effort by Pakistani elites to "recover" Kashmir has been a critical source of tension, resulting in several wars, a nuclear crisis, an ongoing insurgency, domestic instability, and deferred economic development. While there has been recent progress in the relationship with India, both before and after the earthquake on October 8, 2005, the dispute continues and will not see a permanent resolution soon. So, we need to examine Pakistan's efforts over the course of time to determine how domestic politics and the meaning of Pakistan's identity have generally overshadowed other ways to conceive of Pakistan's interests.[13]

Pakistan's efforts to unite with Kashmir have ranged from verbal encouragement, diplomatic cover, money, arms, personnel, bases, indirect fire (artillery), to, ultimately, war (Byman et al. 2001; Chalk 2003). Infiltration has continued at varying levels ever since the boundary was drawn. Rather than merely happening on Pakistani territory, unmarked by state authorities, elements of the government, especially the Army and the Inter-Services Intelligence Directorate (ISI), have played a leading role in coordinating these efforts. "Kashmiri Muslim militants themselves have given countless testimonials of the Pakistan Army's assistances; and the circumstantial evidence—even when one discounts the inevitable distortion and exaggeration coming from the Indian side—seems pointed overwhelmingly in this direction" (Wirsing 1994, 119). This effort is not just an attempt to annoy India, for Pakistan has fomented violence not only against India but also against Kashmiri groups that seek independence rather than union with Pakistan (Bose 1999, 155).

Kashmir and Pakistan's Politics

Our focus on the content of identity and the role of identities in political competition helps to explain Pakistan's policy toward Kashmir. Specifically, because Pakistan defines itself as a Muslim country, Kashmir plays a vital role in its self-image. Given Pakistan's diversity, Kashmir is one of the few issues upon which all Pakistanis agree (Malik 2001, 226). Most Pakistanis share religious ties, broadly defined, with the Muslims of Kashmir. Most Pakistanis and most of the population of the Kashmir Valley are Sunnis, though neither population is entirely homogeneous in the form of Sunni Islam they follow. This matters, not necessarily because Pakistanis inherently identify with the plight of Kashmir. Instead, it may matter because politicians can either use the Kashmir issue to prove their Islamic credentials, or key groups that are devoutly interested may have enough sway to push politicians to take strong stands. Indeed, Marc Gaborieau (2002, 45) has argued that the politics of religion can be "characterized as outbidding: by putting the stakes higher and higher, the religious groups compelled the modernizing elites to concessions on the religious nature of the State." As politicians are pushed to take strong stands on Islamic issues domestically, they may also be pushed toward aggressive support on behalf of the Kashmiris.

However, not all groups in Pakistan have a shared interest in unifying Kashmir. There is evidence that Pakistani Sindhis and Balochs, who stand to lose from both the continued tension with India and in the event of the accession of Kashmir, generally reject Pakistan's Kashmir policy. The Sindhis may be more interested in better relations with India than in the Greater Pakistan project (Shah 1997, 83). Indeed, Sindhis have in the past had a rival irredentist project in mind—the creation of an independent Sindhi state from Indian and Pakistani territories. The Balochs are not in favor of the irredentist effort either (Shah 1997, 107). These groups have no ethnic ties to the contested territories and compete with Punjabis and Pushtuns for state resources. However, Sindhis and Balochs have been less central to the calculations of Pakistani leaders.

So, why do the Punjabis and Pushtuns care about Kashmir? Given the importance of Punjabis in both democratic and military regimes, any serious politician must appeal to their priorities, which include acquiring Jammu and Kashmir. Punjabis have ethnic reasons to care about Kashmir.[14] First, Punjab is the closest part of Pakistan to Kashmir, leading to increased contact and overlapping settlement patterns. This has apparently led to a shared sense of a "blood relationship," where they see each other as kin (Shah 1997, 145). Further, many of the soldiers who died in the struggle for Kashmir were from Punjab,[15] deepening the emotional investment in irredentism. Pushtuns also play a key role as they are heavily represented in the military and the civil service. Their religious ties to the Muslims of Kashmir are not contradicted by other competing interests, as in the case of the Balochs and Sindhis. In the

Pushtun case, geography, bureaucratic interests, and religious ties all push in the same direction.

What is abundantly clear is that the military and particularly the ISI have had a strong and continuing interest in irredentism. While religion has always played a significant role in Pakistan since it was founded to provide a home for South Asia's Muslims, a fundamentalist variant became more important over time, particularly as the war in Afghanistan in the 1980s developed and became defined as an Islamic war. The Inter-Services Intelligence Directorate became deeply involved in the region's religious politics. Further, the current government has strong ties to these policies. The current President, Pervez Musharraf, was the Army chief of staff during the Kargil crisis. The prime minister fired Musharraf in the aftermath of the conflict, and he responded by leading a successful coup.

Two recent developments have apparently altered Musharraf's domestic political strategy and Pakistan's foreign policy: increased dependence on U.S. support and the development of a domestic interest group desiring better relations with India. The events of 9/11 have increased the pressure on Musharraf's government to reduce its support for Islamic fundamentalist groups in neighboring countries.[16] He has faced a critical dilemma—whether to support the United States and its war against Al Qaeda, which has ties to the ISI and Islamic parties in Pakistan and Kashmir, or to continue to rely upon fundamentalist parties and segments of the military. For much of the time since September 2001, it seems that Musharraf has tried to have it both ways—supporting the United States in its Afghan campaign but continuing support for the insurgents in Kashmir. This strategy has been unsustainable, as it has had two effects: increasingly violent opposition from within Pakistan and deepening the role of the United States in Pakistan.

Second, the balance of interests has changed in Pakistan. For much of Pakistan's history, there has been only a weak counterirredentist coalition. Recently, Pakistani business leaders have changed their views toward the regional and international economies, acknowledging that irredentism and economic development are a tradeoff—they could have one but not the other. Indeed, the peace dividend could be quite substantial, potentially producing pipelines and other infrastructure linking Pakistan and India to each other and to the rest of the region (Siddiqi 2004). Op-ed sections of Pakistani newspapers have articulated this realization, as the opportunity costs of lost trade have become obvious with India's increasingly dynamic economy.[17] Recent efforts to develop an Asian free trade area have excluded Pakistan, due to

India's insistence.[18] Consequently, better relations with India not only imply better access to India's market but also to the rest of Asia as well. The best evidence linking Kashmir and free trade is that the meeting of the South Asian Association for Regional Cooperation to create the South Asian Free Trade Agreement occurred on January 4, 2004, at the same time as Pakistan and India agreed to reduce tensions over Kashmir.

Thus, the domestic politics of irredentism has changed moderately, with the relative decline in power of pro-irredentist forces and the increased articulation of anti-irredentist interests. This gamble, Musharraf shifting his political base from the more extreme elements to the more cooperation-minded, may help to explain recent events—the steps to reduce tensions with India, the surprising cooperation on a South Asian Free Trade Agreement, and the attempts to assassinate Musharraf. This delicate balancing act[19] provides further evidence that any politician in Pakistan faces extremely difficult choices as there continues to be strong pressure to support the cause of uniting Kashmir with Pakistan.

Competing Accounts Fall Short

Most of the competing explanations fail to account for Pakistan's continued irredentism. The only alternative account that travels is the role of international borders. Pakistan has never been restrained by international norms, so that argument might shed some light, because the boundary between India and Pakistan has never been accepted or considered legitimate. It is still seen as a cease-fire line, rather than as the legitimate line demarcating the two countries. Thus, Pakistan is free to engage in irredentism. Of course, this only speaks to opportunity, not motivation. Further, it begs the question of why the two countries have not agreed to the border, putting the cart before the horse in an important sense.

Clearly, the imperatives of the international environment cannot explain, until perhaps recently, Pakistan's aggressive efforts. If countries engage in offensive actions when there is an apparent window of opportunity, Pakistan can only be considered an inept burglar at best. India has always been far stronger than Pakistan, so that any assertive action is likely to fail. Only with the advent of its nuclear arsenal, deterring serious Indian retaliation, can we say that Pakistan has a permissive environment to engage in low-level aggression by supporting insurgents in Kashmir. Still, Pakistan's efforts have been quite costly. The Kargil crisis, which represents Pakistan's most aggressive effort of the past two decades, ultimately risked nuclear war, and the gains on the ground were reversed in part due to international pressure. Thus, even though the nuclear standoff might permit more low-level support, it ultimately creates an international audience that is most concerned with any Pakistani assertiveness.

The regional dynamics after 9/11 have created a more restrictive environment. Even though the United States is more dependent on Pakistan than ever before, Pakistan cannot take advantage of this vis-à-vis Kashmir since the insurgents in Kashmir appear to be tied to Al Qaeda. Even if they do not have real ties to Bin Laden, they are viewed as part of a larger threat of Islamic fundamentalism. India has been most successful in framing the conflict in this way. Still, Pakistan has been reluctant to give up its quest.

Past failure clearly has not deterred Pakistan. Its record of war with India is one of failure. Despite repeatedly losing wars and expending resources on a long but not terribly successful insurgency, Pakistan has continued its efforts. It has paid tremendous costs for these efforts, in blood, treasure, and isolation, yet annexation of Kashmir remains very much in the imagination.

Democracy fails to account for the patterns here. While Pakistan has hardly been a stable democracy at any point in time, when its leaders were elected, they behaved very similarly to the generals of the military regimes. In both recent democratic periods, Pakistan became quite aggressive in its support for (or manipulation of) the insurgents in Pakistan. During her government, Benazir Bhutto was apparently compelled by political competition to take strong stands in favor of Kashmiri separatism. "As the conflict in Kashmir intensified, opposition parties continued to outbid Benazir on the question of Kashmir, leading her to ratchet up her inflammatory political rhetoric" (Ganguly 2001, 92). The Kargil crisis, it should be noted, occurred during the most recent elected government of Nawaz Sharif. Thus, regime type by itself is not much of a constraint.

Finally, Pakistan has not been restrained by its own separatism. Despite already having lost half of its population to secession (Bangladesh), Pakistan remains multiethnic, with limited control over its own territory, and with potentially multiple separatist groups. Neither the Sindhis nor the Balochs are enchanted with Pakistan or its focus on Kashmir. Yet, Pakistan has not tried to create a regional environment that would reduce support for secession. Indeed, it has done the opposite, giving India yet more incentive to support groups that aim to divide Pakistan.

Pakistan's efforts to recover Kashmir since 1947 have been costly, not only in terms of short-term spending on arms and personnel, but also in terms of opportunity costs over the long run. These resources plus a decent relationship with India might have made a real difference in the lives of Pakistanis and in the development of the country. Instead, Pakistan is one of the poorest countries, with a terrible record of political performance—alternating military leaders with corrupt democratic ones. Not all of this can be traced to the Kashmir obsession, but clearly the irredentist mission has not been to the benefit of Pakistanis. Only now are some interest groups seeing this and lobbying the government. The problem is that Pakistani leaders need to develop a cohesive national identity focused on something more than antipathy to India and the nursing of old wounds.

Findings

This brief tour of irredentism, past and present, actual and potential, has provided some evidence to suggest that the dynamics that we find in Eastern Europe and the former Soviet Union also matter elsewhere. Table 7.1 might oversimplify the case studies, but it helps to illustrate the basic trends.

Borders perform as well as democracy for explaining the occurrence of irredentism, and each performs better than external pressures, the weight of history, vulnerability or democratization. Arguments focusing on borders and on regime type explain roughly two-thirds of our cases. Borders do matter, we suspect, more because they shape the nationalisms in play than because of the normative deterrent, and we return to this in the next chapter.

Regime type—that is, democracy—is associated with more peaceful policies in most of our cases, coinciding with assertions about the pacific nature of democracies.[20] However, the democratic credentials of several states were suspect in the early days of the postcommunist transition, including Romania's. Given the antidemocratic practices of several states, it is hard to say that elections or the rule of law restrained them, particularly Russia under Yeltsin and Putin. On the other hand, democratization fared poorly as a competing account, inasmuch as several states moving to democracy did not engage in aggression. Most notably, several with troubled transitions—Albania, Romania, and Russia—chose peace.

Most of the remaining arguments are wrong more often than they are right. Clearly, states are deterred by neither external pressures nor unfavor-

TABLE 7.1   Irredentist Foreign Policies: Which Explanations Fit the Cases?

	Interstate borders	External pressures	Legacy	Deterrence	Vulnerability	Democracy	Nuanced Democratization	Nationalism
Albania	Confirm	Confirm	Disconfirm	Confirm	Disconfirm	Disconfirm	Confirm	Confirm
Armenia	Confirm	Mixed	Confirm	Disconfirm	Disconfirm	Disconfirm	Confirm	Confirm*
Croatia	Confirm	Disconfirm	Disconfirm	Confirm	Disconfirm	Confirm	Confirm	Confirm*
Greece	Disconfirm	Disconfirm	Confirm	Disconfirm	Disconfirm	Confirm	Confirm	Confirm
Hungary	Confirm	Confirm, after 1993	Confirm	Confirm	Confirm	Confirm	Disconfirm	Confirm
Ireland	Disconfirm	Mixed	Confirm	Mixed	Disconfirm	Disconfirm	N.A.	Confirm
Pakistan	Confirm	Mixed	Disconfirm	Disconfirm	Disconfirm	Confirm	Confirm	Confirm
Romania	Confirm	Confirm, after 1993	Disconfirm	Disconfirm	Disconfirm	Confirm, after 1996	Disconfirm	Confirm
Russia	Disconfirm	Disconfirm	Disconfirm	Disconfirm	Confirm	Confirm	Disconfirm	Confirm
Serbia	Confirm	Disconfirm	Disconfirm	Mixed	Disconfirm	Confirm	Confirm	Confirm
Turkey	Disconfirm	Disconfirm	Confirm	Confirm	Disconfirm	Disconfirm	Confirm	Confirm
Total	7 C 4 D	3 C 5 D 3 M	5 C 7 D	3 C 7 C 2 M	3 C 9 D	7 C 4 D	6 C 4 D	11 C

*Confirms (C) means the case fits the particular theory. Disconfirm (D) means the case does not fit the theory. Mixed (M) means that the case does not provide clear evidence one way or the other. N.A. means not applicable.

** In these two cases, xenophobic nationalisms should have deterred irredentism, except that the powerful positions of the kin made ethnic cleansing a preferred option.

able balances of power. It might be the case that the European Union success-fully cajoled potential members to behave well at the end of the 1990s, but this fails to account for restrained foreign policies earlier on. International pressures also fail explain the patterns of aggression and restraint seen in the cases discussed in this chapter. Membership in NATO did not stop Greece and Turkey from their Cyprus campaigns, for instance, nor have significant international pressures assuaged Pakistan's Kashmir obsession. Similarly, in-tent irredentists are not deterred by unfavorable strategic situations. They at-tack stronger countries, as demonstrated by Somalia (Saideman 1998) and Pakistan, and engage in aggression against possible allies despite greater threats, as in the case of Croatia. As important, again because silent dogs are often ignored or underappreciated, leaders of stronger countries—Romania and Russia—frequently refrained from irredentism despite the opportunities. Relative power also does not account for Serbia's selective irredentism, as Macedonia and Slovenia would also have been outgunned.

Neither histories of failed irredentism nor vulnerability provided much il-lumination. While the former was offered as an explanation of Hungarian re-straint in a few interviews, it did not apply in a systematic way. Pakistan has not yet been deterred by its previous failures, and history served as a well-spring of symbols for Croatia, rather than as a set of lessons that might inhibit aggression. Vulnerability performs quite poorly. Rather than Somalia's serv-ing as an exception—the only state not vulnerable to irredentism could then engage in it—most irredentist states faced their own separatist threats. Most relevant for today, Pakistan continues to seek Kashmir while worried about the threat of Greater Afghanistan. Likewise, Ireland, as a country that faces no separatist threat of its own, could have supported elements in Northern Ireland more energetically but refrained.

The kin play a complex role, as table 7.2 indicates. Whether or not the rele-vant kin are in power goes a long way to predicting whether a state will en-gage in irredentist foreign policies.

The activities and inclinations of the kin seem to matter, but not as consis-tently, while the risks they face do not seem to affect what the mother country is likely to do. Neither the power nor the interests of the kin seem to be neces-sary conditions, but they seem to be jointly sufficient. That is, a state is likely to be irredentist if the kin are irredentist or powerful, but not necessarily both.

We find that a focus on the nature of nationalism and its role in each do-mestic political system provides a better account than any of the others. Poli-

TABLE 7.2   The Role of Kin

	Irredentist	Endangered	Powerful
Albania	Disconfirms	Disconfirms	Confirms
Armenia	Confirms	Confirms	Confirms
Croatia	Confirms	Confirms	Confirms
Greece	Mixed	Mixed	Disconfirms
Hungary	Confirms	Mixed	Confirms
Ireland	Disconfirms	Disconfirms	Confirms
Pakistan	Confirms	Confirms	Confirms
Romania	Disconfirms	Disconfirms	Confirms
Russia	Mixed	Disconfirms	Confirms
Serbia	Confirms	Confirms	Disconfirms
Turkey	Confirms	Confirms	Disconfirms
Total	6 Confirm	5 Confirm	8 Confirm
	3 Disconfirm	4 Disconfirm	3 Disconfirm
	2 Mixed	2 Mixed	

ticians chose to engage in dangerous courses of action when their constituencies consisted of those with strong interests in the kin abroad and those who would prefer continued or increased international isolation. To make such coalitions work, the nationalism in play must strongly identify domestic constituents with kin abroad. If the nationalism is so xenophobic as to be intolerant of both kin and others, then politicians will find irredentism to be unattractive from the standpoint of domestic politics, not just international costs.

The mini-cases in this chapter help to flesh out the patterns that we saw in our earlier chapters. Leaders will engage in costly, even self-destructive, campaigns of aggression to bring in "lost kin" under some circumstances, but they acquiesce in other situations. In the next chapter, we develop the implications of these case studies for both a better understanding of the international relations of ethnic conflict and for policymakers as they confront one of the most significant threats to peace.

NOTES TO CHAPTER 7: WAR AND PEACE IN EASTERN EUROPE, THE FORMER SOVIET UNION, AND BEYOND

1. The literature is vast, but some key works are Doyle (1986), Chan (1984), Russett (1993), Lake (1992), Bueno de Mesquita et al. (1999), and Gartzke (2000).

2. See Snyder (1991, 1999), Mansfield and Snyder (1995), and Mansfield and Snyder (2005).

3. See Touval (1972), Jackson and Rosberg (1982), Herbst (1989), and Zacher (2001).

4. See Saideman (1997, 2001, 2002).

5. For a discussion of the costs of these policies, see Angjeli (1999).

6. Judah (2001) documents, at best, ambivalent support for the NLA among Macedonia's Albanian population.

7. See also Austin (2004).

8. ICG (2004, 11), citing an interview with Reuters.

9. Horowitz (1985) noted this obstacle to irredentism.

10. Italics added. The text is from an official website of Ireland's government: www.taoiseach.gov.ie/attached_files/html%20files/Constitution%20of%20Ireland%20(Eng)Nov2004.htm.

11. Cox (1985) provides the foundation for this section. We owe John McGarry a debt for suggesting this piece to us.

12. For a variety of theories applied to this conflict, see Paul (2005).

13. To be clear, the dynamics involved implicate not only Pakistan but also India and actors within Kashmir. For the sake of comparison with the other irredentist countries, we focus on Pakistan here.

14. Additionally, Punjab depends on water flowing through Jammu and Kashmir; Pakistani control of these territories would reduce vulnerability to India (Malik 2001, 208).

15. *The Economist*, March 13, 2004.

16. China, a key ally, is among these countries owing to its own problems with separatists supported by groups related to Al Qaeda; *The Economist*, March 13, 2004.

17. For example, see *Dawn*, March 13, 2003.

18. Shahid Javed Burki, "Keeping Out Pakistan?" *Dawn*, October 21, 2003.

19. For a recent assessment, see Ayres (2004).

20. It is important to note that most arguments about democratic peace focus on dyads: joint democracy leads to peace, but democracies do war with nondemocracies (Bueno de Mesquita et. al 1999; Gartzke 2000; Gelpi 1997; Lake 1992; Russett 1993).

8

Findings and Implications

We know more about war than we know about peace, more about killing than we know about living.
— OMAR N. MRADLEY

W E H A V E S E E N B O T H M O R E A N D L E S S V I O L E N C E in the aftermath of communism in Eastern Europe and the former Soviet Union than we might have otherwise expected. Armenia and Azerbaijan continue to be mired in their conflict, reducing their ability to make a successful transition. Yugoslavia, once one of the most developed and progressive countries in the region, produced the most violence Europe has seen since World War II. Most of the successors to the now-dead federation lag far behind the rest of Europe politically, economically, and otherwise. Hungary, to little surprise, has made the easiest move to democracy and integration to Europe, although its foreign policies have perhaps been the most annoying. Depending on one's perspective, Romania has been a failure or dramatic success. Corruption remains high, economic development is behind, and the politics of the system still seem less mature than its neighbors, yet Romania has not engaged in aggression. Its foreign policies are largely a pale imitation of Hungary's. Finally, Russia, despite initial fears, severe economic dislocations, and major political crises, remains the same size as when the Soviet Union collapsed. The big bear has not eaten its smaller and weaker neighbors. Even as Russia has become more confrontational of late, the Near Abroad does not seem to be a priority. Moreover, as the previous chapter demonstrates, the dynamics that we find to be crucial in Eastern Europe also matter elsewhere—in Western Europe and Asia, for instance. Irredentism serves as a significant cause of violence around the globe, but it is restrained less by international pressures than by domestic politics, including xenophobia.

This research has both confirmed beliefs about the international politics of ethnic conflict and surprised us about some of the dynamics of nationalism. The forces motivating leaders, publics, and states are more complicated than past analyses suggested. Yet, there are several dynamics resonating throughout the cases that serve as keys for understanding the future behavior of these and other countries.

The purpose of this chapter is to develop the implications of this project for future research and for the development of foreign policies. We first consider the arguments that we have confronted, particularly the role of boundaries and of international pressures, reinterpreting the roles they play in constraining aggressive foreign policies. Next, we consider what a nuanced view of nationalism might add to our understanding of war and peace and of ethnic conflict in general. The final section develops some of the broader implications for policymakers.

Competing Accounts: Relevant Factors, Different Dynamics

While we find that the alternative theories fall short of accounting for the conditions under which countries engage in costly efforts to (re)gain "lost territories," we discovered some new dimensions to these arguments that might extend their relevance. Boundaries matter greatly, but not as a normative constraint. Rather, they serve to shape identities, affecting the ties between peoples. Conditionality processes do matter, but we need to be clear about their limits. Ultimately, the EU and other organizations may matter more for shaping how decisions are made rather than serve as a set of costs. Vulnerability arguments are not particularly helpful in determining which states engage in war, inasmuch as the continual pattern is of politicians worrying about their political futures, not their countries' destinies. Relative power may matter in shaping outcomes, but not in the choices leaders and publics make.

Boundaries: Defining Identity, Not Aggression

While much of the conflict after the collapse of communism was across intrastate boundaries rather than interstate ones, our studies suggest that the key force at work here was not the dissuasive power of international norms, but rather the impact that borders make on identities. That is, countries willing to engage in aggression were not deterred by international norms against aggression or boundary-changing. One of the arguments by Germany and others was that recognition of the seceding republics would internationalize the Yugoslav conflict and thus deter further aggression, but this optimism proved unfounded. The wars ended only when Croatia conquered Serb-held territories and when the Croatia-Bosnia alliance, along with NATO bombing, pushed Bosnia's Serbs into a corner. To say that war was possible in Yugoslavia because the aggression occurred across interrepublican boundaries rather than international ones leaves us wondering why there was relatively little war among former Soviet republics. Moreover, in the early days of Moldovan independence, boundary norms were not widely discussed as Romania considered reunion.

Yet boundaries have mattered, but in a much deeper and more lasting way than one would expect from a focus on norms.[1] What it means to be Hungarian, Romanian, Russian, Armenian, Serb, or Croat critically depends on the larger political context. It used to be the case that Hungarians ruled over a large, multiethnic empire, but the Treaty of Trianon ended that, creating one of the most homogeneous states in Europe. Over the course of the twentieth century, and particularly after 1956, Hungarians within Hungary developed a shared sense of being Hungarian. It focused not only on language, which Hungarians throughout the Carpathian basin share, but also on the experiences of living within a particular territory. For Hungarians, it matters whether or not one experienced post-1956 communism within Hungary. That experience, delimited by international boundaries, has created a sense of *us* that applies rather narrowly. As a result, Hungarians outside of Hungary are important, deserving of good treatment where they *reside*, but not quite part of the Hungarian nation-state.

Likewise, Romanian identification with Moldovans, and vice versa, is actually rather weak. There is, again, some kinship, some identification of a shared identity, but there are also important distinctions drawn between the two. Romanians share a variety of stereotypes about Moldovans, so that even as public policy causes Moldovans to go to universities in Bucharest, they take home to Moldova experiences of discrimination.[2] While Romanians see reunion as inevitable, they are not sufficiently motivated to do anything significant about it in the short term.

Russia faces a different situation, similar to Hungary in 1920. Russia existed within this set of boundaries for the first time in 1991, for the original

state of Russia even before its expansion in the 1800s always included significant portions of Ukraine and Belarus. The collapse of the Soviet Union meant
also the disintegration of the old Russian Empire, leaving Russians ponder-
ing what it meant to be Russian with twenty-five million Russians left on the
outside. As chapter 6 demonstrates, this has led to much debate and confusion, rather than assertion or aggression.

Key leaders and constituencies within Croatia viewed the Croats in Bosnia
as an integral part of the whole community of Croats. Residing in a single
state helped to maintain this view as they largely shared the same experiences—both the World War II conflicts and the various efforts to reassert
Croatian identity under Tito. Certainly, Croats do not share a singular vision
of what it means to be Croatian, but clearly, for Tudjman and others in power
in the 1990s, the Croatian nation was not and should not be divided by republican boundaries.

While Serbs of Serbia have drawn some distinctions over the course of
time among the different Serb populations of Yugoslavia, they did see the
Serbs as sharing a common fate—and a common destiny to govern and even
dominate the federation. Indeed, this goes beyond identity to basic political
demography—that democracy would facilitate Serb influence in Yugoslavia
or in reduced Yugoslavia. There was no need to cleanse Yugoslavia or Serbia
of the ethnic others. Ethnic cleansing, as discussed in chapter 2, was a tactic,
rather than the long-professed goal of Serb nationalists.[3]

Like Croatians, Armenians defined their identity in terms of a shared set
of experiences—primarily the Turkish genocide, but also the experience of
living under Russian-dominated communism. Boundaries inside the USSR
had been political playthings that often moved at the whim of leaders in
Moscow, usually to advance central communist control—a tactic that, in the
Caucasus, tended to exacerbate ethnic identities and the distinction between
Armenians and Turkic Azeris. The immediate spark of the conflict over
Karabakh began in events of the late 1980s, but those events created the
conflagration they did only because Armenians were so willing to quickly
and widely interpret them in terms of their shared historical experience of
victimhood.

Greece and Turkey's experiences with Cyprus are perhaps the strongest
illustrations of the limitations that territory places on identities and their
ability to support irredentism. Cypriot territory has never been a part of either Greece or Turkey in their modern incarnations, and while both countries share an ethnic affinity for their kin on the island, those links were not

close enough in either home population to support serious efforts at political unification. When the Greek government tried irredentism anyway, it was summarily thrown out of power. Turkey's efforts, while aggressive on the ground, have fallen short of political unity, and there seems to be no great groundswell of support for serious irredentism. Ultimately, Greek and Turkish identities have seemed to matter more on the island than on either mainland (with respect to the Cyprus issue), a function in part of the geographical isolation of Cyprus from both "mother countries."

The cases of Albania and Ireland seem to support this. Both care a great deal about their kin in the neighboring territory but have come to see the kin as not quite "us." There is little support for Greater Albania, inasmuch as the Kosovars are seen as a distinct people, despite the shared ties. The Irish seem to consider the experiences of the conflict in the North to have created a division between themselves and those in the north. Violence in the north, coupled with peace and prosperity in the south, have caused some to wonder whether a serious cultural divide has grown up between the two—a position strengthened by an earlier divide between visions for Ireland's future that ended up coinciding with the geographical boundary line.

Yet international borders do not sever all identity links. There are enough Somalis and Pakistanis identifying with kin to make significant sacrifices. The former may be due to the nomadic nature of some of the groups involved, or because, for the Ogaden at least, the prospective gains in relative power amplify the shared sense of identity. For Pakistan, it may be that the continued conflict, from 1947 to the present, has reinforced the shared sense of identity. Boundaries can influence identities, but they are not the sole determinants of who is perceived as "us" and who is the relevant other. Still, we need to pay more attention to how international boundaries matter in influencing the content of nationalisms—what the shared experiences are that define who belongs to the nation and who does not.

Conditionality and International Pressures

We must be clear—international pressures do matter, and efforts by international organizations to shape the behavior of newcomers can be quite important. Hungary and Romania went to a great deal of effort to accommodate NATO and EU demands. The international community, as Thomas Ambrosio (2001) rightly points out, largely determines whether an irredentist effort will be successful, but not whether one takes place. The record of irredentism is generally one of self-destruction—and usually the likely costs can be anticipated. That is, it is known that the international community has been and is likely to impose costs on countries seeking to engage in aggression to unify neighboring territories, but these costs do not deter leaders who are committed to these courses of action. These costs are one factor, but politicians must look to their domestic standing first and foremost.

Those who argue for the power of international institutions seem to forget that international engagement has not only benefits but costs as well.[4] Some politicians have paid more attention to those who are hurt by integration with the international economy, and these constituents (whether voters, campaign contributors or members of the security apparatus) have common cause with others who seek policies that are likely to antagonize outsiders. Milosevic was not the only politician to discover that economic transformation, as required by international and regional organizations, would be quite painful. Therefore, we need to pay attention to the domestic politics of accession—who benefits, who gets hurt, and who has the power.

Still, membership matters. Politicians, as Milada Vachudova notes (2005), gained or lost votes, depending on whether they were seen as facilitators or obstacles to membership.[5] These processes made it harder for politicians to argue that their nationalist courses had no consequences. But the key remains this—not all leaders saw membership as the ultimate goal for their countries and not all constituents did either. We see in Europe (and elsewhere) different combinations of interests, with some making integration the highest priority and others finding other objectives to be more important.

Instead, membership in NATO and particularly the EU will matter deeply by changing who makes the decisions and who are the primary constituents. If the European Court becomes the Supreme Court of Europe, overruling the legislation and implementation occurring within individual states, then real decision making will have moved, changing what governments do. If regulations for language policy are made in Brussels, rather than Bucharest, then the content of policy will change—if the locals are willing to implement the new laws.

We remain Euro-skeptics at this point because borders matter in a second fundamental way: they determine the constituencies—the pools of potential voters—for politicians. Ultimately, politicians are going to respond to their domestic audiences, and their domestic audiences are going to focus on the issues that directly concern themselves. There is already a lively debate about the EU's democratic deficit,[6] and we have seen events over the past couple of years shake Europe's confidence in the inevitability of EU institutionalization. France's rejection of the EU Constitution is particularly challenging, given that country's leading role in the development of the EU throughout its history. There is no doubt that the EU, and NATO to a lesser extent, will matter a great deal in shaping Europe's destiny. Yet, we need to keep in mind its limits:

- There is still no common foreign policy.
- Countries are willing to forgo the benefits of membership if other priorities matter more, as Bosnia, Croatia, and Serbia demonstrated throughout the 1990s; all are only now starting to comply with international pressures.
- Members are willing to sell out the principles of the organization if a compelling domestic need arises, as Greece's successful sponsorship of Cyprus attests.
- Hard bargaining will continue to be the order of the day, which again leads to compromises over values, with the rest of the EU submitting to Greece on Macedonia and Cyprus to win votes on other issues.

Finally, the EU is limited to Europe, although the definition of Europe is still up for grabs. If the temptation to join Europe has played any role in taming aggressive foreign policies, this is limited to one continent. In the rest of the world, there is no institution with the resources and level of integration to provide as strong of a lure. While integration with India's vibrant economy may tempt Pakistan to reduce its irredentism, the path is uncertain and cooperation is hardly inevitable.

Before moving on, we should address an alternative means by which the EU might affect Eastern Europe and the former Soviet Union: socialization. Many scholars have argued it is not just the immediate gains and costs of EU membership that have altered how the new members behave, but that these efforts have gone much further and deeper by teaching and persuading them of the correct way, the European way, of behaving (Cronin 2002; Linden 2002; Schimmelfennig 2003). We have primarily examined conditionality rather than socialization since the latter is a longer-term process by far.

It might seem unfair to argue against socialization in the first decade after the Cold War, since it is too early to be a fair test. Indeed, it is too early to tell in many places whether the promises made to the EU on the way to accession were sincere expressions of preferred paths of reform or just telling the EU what it wanted to hear. It is also unclear whether these new norms can overcome domestic political preferences when the two forces meet. Moreover, for the question at hand, it seems that socialization would only be able to account for restraint by Hungary and Romania. It is very hard to believe that outside actors have successfully persuaded or taught Russia to restrain its foreign policies, given the violence used in Chechnya or the antidemocratic steps taken by President Putin at various points in time.[7]

Vulnerability

We have not spent much time on the vulnerability argument in the first two chapters of this book, since we had already shown elsewhere (Saideman 2001) that this argument does not hold up. Therefore, it is not terribly surprising that states act hypocritically—criticizing acts that they themselves take. The most obvious example is Romania, which is very sensitive to any interest shown by Hungary in the plight of the Hungarians in Romania, yet is quite attentive to the condition of Romanian-speakers in Moldova. Despite Romania's own history as a victim of irredentism and continually stated fear of Hungary's darker motives, Romania has essentially borrowed Hungary's techniques and applied them to Moldova. Romania has passed legislation similar to Hungary's much ballyhooed Status Law to give benefits to Romanian-speakers of Moldova. Likewise, each country has a governmental office dedicated to the monitoring of its kin abroad.

Croatia, despite waging a war against Serbian irredentism, became Serbia's partner in Bosnia as they sought to divide the republic between them. This effort undercut Croatia's legitimacy, it weakened its complaints against Serbia's aggression, and it diverted resources from the defense of its integrity. Serbia fought in the name of self-determination in Bosnia and Croatia and of territorial integrity a few years later in Kosovo. In these circumstances, these are logically contradictory claims. To deny Kosovar Albanians the right to choose their political destiny while arming Serbs in Croatia to defend their political rights is the height of hypocrisy. Serbia was clearly not constrained by the separatism it faced within its own republic.

Armenia has held onto territory that is convenient for governing Nagorno-Karabakh—a land bridge—despite having weak historical claims and no real demographic grievance. It thereby weakens its own claims since territorial claims need not be based on demographic facts—the essence of Armenia's claim to Karabakh. History has likewise been selectively used, and at times Armenia has turned down deals involving territory that was formerly dominated by Armenians, because it now contains too many Azeris!

Hypocrisy is not new to international relations.[8] We are not surprised by it, and we often do not even notice it. Yet, it is important here to note that fears of setting precedents and concerns about appearing hypocritical are not nearly as powerful as fans of international norms would have us believe.[9] States are not going to submit to the international community's sense of appropriate behavior, at least in the realm of ethnic politics, if they face a compelling interest to do otherwise. It is also clear that the short run matters more than the long run in determining today's political choices. Undermining an international regime or refusing to support the development of a new one poses long-term consequences, but politicians and their publics focus on today's issues, not tomorrow's costs and choices.

Power and Outcomes

Ambrosio (2001) argues that the international community and the likelihood of success dissuades irredentism. This follows from a broader discussion about the role of power in international relations. The problem is that strength or weakness may not determine a country's preferences or the interests of politicians. Rather, relative power determines outcomes. Repeatedly, weaker countries have attacked stronger ones, as in the cases of Armenia, Greece, and Pakistan. Moreover, strong states frequently refrained from taking advantage of the weaker ones, as Romania did not attack Moldova, and, most notably, Russia has not openly attacked its weaker neighbors. Instead, we have repeatedly seen weaker states punished for their temerity—with Pakistan as the poster child for failed irredentist efforts, losing war after war and suffering international isolation for its efforts. Armenia stands out as a weak state that won its war, but exemplifies the term "pyrrhic" victory. The purpose of this book is not to argue that deterrence always fails or that deterrence theory is wrong, but the cases here do suggest that we need to be concerned about overestimating the power of threats when politicians focus on their internal audience more than the external one.

Nuances of Nationalism

In the course of this research, we found that nationalism was more complex than the simple sharing of key attributes such as language. In previous work (Saideman 2001), ethnic ties seemed to be sufficient for explaining the sides countries took in other states' conflicts. Here, we found out that the content of nationalisms matter, this content changes over time, and even nationalist populaces are sensitive to the costs.

It was necessary to take seriously the content of nationalisms—the beliefs and attitudes defining who is the us, who are the relevant others, the strength of feelings about the various communities—to understand why some groups and countries take strong stands on behalf of kin abroad while others cared, but not enough to exert themselves as much. We found that there generally exist hierarchies of identifications with various other groups that place them on a spectrum from most *us*-ness to most *other*-ness. This comes as little surprise, since social identity theorists have been saying the same thing for years,[10] but the implications for foreign policy are novel and important.

Kin outside the country are close to the group inside but not always identical. That is, ties exist, but there is rarely complete identification with the brethren beyond the border. They may share languages, religion and race, but they do not share the same history or the same experiences. For some groups within a state, the kin outside may actually be seen as more important and more a part of the group than other groups within the state. Croatian elites certainly saw Croats in Bosnia as being more tied to themselves than to Serbs in Croatia.

Talking to Hungarians in Hungary and Romania has helped to clarify some of this, inasmuch as Hungarians in Hungary care a great deal about Hungarians in Romania, but not as much as they care about themselves and not as much as they are concerned with Romanians in either country. That is, Hungary's Hungarians want their kin to do well, but to stay put. They certainly do not want to do anything that would increase the heterogeneity of their country, especially if it would mean more Romanians.

As a result, we have come to focus on two dimensions of the content of any nationalism—who are identified as the relevant us, the key others, and where in between some people may be, and how tolerant a group is of the other. This moves us past the distinction between ethnic and civic nationalisms as some ethnic nationalisms are more acceptant of the existence of other groups residing in their midst. True, most civic nationalisms are tolerant of heterogeneity, but we need to take seriously how ethnic nationalisms and nationalists might vary. Some nationalists might care more about the kin abroad than the possibility of including more members of other groups, while other nationalists might care a great deal more about the "threat" of increased diversity rather than the plight of kin.

Once we begin to focus on the stuff inside a particular nationalism, it quickly becomes apparent that the meanings, the rankings, and all the rest can vary over time. It is true that the constructivist approach to identity has stressed that nationalisms are socially constructed—the product of interactions over time, leaving room for politicians to manipulate identities but not create them out of thin air.[11] Yet, as we study the impact of nationalism upon conflict, we tend to focus on static notions of the national identities that are in play and consider whether someone is more or less nationalist, rather than what the content of the nationalism might stress.

What it means to be Hungarian today is significantly different from what it meant to be Hungarian sixty years ago. The 1956 revolution and the Soviet response altered what it meant to be Hungarian—that event and the subsequent repression have shaped who Hungarians feel are, indeed, Hungarian and those who are less Hungarian. Since 1991, Russians have faced an identity crisis, one that is very different from Russian identity issues of the early twentieth century, and one that has not yet been resolved. It seems certain that the Karabakh conflict—approaching twenty years old as of this writing—has shaped the identity of Armenians and given them a powerful new set of shared experiences by which they will understand their future. Greeks, Turks, Romanians, and Moldovans—all have been shaped by powerful events in the last fifty years that have taken some possibilities off the table and opened up new ones. The history of nationalism in the latter half of the twentieth century is a demonstration of the power of nations to reshape who they are and how they think of themselves in response to new opportunities and new threats.

Despite our emphasis on nationalism as a motivation, we also need to be clear that people are actually less willing to sacrifice on behalf of their nation than generally advertised. A consistent theme throughout the cases is that costs do matter. Constituents will respond to the appeals of nationalists more enthusiastically if they are promised that the costs will be low. During Serbia's first elections, Milosevic tried to portray himself as a moderate, arguing that the other, more rabid nationalists on the slate were more likely to risk war. Hungary's Socialist Party was able to score points in various debates whenever the more nationalist Fidesz Party proposed policies that would cost Hungarians tax dollars that could be spent at home. Russia's Zhirinovsky has never gained a strong following in large part because Russia's domestic troubles seem much more pressing to most Russians than those of their kin in the near abroad. Despite the strong emotional appeal that often exists toward one's kin abroad, most people are more interested in themselves than in others and prefer not to expend significant resources on somebody else. This becomes increasingly clear when we compare the effects of a successful irredentist effort to immigration below. To be clear, costly policies are still possible for three reasons:

- Those desiring the dangerous strategy may not be paying the bills with their money or blood;
- Supporters of expensive efforts may simply expect to benefit more than they pay;
- Constituents may be sold by promises of aggression on the cheap.

Domestic Dynamics of Irredentism

In the course of this research, it became increasingly clear that there is a natural barrier to irredentism in most countries—xenophobia. The inclusion of new people into one's society has political, economic, and social costs that most would like to avoid. Any successful effort at irredentism would produce an effect similar to a massive wave of immigration. Union, if realized, would alter the demographic balance of the state and include within the society many more individuals seeking the benefits of citizenship. Below, we sketch out some of the anticipated consequences that serve as deterrents.

The inclusion of large numbers of newcomers would alter the political balance of any country. It is highly unlikely that the new citizens would perfectly reflect the distribution of political attitudes already in the country. Therefore, the wave of new citizens would be a boon to some and a bane for others. The Somali invasion of Ethiopia in 1977, had it concluded successfully, would have increased the Ogaden population of Somalia. This would have enhanced the power of that clan and of the clan-family to which it belonged, but it would have made the remaining clan-families relatively weaker. Hungarians abroad were seen to be more likely to vote for the center-right Fidesz Party, so the Socialists have been less enthusiastic about dual citizenship. Donald Horowitz (1985) pointed out long before the Kosovo conflict that Albania's interest in a Greater Albania is modest at best because including the Kosovar Albanians would upset the existing balance between different kinship groups in Albania.

On the other hand, there would also be those who would benefit from the change in the domestic balance of power. The already mentioned Ogaden would see their power increase in a Greater Somalia. Right-wing Croats would have cemented their control had they been successful in bringing into Croatia the parts of Bosnia inhabited by like-minded Croats. Inclusion of Serb nationalists from Croatia and Bosnia into a Greater Serbia would have created an indebted class of constituents for the more nationalist parties in Serbia. One reason Armenia's irredentism in Karabakh has gone on so long is that the political classes in Karabakh successfully seized power in Armenia proper, transferring those attitudes to the center of policymaking.

The economics of irredentism also serve as a deterrent. Increasing the number of citizens means not only diluting one's political power but also stretching the welfare state to include new beneficiaries. Constituents may be reluctant to support irredentism because it will mean that their tax dollars will go to other people rather than to themselves. The experience of Germany in the 1990s may discourage potential irredentists, since the costs of incorporating and transforming East Germany were staggering, even when borne by one of the world's richest countries.[12] It should not be surprising that Romania's enthusiasm for bringing Moldova back into the fold was greatest at the outset of the post–Cold War era, when Moldova was either even or ahead of Romania economically. This interest in Moldova has declined as Romania's economy has grown while Moldova's has regressed. Similarly, Ireland amended its constitution, largely ruling out a Greater Ireland, in 1998 after the Celtic Tiger had zoomed past Northern Ireland and much of Western Europe. Hungarian voters seem to shrink from serious efforts to help their kin when the expense becomes significant and obvious.

Last, xenophobia in this context most clearly refers to fear and/or dislike of foreigners. Not only would successful unification produce political and economic shocks, but it could also produce social stress. Notwithstanding the reality that many states, particularly those in Europe, desperately need new immigrants owing to declining populations, foreigners are not welcome.[13] Even before 9/11, right-wing parties were on the rise in France, Italy, and elsewhere, largely focused on immigration. Anti-immigration sentiments exist in all countries that receive immigrants, and this is nothing new. The key here is that if a country expands its territory to include lost kin and lost territories, it has an impact similar to immigration. Because the kin abroad are seen as being similar but not identical to the citizens of the homeland, many individuals would prefer them to remain on the other side of the border. These kin are seen as having different experiences and values—they are simply different. Romanian attitudes toward Moldova are shaped in large part by their attitudes toward Moldovans, whom they see as backward kin and treat as such. Hungarian voting behavior seems to reflect this general pattern, as the referendum on dual citizenship as well as the 2001 election turned, in part, on issues of immigration and spending on outsiders.

While differences among kin provide one obstacle to irredentist efforts, hate or fear of the truly foreign also serve as an impediment to irredentism. Because the targeted territories are usually inhabited by non-kin groups and because the history of losing the territories usually involved these others, successful irredentism might mean the inclusion of not only kin but of hated out-groups in the new state. To repeat the line of a Hungarian residing in Romania, "To kill Hungary, give it Transylvania."[14] Hungarians simply do not like Romanians, so the prospect of incorporating millions of Romanians serves as a formidable obstacle to any irredentist effort. The politics of the Status Law turned, in part, on the prospect of Romanian immigration. Romanians feel similarly about the Russophones residing in Moldova. The historic antagonism between Russia and Romania means that Romanians identify Russian speakers as adversaries, not potential partners. Because the Russophones reside not only in the Transnistria region of Moldova but also in the cities, any serious effort to annex Moldova, even only the western part, would mean the inclusion of many Russophones.

Xenophobia works to inhibit foreign aggression in another way. To be a nationalist does not necessarily require an assertive foreign policy, but rather can mean targeting domestic groups. The Greater Romania Party focuses most of its attention not on Greater Romania, but on a purer Romania. The party's newspapers regularly editorialize about Roma, Jews, Muslims, Hungarians, and homosexuals, not the plight of Romanian-speakers in Moldova. Many Russian nationalists, Zhirinovsky included, have likewise spent much time focusing on the foreign enemy within rather than the estranged kin abroad. This book raises the possibility that forces that might be bad for domestic politics might be good for international peace and regional stability. This is not to say that we recommend emphasizing hate, but we need to understand that trade-offs may exist.

Of course, there is a way to be irredentist and yet preserve homogeneity—ethnic cleansing (Mann 2005). While we argue in chapter 2 that Croatia and Serbia would have accepted multiethnic hunks of Bosnia if gained peacefully, it is clear that ethnic cleansing was pursued during the war to create homogeneous territories that would easily fit into Greater Croatia and Greater Serbia. Again, this seems to have been pursued to create defensible territories, necessary in war, rather than due to the desire to create a homogeneous country. Serbia's efforts to hold onto Kosovo and Vojvodina indicate that homogeneity was not Milosevic's goal. Croatia did not try to cleanse Zagreb of the Serb population there, only the contested regions. Armenia largely succeeded in cleansing not only Karabakh itself but also the Azeri-populated Lachin corridor, to homogenize the territory as much as possible and avoid having to live with people perceived as Turks. The ability to engage in ethnic cleansing means that heterogeneous lost territories need not be a deterrent if the will to use sufficient violence is strong enough. Scholars are increasingly focused on why some individuals and governments are more willing to engage in large-scale atrocities.[15] Because the "kin" were very influential in the policy process in Armenia and Croatia, their cleansing efforts may be less surprising. In such cases, the enthusiasm and self-interest of those making decisions may permit or facilitate the step toward cleansing.

Before even considering the potential external costs that might be imposed upon a country that pursues irredentism, the calculus is pretty clear. Most countries do not engage in irredentism because it would upset the existing order domestically. While international opposition may or may not be certain (Ambrosio 2001), the internal dynamics are quite straightforward. Successful irredentism would produce winners and losers, even if war were not required. However, as in the case of many other public-policy questions (Olson 1965), the potential winners are often smaller and far more certain about their likely concentrated benefits, the potential losers are quite large, and the costs may appear to be diffuse. This means that it is possible for the irredentist camp to win, as they can be easier to organize than the anti-irredentist coalition.

Nationalism and Foreign Policy

Most of the literature on nationalism and foreign policy focuses on minorities and their impact. Specifically, there is an extensive literature on diasporas and their impact on the foreign policies of their host states,[16] but the identities of majorities and their implications have largely been ignored. In our previous work, we do consider the ethnic identities of relevant constituencies (Saideman 2001), focusing somewhat on the identification of us and them, but we did not consider the importance of tolerance and intolerance. That is, xenophobia was largely ignored. While there have been more efforts of late to consider identity and foreign policy (Prizel 1998; Telhami and Barnett 2002; Woodwell 2007), we need more efforts here to understand how the identifications of individuals, groups, and states with and counter to others shape not only their perceptions but also their actions. Thus, this book is part of a larger movement (Posner 2004, 2005; Abdelal et al. 2006; Chandra 2006) in political science to take seriously the content of identities and their implications for political behavior. Here we have shown that these identities matter in the international realm, shaping the proclivity for war or peace.

This book is part of a larger trend since the end of the Cold War to understand the sources of ethnic strife with an increased focus on how borders do not serve as barriers to influence. While ethnic conflict is not as contagious as often averred (Lake and Rothchild 1998), it is clear that dynamics in one country to affect the outcomes in the next. Cetinyan (2002) and Jenne (2004, 2006) show that the concern and power of the mother country greatly determine demands of an ethnic group and its treatment by its host government. Here, we have identified factors that shape the behavior of the mother country—coalitions favoring integration or isolation, the content of the nationalist identity—that fill in a missing hole in the "triadic nexus." In earlier work (Saideman 1997, 2001), we found that external support occurred when relevant constituents in one state had ties to combatants in another. Here, we find that ties are not enough, because the consequences of support are much more significant. Rather than rhetoric, recognition, arms, or bases, there is a real likelihood of war and a possibility of altering the political system with the incorporation of kin. Thus, support of ethnic brethren abroad is more likely than irredentism—not because of norms or institutions, but as a result of the implications for the mother country's domestic dynamics. Supporting secession is similar but not identical to engaging in irredentism.

Policy Implications

How do politicians react to the imperatives of nationalism? One of the challenges of social science is that there is rarely one way to respond to political stimuli, and we found this to be the case here as well. Two questions motivated our research: does a politician have to be a nationalist to win and stay in office and, if so, what does it take to be a successful nationalist? It turns out that the second question is very challenging, not only for analysts but for politicians as well, inasmuch as they have to figure out how to appease constituents who care a great deal about their identities and even their kin without alienating other key constituents. We discovered two strategies to reducing the salience of the kin issue: by improving the condition of the kin abroad, and by diverting the attention of nationalists toward other targets.

The various efforts by Hungarian politicians to protect the kin abroad via bilateral treaties, the Status Law, and the like seemed to be aimed at two targets, both the domestic audience, to show that they are good nationalists, and that kin. The better the treatment the kin faced, the less important they are on the domestic agenda. Hungary has expended considerable political capital in its effort to improve the condition of the kin, trying to rally regional organizations to the cause. It is hard to tell whether the aim is sincere—that politicians really care about the kin, or whether each side in Hungary's political system is using the kin issue and the surrounding complications in their competition with each other.

In Russia, there appeared to be ample opportunities for ethnically entrepreneurial politicians such as Vladimir Zhirinovsky to make political hay out of the conditions of Russians abroad, especially in the Baltic states, where severe discrimination took hold. But this failed in large part because the Russian population could not decide whether Russian-speakers in the Baltic States "counted" as Russians or not. Moreover, as Russia has developed following the fall of communism, power has been increasingly concentrated in the presidency, with the Duma as little more than a "talk shop," especially on foreign-relations issues. Zhirinovsky, or any other Russian nationalist candidate, would thus have to win the presidency, not merely seats in the Duma—and there is not nearly enough of a constituency that cares about Russians abroad to support such an outcome. This power structure, combined with confusion of Russia's identity links to Russians in neighboring countries and severely pressing economic problems at home, have conspired to keep an aggressive Russian nationalist foreign policy off the table. However, more recently (May 2007), conflicts within Estonia have gained Vladimir Putin's attention. Still, the dispute has not escalated, and there does not seem to be a lot of impetus within Russia to exacerbate the conflict.

The second tactic is to focus the passions of nationalists on domestic audiences. Since the end of the Cold War, Romanian politicians have used a variety of domestic "others" as their targets. To be a successful nationalist in the Romanian context meant anti-Semitic statements, anti-Roma policies, and hostility to Hungary and Hungarians. While international pressure has muted some of this, with Vadim Tudor's questionable turn toward "philo-Semitism," other groups become more convenient for nationalists: gays, Muslims, and immigrants. In elections and in the newspapers, the plight of Romanian-speakers in Moldova gets far less play than these other issues, which are the favorites of the nationalists. The domestic payoff for aggression abroad is relatively modest, since nationalists can prove their credentials using xenophobia at home. While this is not good for minority relations in Romania, it may help to explain the stability that exists between Romania and Moldova. Thus, xenophobia may be good for regional relations despite its damage domestically.

What can policymakers learn from this book? Because irredentism is a significant cause of war, both before and after the Cold War, and because nationalism has been viewed as a source of regional instability, this study may shed some light on what governments can and cannot do. We focus here on two inferences we can draw from this project on the limits of external pressures and the content of nationalisms.

We have found consistent evidence that the impact of international organizations is overrated. Despite the best efforts of the most powerful and coherent international organizations, politicians will act in their best interests even if it means ostracism or other costs being borne by the society. Therefore, we need to be humble about what outside actors can do. This does not mean that external intervention cannot work, but that moderate efforts are unlikely to work and that all efforts need to take domestic political dynamics into account. Clearly, the accession process to NATO and the EU did and does matter, and membership will affect the new democracies for the long term. However, we ought not to expect leaders to engage in policies that endanger their domestic positions solely to appeal to outside actors. Carrots and sticks are unlikely to work in the short term if politicians face stronger incentives from domestic audiences—the folks who determine who governs. Understanding the limits of international pressures is an important lesson for policymakers to take seriously.

There is some good news in the long term. Because irredentism tends to occur when there are enough individuals and groups that might want to be less integrated with the world economy—the natural coalition partners of sincere nationalists—economic growth can alter the pattern of interests, making international integration favored by more. Unfortunately, the likely outcome of accession for Eastern Europe will not be the same as Ireland's experience. Ireland received a great deal of EU funding. Ireland and others in similar positions have sought to protect their "entitlements" so that the new members to the EU will receive far less. In Eastern Europe, economic growth, then, is perhaps less likely to be as dynamic as it was in the Celtic Tiger, leaving many in these countries wondering what the benefits of less sovereignty might be. Indeed, over time a deficit between benefits and costs of membership might create a nationalist backlash, leading to greater xenophobia, withdrawal, or even aggression based on scapegoating. As the different cases in this book illustrate, political developments seldom move in a single direction. Indeed, we need to be wary of arguments that posit trends in particular directions, for identities and politics fluctuate over time.

Policymakers need to take a more nuanced approach to the nationalisms they see around the globe. While the distinction between ethnic and civic has some use, even ethnic nationalisms vary quite considerably not only in their intensity but also in their foreign policy implications. Not all ethnic nationalisms lead to aggressive foreign policies. More attention needs to be paid to who is targeted and who is ignored when nationalists appeals are made—as each claim about who is us defines the relevant other. This may pose some nasty trade-offs, in that it may make sense *not* to discourage some ethnic extremism, such as anti-immigration sentiments, if it means less aggression toward the neighbors. Hate and fear may have some useful, positive qualities in that they may inhibit destructive foreign policies. Thus, there may be a trade-off between domestic insecurity and international instability. While this may be quite disturbing, it may also be true, so policymakers could face the dilemma of which one poses a greater threat.

On a more positive note, if the risk of including more "others" in their society deters irredentism, then encouraging internal migration to create more heterogeneous populations along contested borders makes sense. Indeed, Romanian dictator Ceausescu forcibly altered the demographics of Transylvania to deter Hungarian irredentism. We are not recommending such measures. Indeed, such measures are likely to exacerbate conflict in the short term. Instead, we suggest encouraging economic development of territories that irredentists might target, inasmuch as this is a less visible way to encourage integration. Indeed, this study is part of a larger literature that belies the notion that intermixing is bad and that group concentration is better for stability.[17] Indeed, while advocates of partition currently have a possible case in Iraq, they must not overlook that the creation of greater homogeneity in the different regions may actually create international conflict by making irredentism more appealing. Instead, fostering the intermingling of different ethnic groups may have real benefits for regional security because of how it plays into people's worst tendencies—xenophobia in the mother state—rather than integration as an idealistic dream.

We find that the crucial dynamics shaping the likelihood of peace, of assertive foreign policies, and of war are those shaping politicians' short-term interests and the longer-term definitions of us and them—nationalisms. Neither one is easy to influence from the outside. While our previous work suggested that cooperation is hard to develop and sustain, this book serves as a cautionary tale about the limits of the international community's ability to shape events.

NOTES TO CHAPTER 8: FINDINGS AND IMPLICATIONS

1. Ron (2003) argues that boundaries matter, but in a different way, since they shape which methods are appropriate or not.

2. These distinctions were reported repeatedly in interviews in Bucharest in 2004.

3. For more on ethnic cleansing, see Mann (2005).

4. Indeed, the antiglobalization movement should make this clear: some groups pay steep penalties for integration. For an article that takes seriously the implications of winners and losers of integration, see Tucker, Pacek, and Berinsky (2002).

5. To be clear, however, the more general pattern is of alternation: incumbents have lost most of the elections in Eastern Europe regardless of their positions or performance. For a review of the literature on postcommunist elections, see Tucker (2002).

6. For a discussion of these issues, see Karp, Banducci, and Bowler (2003).

7. Mendelson (2002). Even under Yeltsin, Russia's democratic credentials could only be considered suspect, given the use of force against the Duma.

8. Indeed, Krasner's book (1999) on sovereignty is entitled *Organized Hypocrisy*.

9. See Kier and Mercer (1996) for an excellent discussion of precedents and military intervention.

10. See, for example, Brewer (1991).

11. See Kaufman (2001) for a discussion of how existing social structures, past histories and elite politicians combine to create dangerous circumstances. Volkan (1999) focuses on the impact of history on identities and the development of hatred.

12. Indeed, Germany significantly revised its immigration laws in the aftermath of reunification to reduce the number of ethnic Germans "returning" (Cordell and Wolff 2007). On the other hand, some economists have argued that Germany's experience

was not so bad and that governments should permit, rather than block, immigration (Sinn 2000).

13. Studies of anti-immigration parties and sentiments suggest that cultural or social resistance is at the core, along with economic concerns (Fetzer 2000; Jackson et al. 2001). For more on anti-immigration sentiments, see McLaren (2003), Pettigrew (1998), and Rudolph (2003), as well as the reports of the European Monitoring Center on Racism and Xenophobia (http://eumc.eu.int).

14. Interview with Tóni Niculescu, executive vice president, Department for European Immigration, Executive Presidency of the Democratic Alliance of Hungarians in Romania (UDMR), May 14, 2004.

15. See Krain (1997), Bax (2000), Rummel (2000), Naimark (2001), Mitchell (2004), Valentino (2004), and Midlarsky (2005).

16. For the most recent work, see Shain (2007).

17. For the argument that intermixing fosters ethnic conflict, see Kaufmann (1996a, 1996b, 1998) and Posen (1993). For the work on the conflict-limiting impact of intermixing, see Gurr (2000), Toft (2002, 2003), Ayres and Saideman (2000), Saideman and Ayres (2000), and Saideman et al. (2002).

Abdelal, Rawi, Yoshiko M. Herrera, Alastair Iain Johnston, and Rose McDermott. 2006. "Identity as a Variable." *American Political Science Review* 4, no. 4: 695–711.

Adamson, Fiona. 2001. "Democratization and the Domestic Sources of Foreign Policy: Turkey in the 1974 Cyprus Crisis." *Political Science Quarterly* 116, no. 2 (Summer): 277–304.

Ahrend, Radiger. 2004. "Accounting for Russia's Post-Crisis Growth." OECD Working Paper 404.

Ambrosio, Thomas. 2001. *Irredentism: Ethnic Conflict and International Politics*. Westport, CT: Praeger.

Anderson, Benedict. 1983. *Imagined Communities: Reflections on the Origin and Spread of Nationalism*. London: Verso.

Andreas, Peter. 2005. "Criminalizing Consequences of Sanctions: Embargo Busting and Its Legacy." *International Studies Quarterly* 49, no. 2: 335–360.

Andrejevich, Milan. 1993. "The Radicalization of Serbian Politics." *RFE/RL Research Report* 2, no. 13: 24.

Angjeli, Anastas. 1999. "The Political Impact and Economic Cost to Albania of the Crisis in Kosovo." *Mediterranean Quarterly* 10, no. 3: 7–14.

Arbatov, Alexei G. 1993. "Russia's Foreign Policy Alternatives." *International Security* 18, no. 2 (Fall): 5–43.

Astourian, Stephan. 1994. "In Search of Their Forefathers: National Identity and the Historiography and Politics of Armenian and Azerbaijani Ethnogeneses." In *Nationalism and History: The Politics of Nation Building in Post-Soviet Armenia, Azerbai-*

jan and Georgia, ed. Doland Schwartz and Razmik Panossian, 41–94. Toronto: University of Toronto Centre for Russian and East European Studies.

Atzili, Boaz. 2006. "When Good Fences Make Bad Neighbors: Fixed Borders, State Weakness, and International Conflict." *International Security* 31, no. 3: 139–173.

Austin, Robert C. 2004. "Greater Albania: The Albanian State and the Question of Kosovo." In *Ideologies and National Identities*, ed. John Lampe and Mark Mazower, 235–248. New York: Central European University Press.

Avery, Graham, and Fraser Cameron. 1998. *The Enlargement of the European Union*. Sheffield, UK: Sheffield Academic Press.

Ayres, R. William. 1997. "Mediating International Conflicts: Is Image Change Necessary?" *Journal of Peace Research* 34, no. 4 (November): 431–447.

Ayres, R. William, and Stephen M. Saideman. 2000. "Is Separatism as Contagious as the Common Cold or as Cancer? Testing the International and Domestic Determinants of Secessionism." *Nationalism and Ethnic Politics* 6, no. 3: 92–114.

Banac, Ivo. 2006. "The Politics of National Homogeneity." In *War and Change in the Balkans: Nationalism, Conflict and Cooperation*, ed. Brad K. Blitz, 30–43. Cambridge: Cambridge University Press.

Barbieri, Katherine, and Gerald Schneider. 1999. "Globalization and Peace: Assessing New Directions in the Study of Trade and Conflict." *Journal of Peace Research* 36, no. 4: 387–404.

Bárdi, Nándor. 2003. "Hungary and the Hungarians Living Abroad: A Historical Outline." *Regio Yearbook: Minorities, Politics, Society*, 121–138.

——. 2004. "The History of Relations Between Hungarian Governments and Ethnic Hungarians Living Beyond the Borders of Hungary." In *The Hungarian Status Law Syndrome: A Nation Building and/or Minority Protection*, ed. Zoltán Kántor et al., 58–86. Sapporo: Slavic Research Center, Hokkaido University.

Barkey, Karen. 2000. "Negotiated Paths to Nationhood: A Comparison of Hungary and Romania in the Early 20th Century." *East European Politics and Societies* 14, no. 3: 497–531.

Barrington, Lowell. 1995. "The Domestic and International Consequences of Citizenship in the Soviet Successor States." *Europe-Asia Studies* 47, no. 5 (July): 731–763.

Bartlett, William. 2003. *Croatia: Between Europe and the Balkans*. London: Routledge.

Batt, Judy. 2005. *The Question of Serbia*. Paris: European Union.

Bax, Mart. 2000. "Warlords, Priests and the Politics of Ethnic Cleansing: A Case Study from Rural Bosnia Hercegovina." *Ethnic and Racial Studies* 23, no. 1: 16–36.

Behr, Michelle, Edina Fata, Anita Kulcsar, Istvan Lassu, and Szilvia Nagy. 2002. "Who Is Hungarian? Attitudes Toward Immigration, Ethnicity and Nationality in Rural Hungary." *East European Quarterly* 36, no. 3 (Fall): 281–299.

Bell, Bowyer J. 1993. *The Irish Troubles: A Generation of Violence, 1967–1992*. New York: St. Martin's.

Bennett, Christopher. 1995. *Yugoslavia's Bloody Collapse: Causes, Course and Consequences*. New York: New York University Press.

Bennett, D. Scott, and Allan Stam. 2000. "*EUGene*: A Conceptual Manual." *International Interactions* 26: 179–204.

Berger, Thomas U. 1998. *Cultures of Antimilitarism: National Security in Germany and Japan*. Baltimore: Johns Hopkins University Press.

Bigler, Robert M. "Back in Europe and Adjusting to the New Realities of the 1990's in Hungary." *East European Quarterly* 30, no. 2: 205–234.

Binnendijk, Hans, and Jeffrey Simon. 1996. "Hungary's 'Near Abroad': Minorities Policy and Bilateral Treaties." *Strategic Forum* 93. Washington, DC: National Defense University Institute for National Strategic Studies.

Biondich, Mark. 2004. "'We Were Defending the State': Nationalism, Myth and Memory in Twentieth-Century Croatia." In *Ideologies and National Identities: The Case of Twentieth-Century Southeastern Europe*, ed. John R. Lampe and Mark Mazower, 55–82. Budapest: Central European University Press.

Bookman, Milica Z. 1994. *Economic Decline and Nationalism in the Balkans*. New York: St. Martin's.

Böröcz, József. 2000. "The Fox and the Raven: The European Union and Hungary Renegotiate the Margins of Europe." *Comparative Studies in Society and History* 42, no. 4: 847–875.

Bose, Sumatra. 1999. "Kashmir: Sources of Conflict, Dimensions of Peace." *Survival* 41, no. 3: 149–171.

Botev, Nikolai, and Richard A. Wagner. 1993. "Seeing Past the Barricades: Ethnic Intermarriage in Yugoslavia During the Last Three Decades." *Anthropology of East Europe Review* 11, nos. 1–2 (Autumn): 27–35.

Bozóki, András. 2002. "The Hungarian Socialists: Technocratic Modernization or New Social Democracy?" In *The Communist Successor Parties of Central and Eastern Europe*, ed. András Bozóki and John T. Ishiyama, 89–115. Armonk, NY: M. E. Sharpe.

Bran, Mirel. 1995. "Romania: Using Nationalism for Political Legitimacy." In *New Xenophobia in Europe*, ed. Bernd Baumart and Adrian Favell, 280–293 London: Kluwer Law International.

Brass, Paul R. 1991. *Ethnicity and Nationalism: Theory and Comparison*. New Delhi: Sage.

Bremmer, Ian. 1994. "The Politics of Ethnicity: Russians in the New Ukraine." *Europe-Asia Studies* 46, no. 2: 261–283.

Brewer, Marilynn. 1991. "The Social Self: On Being the Same and Different at the Same Time." *Personality and Social Psychology Bulletin* 17, no. 5: 475–482.

Brown, David. 1999. "Are There Good and Bad Nationalisms?" *Nations and Nationalism* 5, no. 2: 281–302.

Brubaker, Rogers. 1996. *Nationalism Reframed: Nationhood and the National Question in the New Europe*. New York: Cambridge University Press.

——. "Migrations of Ethnic Unmixing in the 'New Europe.'" *International Migration Review* 32, no. 4: 1047–1065.

Brubaker, Rogers, and Frederick Cooper. 2000. "Beyond 'Identity.'" *Theory and Society* 29: 1–47.

Brusstar, Jim, and Ellen Jones. 1995. "The Outlook for Russian Foreign Policy: Great Power Restoration." *Strategic Forum* 52. Washington, DC: National Defense University Institute for National Strategic Studies.

Brzezinski, Zbigniew. 1994. "The Premature Partnership." *Foreign Affairs* 73, no. 2: 67–82.

Bueno de Mesquita, Bruce, James D. Morrow, Randolph M. Siverson, and Alastair Smith. 1999. "An Institutional Explanation of the Democratic Peace." *American Political Science Review* 93, no. 4: 791–808.

Bueno de Mesquita, Bruce, Alastair Smith, Randolph M. Siverson, and James D. Morrow. 2003. *The Logic of Political Survival*. Cambridge, MA: MIT Press.

Bugajski, Janusz. 2000. "Nationalist Majority Parties: The Anatomy of Ethnic Domination in Central and Eastern Europe." In *The Politics of National Minority Participation in Post-Communist Europe: State-Building, Democracy, and Ethnic Mobilization*, ed. Jonathan P. Stein, 65–101. Armonk, NY: M. E. Sharpe.

Bumci, Aldo. 2003. "Regional Perspectives for an Independent Kosovo—Albanian and Macedonia." In *Understanding the War in Kosovo*, ed. Florian Bieber and Židas Daskalovksi, 283–301. London: Frank Cass.

Bunce, Valerie. 1999. *Subversive Institutions: The Design of Socialism*. Cambridge: Cambridge University Press.

Burg, Steven L., and Paul S. Shoup. 1999. *The War in Bosnia-Herzegovina: Ethnic Conflict and International Intervention*. Armonk, NY: M. E. Sharpe.

Byman, Daniel L., Peter Chalk, Bruce Hoffman, William Rosenau, and David Brannan. 2001. *Trends in Outside Support for Insurgent Movement*. Los Angeles: Rand Corporation.

Carment, David, and Patrick James. 1995. "Internal Constraints and Interstate Ethnic Conflict: Toward a Crisis-Based Assessment of Irredentism." *Journal of Conflict Resolution* 39, no. 1: 82–109.

——. 1997. "Secession and Irredenta in World Politics: The Neglected Interstate Dimension." In *Wars in the Midst of Peace: The International Politics of Ethnic Conflict*, ed. David Carment and Patrick James, 194–231. Pittsburgh: University of Pittsburgh Press.

Carment, David, Patrick James, and Zeynep Taydas. 2006. *Who Intervenes: Ethnic Conflict and Interstate Crisis*. Columbus: Ohio State University Press.

Carpenter, Ted Galen, and Pavel Kislitsyn. 1997. "NATO Flashpoint No. 2: The Border Between Hungary and Serbia." Washington, DC: Cato Institute.

CEDIME (Center for Documentation and Information on Minorities). 2001. "Hungarians of Romania." www.greekhelsinki.gr/english/reports/CEDIME-Reports-Minorities-in-Romania.html. Accessed August 20, 2004.

Ceh, Nick, and Jeff Harder. 2004. "Imagining the Croatian Nation." *East European Quarterly* 38, no. 4: 409–417.

Cetinyan, Rupen. 2002. "Ethnic Bargaining in the Shadow of Third-Party Intervention." *International Organization* 56, no. 3 (Summer): 645–678.

Chalk, Peter. 2001. "Pakistan's Role in the Kashmir Insurgency." *Jane's Intelligence Review*, September 1, 2001.

Chan, Steve. 1984. "Mirror, Mirror on the Wall . . . Are the Free Countries More Pacific?" *Journal of Conflict Resolution* 28, no. 4: 617–648.

Chandra, Kanchan. 2006. "What Is Ethnic Identity and Does It Matter?" *Annual Review of Political Science* 9: 397–424.

Charlton, Angela. 1999 (September 19). "Russian Premier Blames International Islamists for Dagestan Fighting." Associated Press.

Chazan, Naomi. 1991. "Irredentism, Separatism, and Nationalism." In *Irredentism and International Politics*, ed. Naomi Chazan, 143. Boulder, CO: Lynne Rienner.

Checkel, Jeffrey, ed. 2005. "International Institutions and Socialization in Europe." Special issue of *International Organization* 55, no. 4.

Chiozza, Giacomo, and Heins Goemans. "International Conflict and the Tenure of Leaders: Is War Still *Ex Post* Inefficient?" *American Journal of Political Science* 48, no. 3 (July 2004): 604–619.

Chirot, Daniel. 2005. "What Provokes Violent Ethnic Conflict? Political Choice in One African and Two Balkan Cases." In *Ethnic Politics After Communism*, ed. Zoltan Barany and Robert G. Moser, 140–165. Ithaca, NY: Cornell University Press.

Clark, David H. 1998. "Rethinking the Logical Conditions of Diversionary Behavior." Paper prepared for presentation at the annual meeting of the International Studies Association, Minneapolis.

Clogg, Richard. 1992. *A Concise History of Greece*. Cambridge: Cambridge University Press.

Clover, Charles. 1999. "Dreams of the Eurasian Heartland." *Foreign Affairs* 78, no. 2 (March–April): 9–13.

Cohen, Lenard J. 1995. *Broken Bonds: Yugoslavia's Disintegration and Balkan Politics in Transition*. 2nd ed. Boulder, CO: Westview Press.

——. 1997. "Embattled Democracy: Postcommunist Croatia." In *Politics, Power and the Struggle for Democracy in South-East Europe*, ed. Karen Dawisha and Bruce Parrott, 69–121. Cambridge: Cambridge University Press.

——. 2001. *The Serpent in the Bosom: The Rise and Fall of Slobodan Milosevic*. Boulder, CO: Westview Press.

Collier, David, and James E. Mahon Jr. 1993. "Conceptual "Stretching" Revisited: Adapting Categories in Comparative Analysis." *American Political Science Review* 87 (4): 845–855.

Colton, Timothy, and Robert Legvold, eds. 1992. *After the Soviet Union: From Empire to Nations*. New York: Norton.

Connor, Walker. 1994. *Ethnonationalism: The Quest for Understanding*. Princeton, NJ: Princeton University Press.

Coogan, Tim Pat. 1996. *The Troubles: Ireland's Ordeal 1966–1996 and the Search for Peace*. Boulder, CO: Roberts Rinehart.

Cooperman, Alan. 1993 (December 15). "Red Army, Voicing Anger, Votes for Zhirinovksy." Associated Press.

Cordell, Karl, and Stefan Wolff. 2007. "Germany as a Kin-State: The Development and Implementation of a Norm-Consistent External Minority Policy Towards Central and Eastern Europe." *Nationalities Papers* 35, no. 2: 289–315.

Cornell, Svante. 1997. "Undeclared War: The Nagorno-Karabakh Conflict Reconsidered." *Journal of South Asian and Middle Eastern Studies* 20, no. 4: 1–24.

——. 1999. "International Reactions to Massive Human Rights Violations: The Case of Chechnya." *Europe-Asia Studies* 51, no. 1: 85–100.

"Council of Europe Ministers Encourage Russian Efforts for Membership." 1994 (November 10). Associated Press.

Cox, W. H. 1985. "Who Wants a United Ireland?" *Government and Opposition* 20: 38–39.

Crawford, Beverly. 1996. "Explaining Defection from International Cooperation: Germany's Unilateral Recognition Of Croatia." *World Politics* 48, no. 4: 482–521.

Croissant, Michael. 1998. *The Armenia-Azerbaijan Conflict: Causes and Implications*. Westport, CT: Praeger.

Cronin, Bruce. 2002. "Creating Stability in the New Europe: The OSCE High Commissioner on National Minorities and the Socialization of Risky States." *Security Studies* 12, no. 1: 132–163.

Crowther, William. 1992. "Romania and Moldavian Political Dynamics." In *Romania After Tyranny*, ed. Daniel N. Nelson, 239–259. Boulder, CO: Westview Press.

——. 1998. "Ethnic Politics and the Post-Communist Transition in Moldova." *Nationalities Papers* 26, no. 1 (March): 147–164.

Csepeli, György. 1997. *National Identity in Contemporary Hungary*. Boulder, CO: Social Science Monographs.

Csepeli, György, and Antal Örkény. 1996. "The Changing Faces of Hungarian Nationalism." *Social Research* 63, no. 1 (Spring): 247–284.

Csergo, Zsuzsa. 2003. "National Strategies and the Uses of Dichotomy." *Regio Yearbook: Minorities, Politics, Society*, 95–101.

——. 2007. *Talk of the Nation: Language and Conflict in Romania and Slovakia*. Ithaca, NY: Cornell University Press.

Csergo, Zsuzsa, and James M. Goldgeier. 2001. "Virtual Nationalism." *Foreign Policy* 126 (July–August): 76–77.

——. 2002. "Hungary's 'Status Law:' A Post-Territorial Approach to Nation Building?" Paper presented at the annual meeting of the American Association for the Advancement of Slavic Studies, November 21–24, Pittsburgh.

——. 2004. "Nationalist Strategies and European Integration." *Perspectives on Politics* 2, no. 1: 21–37.

Curtis, Glenn E., ed. *Armenia, Azerbaijan, and Georgia: Country Studies*. 1995. Washington, DC: Federal Research Division, Library of Congress.

——. *Russia: A Country Study*. 1996. Washington, DC: Federal Research Division, Library of Congress.

Daniszewski, John. 2001 (April 30). "A Desperate, Destitute Nation Deserts Itself." *Los Angeles Times*.

Datculescu, Petre. 1992. "Social Change and Changing Public Opinion in Romania After the 1990 Election." In *Romania After Tyranny*, ed. Daniel N. Nelson, 127–148. Boulder, CO: Westview Press.

Dauderstädt, Michael, and Britta Joerissen. 2004. "The European Policy of Left-Wing Parties in Post-Communist Accession Countries." Working Paper, Friedrich Eerbt Stiftung. http://library.fes.de/pdf-files/id/02603.pdf. Accessed September 3, 2007.

David, Steven R. 1991. *Choosing Sides: Alignment and Realignment in the Third World.* Baltimore: Johns Hopkins University Press.

Davis, David R., and Will H. Moore. 1997. "Ethnicity Matters: Transnational Ethnic Alliances and Foreign Behavior." *International Studies Quarterly* 41, no. 1: 171–184.

de Waal, Thomas. 2003. *Black Garden: Armenia and Azerbaijan Through Peace and War.* New York: New York University Press.

de Witte, Bruno. 2002. "Politics Versus Law in the EU's Approach to Ethnic Minorities." In *Europe Unbound: Enlarging and Reshaping the Boundaries of the European Union,* ed. Jan Zielonka, 137–160. London: Routledge.

Deegan-Krause, Kevin. 2004. "Uniting the Enemy: Politics and the Convergence of Nationalisms in Slovakia." *East European Politics and Societies* 18, no. 4: 651–696.

Deets, Stephen. 2006. "Reimagining the Boundaries of the Nation: Politics and the Development of Ideas on Minority Rights." *East European Politics and Societies* 20, no. 3: 419–446.

Deets, Stephen, and Sherrill Stroschein. 2005. "Dilemmas of Autonomy and Liberal Pluralism: Examples Involving Hungarians in Central Europe." *Nations and Nationalism* 11, no. 2: 285–305.

Demuryan, Avet. 2000 (May 20). "Attempts to Undermine Armenia's Territorial Integrity Are Inadmissible, Say Members of Armenia's Parliament." *RIA Novosti.*

DeRouen, Karl. 1995. "The Indirect Link: Politics, the Economy, and the Use of Force." *Journal of Conflict Resolution* 39, no. 4: 671–695.

Diez, Thomas. 2002. "Why the EU Can Nonetheless Be Good for Cyprus." *Journal on Ethnopolitics and Minority Issue in Europe* 2. www.ecmi.de/jemie/download/Focus2-2002_Diez.pdf. Accessed October 23, 2007.

Diez, Thomas, Stephan Stetter, and Mathias Albert. 2006. "The European Union and Border Conflicts: The Transformative Power of Integration." *International Organization* 60, no. 3: 563–594.

Dimitrijević, Vojin. 2000. "The International Community and the Yugoslav Crisis." In *The Road to War in Serbia: Trauma and Catharsis,* ed. Nebojša Popov, 633–660. Budapest: Central European University Press.

Djilas, Aleksa. 1993. "A Profile of Slobodan Milosevic." *Foreign Affairs* 72, no. 3: 81–96.

———. 1995. "Fear Thy Neighbor: The Breakup of Yugoslavia." In *Nationalism and Nationalities in the New Europe,* ed. Charles A. Kupchan, 100–101. Ithaca, NY: Cornell University Press.

Dodd, Clement. 1999. "A Historical Overview." In *Cyprus: The Need for New Perspectives,* ed. Clement Dodd, 1–15. Huntingdon, UK: Eothen Press.

Doyle, Michael. 1986. "Liberalism and World Politics." *American Political Science Review* 80, no. 4: 1151–1169.

Elliott, Sydney, and W. D. Flackes. 1999. *Conflict in Northern Ireland: An Encyclopedia.* Denver: ABC-CLIO.

Enyedi, Zsolt, Zoltán Fábián, and Endre Sik. 2004. "Is Prejudice Growing in Hungary? Changes in Anti-Semitism, Anti-Roma Feeling and Xenophobia over the Last Decade." TÁRKI Social Report Reprint Series 21. Budapest: TÁRKI.

European Commission. 1996. *Central and Eastern EUROBAROMETER*. Brussels: EU Directorate for Information, Communications, Culture.

European Commission. 2001. *Enlargement Strategy Paper: Report on Progress Towards Accession by Each of the Candidate Countries*. www.europarl.europa.eu/meetdocs/committees/afet/20020325/700700en.pdf.

Farer, Tom J. 1979. *War Clouds on the Horn of Africa: The Widening Storm*. New York: Carnegie Endowment for International Peace.

Fearon, James D. 1998. "Commitment Problems and the Spread of Ethnic Conflict." In *The International Spread of Ethnic Conflict*, ed. David A. Lake and Donald Rothchild, 107–126. Princeton, NJ: Princeton University Press.

Fedor, Helen, ed. 1995. *Belarus and Moldova: Country Studies*. Washington, DC: Federal Research Division, Library of Congress.

Fetzer, Joel S. 2000. "Economic Self-interest or Cultural Marginality? Anti-immigration Sentiment and Nativist Political Movements in France, Germany and the USA." *Journal of Ethnic and Migration Studies* 26, no. 1 (January): 5–23.

Fowkes, Ben. 1997. *The Disintegration of the Soviet Union: A Study in the Rise and Triumph of Nationalism*. New York: St. Martin's.

Fox, Jon E. 2007. "From National Inclusion to Economic Exclusion: Ethnic Hungarian Labour Migration to Hungary." *Nations and Nationalism* 13, no. 1: 77–96.

Foye, Stephen. 1995. "Russia and the 'Near Abroad.'" *Post Soviet Prospects* 3, no. 2 (December): 1–6.

Frazer, Graham, and George Lancelle. 1994. *Absolute Zhirinovsky*. New York: Penguin Books.

Freyberg-Inan, Annette. 2002. "Which Way to Progress? Impact of International Organizations in Romania." In *Norms and Nannies: The Impact of International Organizations on the Central and East European States*, ed. Ronald Linden, 129–164. Lanham, MD: Rowman & Littlefield.

Friedman, Brian. 1992 (January 23). "Russia Intensified Dispute with Ukraine." Associated Press.

Fuller, Elizabeth, 1988. "Moscow Rejects Armenian Demands for Return of Nagorno-Karabagh," *Radio Liberty Research Bulletin* 91/88 (February 29).

Gaborieau, Marc. 2002. "Religion in the Pakistani Polity." In *Pakistan: The Contours of State and Society*, ed. Soofia Mumtaz, Jean-Luc Racine, and Imran Anwar Ali, 45. Karachi: Oxford University Press.

Gagnon, V. P. 1994. "Ethnic Nationalism and International Conflict: The Case of Serbia." *International Security* 19, no. 3: 130–166.

——. 2004. *The Myth of Ethnic War: Serbia and Croatia in the 1990s*. Ithaca, NY: Cornell University Press.

Gallagher, Tom. 1995. *Romania after Ceauşescu: The Politics of Intolerance*. Edinburgh: Edinburgh University Press.

Ganguly, Sumit. 2001. *Conflict Unending: India-Pakistan Tensions Since 1947*. New York: Columbia University Press.

Gartzke, Erik. 2000. "Preferences and the Democratic Peace." *International Studies Quarterly* 44, no. 2: 191–212.

Garvin, Tom. 1996. *1922: The Birth of Irish Democracy*. New York: St. Martin's.

Geertz, Clifford. 1963. "The Integrative Revolution: Primordial Sentiments and Civil Politics in the New States." In *Old Societies and New States: The Quest for Modernity in Asia and Africa*, ed. Clifford Geertz, 255–310. London: Free Press.

Gellner, Ernest. 1983. *Nations and Nationalism*. Ithaca, NY: Cornell University Press.

Gelpi, Christopher. 1997. "Democratic Diversions: Governmental Structure and the Externalization of Domestic Conflict." *Journal of Conflict Resolution* 41, no. 2: 255–282.

Gleason, Gregory. 2001. "Inter-State Cooperation in Central Asia from the CIS to the Shanghai Forum." *Europe-Asia Studies* 53, no. 7: 1077–1095.

Gleditsch, Kristian S., and Michael S. Ward. 1997. "Double Take: A Reexamination of Democracy and Autocracy in Modern Polities." *Journal of Conflict Resolution* 41, no. 3: 361–383.

Goati, Vladimir. 1992. "Visepartijski mozaik Srbije" (Multiparty Mosaic of Serbia). In *Radanje Javnog Mnjenna I Politickih Stranaka* (Emergence of Public Opinion and Political Parties), ed. Miroslav Pecujlic, Vladimir Milic and Srbobran Brankovic, 160–190. Belgrade: Institute for Political Studies.

Goldenberg, Suzanne. 1994. *Pride of Small Nations: The Caucasus and Post-Soviet Disorder*. London: Zed Books.

Goldstein, Ivo. 1999. *Croatia: A History*. Montreal: McGill-Queen's University.

Goltz, Thomas. 1993. "Letter from Eurasia: The Hidden Russian Hand." *Foreign Policy* 92 (Fall): 92–117.

Gow, James. 1992. *Legitimacy and the Military*. New York: St. Martin's.

——. 2003. *The Serbian Project and Its Adversaries: A Strategy of War Crimes*. London: Hurst and Company.

Gurr, Ted Robert. 1993. *Minorities at Risk: A Global View of Ethnopolitical Conflicts*. Washington, DC: U.S. Institute of Peace Press.

——. 2000. *Peoples Versus States: Ethnopolitical Conflict and Accommodation at the End of the 20th Century*. Washington, DC: U.S. Institute of Peace Press.

Haddock, Bruce, and Ovidiu Caraiani. 1999. "Nationalism and Civil Society in Romania." *Political Studies* 48: 258–274.

Hagan, Joe. 1994. "Domestic Political Systems and War Proneness." *Mershon International Studies Review* 38, no. 2 (October): 183–207.

Hale, Henry. 2004. "Divided We Stand: Institutional Sources of Ethnofederal State Survival and Collapse." *World Politics* 56, no. 2: 165–193.

Hall, John A., ed. 1998. *The State of the Nation: Ernest Gellner and the Theory of Nationalism*. Cambridge: Cambridge University Press.

Haraszti, Miklos. 1998. "Young Bloods: Hungary's Election Results Promise a New Taste of Political Salami." *Transitions* 5, no. 7: 48–53.

Heldt, Birger. 1999. "Domestic Politics, Absolute Deprivation, and the Use of Armed Force in Interstate Territorial Disputes, 1950–1990." *Journal of Peace Research* 43, no. 4: 451–478.

Hendrickson, Ryan C. 2002. "Clinton's Military Strikes in 1998: Diversionary Uses of Force?" *Armed Forces and Society* 28, no. 2: 309–332.

Herbst, Jeffrey. 1989. "The Creation and Maintenance of National Boundaries in Africa." *International Organization* 43, no. 4: 673–692.

Herzig, Edmund. 1990. "Armenians." In *The Nationalities Question in the Soviet Union*, ed. Graham Smith, 248–268. London: Longman.

Hislope, Robert. 1996. "Intra-ethnic Conflict in Croatia and Serbia: Flanking and the Consequences for Democracy." *East European Quarterly* 30, no. 4 (Winter): 471–494.

Hoare, Attila. 1997. "The Croatian Project to Partition Bosnia-Hercegovina, 1990–1994." *East European Quarterly* 31, no. 1 (March): 121–138.

Hockenos, Paul. 2003. *Homeland Calling: Exile Patriotism and the Balkan Wars*. Ithaca, NY: Cornell University Press.

Hoffman, David. 2002. *The Oligarchs: Wealth and Power in the New Russia*. New York: Perseus.

Holbrooke, Richard C. 1998. *To End a War*. New York: Random House.

Hopf, Ted. 1992. "Managing Soviet Disintegration: A Demand for Behavior Regimes." *International Security* 17, no. 1: 44–75.

Horowitz, Donald L. 1985. *Ethnic Groups in Conflict*. Berkeley: University of California Press.

——. 1991. "Comparing Democratic Systems." *Journal of Democracy* 1, no. 4 (Fall): 73–79.

Hughes, James, and Gwendolyn Sasse. 2003. "Monitoring the Monitors: EU Enlargement Conditionality and Minority Protection in the CEECs." *Journal on Ethnopolitics and Minority Issues in Europe* 1. www.ecmi.de/jemie. Accessed September 7, 2007.

Huth, Paul K. 1988. *Extended Deterrence and the Prevention of War*. New Haven: Yale University Press.

Huth, Paul. 1999. "Deterrence and International Conflict: Empirical Findings and Theoretical Debates." *Annual Review of Political Science* 2: 61–84.

Iams, John. 1992 (May 21). "Russian Parliament Calls Crimea Transfer Illegal, But Urges Negotiation." Associated Press.

Ieda, Osamu. 2004. "Post-Communist Nation Building and the Status Law Syndrome in Hungary." In *The Hungarian Status Law Syndrome: A Nation Building and/or Minority Protection*, ed. Zoltán Kántor et al., 3–57. Sapporo: Slavic Research Center, Hokkaido University.

Imholz, Kathleen. 1999. "Wrong on Albania." *Foreign Affairs* 78, no. 1: 135–136.

Institutul pentru Politici Publica (Institute on Public Policy). 2003. *Intoleranţă, Discriminare Autoritarism: În Opinia Publică* (Intolerance, Discrimination and Authoritarianism in Public Opinion). Bucharest: Institute on Public Policy.

Interfax. 1999 (June 4). "Unity Bloc Secures Majority in Armenian Parliament."

International Crisis Group (ICG). 2004. "Pan-Albanianism: How Big a Threat to Balkan Stability?" *ICG Europe Report* 153: 1–45.

Iordachi, Constantin. 2002. "Is There a Road to Greater Romania? Moldova, Romania, and the Protracted Politics of Unification." *Romanian Journal of Society and Politics* 2, no. 1: 136–140.

——. 2004. "Dual Citizenship and Policies Toward Kin-Minorities in East-Central Europe: A Comparison Between Hungary, Romania, and the Republic of Moldova." In *The Hungarian Status Law Syndrome: A Nation Building and/or Minority Protection*, ed. Zoltán Kántor et al., 239–269. Sapporo: Slavic Research Center, Hokkaido University.

Isachenkov, Vladimir. 2000 (February 25). "Putin Opens Campaign, Promising Strong State and Low Taxes." Associated Press.

Isakovic, Zlatko. 2000. *Identity and Security in Former Yugoslavia*. Aldershot, UK: Ashgate.

Ishkhanian, Rafael. 1991. "The Law of Excluding the Third Force." In *Armenia at the Crossroads: Democracy and Nationhood in the Post-Soviet Era*, ed. Gerald J. Libaridian, 10–38. Ithaca, NY: Cornell University Press.

Iwaskiw, Walter R., ed. 1995. *Estonia, Latvia, and Lithuania: Country Studies*. Washington, DC: Federal Research Department, Library of Congress.

——. 1999. *National Minorities and the European Nation-State System*. Oxford: Oxford University Press.

Jackson, James S., K. T. Brown, T. N. Brown, and B. Marks. 2001. "Contemporary Immigration Policy Orientations Among Dominant-Group Members in Western Europe." *Journal of Social Issues* 57: 431–456.

Jackson, Robert H., and Carl G. Rosberg. 1982. "Why Africa's Weak States Persist: The Empirical and the Juridical in Statehood." *World Politics* 35, no. 1: 1–24.

Jackson Preece, Jennifer. 1997. "National Minority Rights vs. State Sovereignty in Europe: Changing Norms in International Relations?" *Nations and Nationalism* 3, no. 3: 345–364.

Jacobson, Sally. 1994 (December 1). "Russia Upsets NATO Plans to Reach Out to Eastern Europe." Associated Press.

James, Patrick, and Athanasios Hristoulas. 1994. "Domestic Politics and Foreign Policy: Evaluating a Model of Crisis Activity for the United States." *Journal of Politics* 56, no. 2: 327–348.

Jervis, Robert, Richard Ned Lebow, and Janice Gross Stein. 1985. *Psychology and Deterrence*. Baltimore: Johns Hopkins University Press.

Jenne, Erin K. 2004. "A Bargaining Theory of Minority Demands." *International Security Quarterly* 48, no. 4 (December): 729–754.

——. 2006. *Ethnic Bargaining: The Paradox of Minority Empowerment*. Ithaca, NY: Cornell University Press.

Joseph, Joseph S. 1997. *Cyprus: Ethnic Conflict and International Politics*. New York: St. Martin's.

Judah, Tim. 2000. *The Serbs: History, Myth and the Destruction of Yugoslavia*. 2nd ed. New Haven: Yale University Press.

——. 2001. "Greater Albania?" *Survival* 43, no. 2: 7–17.

Kántor, Zoltán, et al., eds. 2004. *The Hungarian Status Law Syndrome: A Nation Building and/or Minority Protection.* Sapporo: Slavic Research Center, Hokkaido University.

Kaplan, Robert. 1993. *Balkan Ghosts: A Journey Through History.* New York: Random House.

Kardos, Gabor. 1995. "The Culture of Conflict." *World Policy Journal* 12, no. 1 (Spring): 102–107.

Karp, Jeffrey A., Susan A. Banducci, and Shaun Bowler. 2003. "To Know It Is to Love It? Satisfaction with Democracy in the European Union." *Comparative Political Studies* 36, no. 3: 271–292.

Katagoshchina, Irina. 2002. "Identity Crisis as a Factor in Migratory Processes in the Post-Soviet Space." *Anthropology & Archeology of Eurasia* 41, no. 1 (Summer): 26–53.

Kaufman, Stuart J. 1994. "The Irresistible Force and the Imperceptible Object: The Yugoslav Breakup and Western Policy." *Security Studies* 4, no. 2: 281–329.

——. 2001. *Modern Hatreds: The Symbolic Politics of Ethnic War.* Ithaca, NY: Cornell University Press.

Kaufmann, Chaim D. 1996a. "Intervention in Ethnic and Ideological Civil Wars." *Security Studies* 6, no. 1: 62–104.

——. 1996b. "Possible and Impossible Solutions to Ethnic Civil Wars." *International Security* 20, no. 4: 136–175.

——. 1998. "Where All Else Fails: Ethnic Population Transfers and Partitions in the Twentieth Century." *International Security* 23, no. 2: 120–156.

Kelley, Judith. 2002. "Membership, Management and Enforcement: European Institutions and Eastern Europe's Ethnic Politics." Paper prepared for presentation at the annual meeting of the American Political Science Association, Boston.

——. 2004a. *Ethnic Politics in Europe: The Power of Norms and Incentives.* Princeton, NJ: Princeton University Press.

——. 2004b. "International Actors on the Domestic Scene: Membership Conditionality and Socialization by International Institutions." *International Organization* 58, no. 3 (Summer): 425–458.

Keohane, Robert, and Joseph Nye. 2001. *Power and Interdependence.* 3rd ed. New York: Longman.

Kettle, Steve. 1996. "Slovakia's One-Man Band." *Transitions* 2, no. 17: 12–15.

Kier, Elizabeth, and Jonathan Mercer. 1996. "Setting Precedents in Anarchy: Military Intervention and Weapons of Mass Destruction." *International Security* 20, no. 4 (Spring): 77–106.

King, Charles. 2000. *The Moldovans: Romania, Russia, and the Politics of Culture.* Stanford: Hoover Institution Press.

——. 2005. "Migration and Ethnic Politics in Eastern Europe and Eurasia." In *Ethnic Politics After Communism*, ed. Zoltan Barany and Robert G. Moser, 166–190. Ithaca, NY: Cornell University Press.

Kingston, Klara. 2001. "The Hungarian Status Law." *RFE/RL East European Perspectives* 3, no. 17, www.rferl.org/reports/eepreport/2001/10/17-031001.asp. Accessed October 23, 2007.

Kiss, Csilla. 2002. "From Liberalism to Conservatism: The Federation of Young Democrats in Post-communist Hungary." *East European Politics and Society* 16, no. 3: 739–763.

Kola, Paulin. 2003. *The Search for a Greater Albania.* London: Hurst & Company.

Kolstø, Pål. 2000. *Political Construction Sites: Nation-Building in Russia and the Post-Soviet States.* Boulder, CO: Westview Press.

Kovács, Mária M. 2005. "The Politics of Dual Citizenship in Hungary." Prepared for the Conference on Dual Citizenship: Rights and Security in an Age of Terror, Munk Centre for International Studies, University of Toronto.

Kozhemyako, Victor. 1999 (January 5). "Interview with Valentin Rasputin." *Sovetskaya Rossiya.*

Kozlovich, Anatoly. 1993 (December 8). "Belarus Parliament Expects Zyuganov or Zhirinovsky to Win Because They Promised to Turn Belarus Into Northwest Territory." *Literaturnaya Gazeta.*

Krain, Matthew. 1997. "State-Sponsored Mass Murder: The Onset and Severity of Genocides and Politicides." *Journal of Conflict Resolution* 41, no. 3: 331–360.

Krasner, Stephen D. 1999. *Sovereignty: Organized Hypocrisy.* Princeton, NJ: Princeton University Press.

Laitin, David. 1998. *Identity in Formation: The Russian-Speaking Populations in the Near Abroad.* Ithaca, NY: Cornell University Press.

——. 1999. "Somalia." In *Civil Wars, Insecurity, and Intervention*, ed. B. F. Walter and J. Snyder, 146–180. New York: Columbia University Press.

Laitin, David D., and Said S. Samatar. 1987. *Somalia: Nation in Search of a State.* Boulder, CO: Westview Press.

Laitin, David, and Ronald Suny. 1999. "Armenia and Azerbaijan: Thinking a Way out of Karabakh." *Middle East Policy* 7, no. 1 (October): 145–175.

Lake, David A. 1992. "Powerful Pacifists: Democratic States and War." *American Political Science Review* 86, no. 1: 24–37.

Lake, David A., and Donald Rothchild, eds. 1998. *The International Spread of Ethnic Conflict: Fear, Diffusion, Escalation.* Princeton, NJ: Princeton University Press.

LeDonne, John P. 1997. *The Russian Empire and the World, 1700–1917: The Geopolitics of Expansion and Containment.* New York: Oxford University Press.

Leeds, Brett Ashley, and David R. Davis. 1997. "Domestic Political Vulnerability and International Disputes." *Journal of Conflict Resolution* 41, no. 6: 814–834.

Levy, Jack. 1989. "The Diversionary Theory of War: A Critique." In *Handbook of War Studies*, ed. Manus I. Midlarsky, 259–288. Boston: Unwin Hyman.

Licklider, Roy. 1995. "The Consequences of Negotiated Settlements in Civil Wars, 1945–1993." *American Political Science Review* 89, no. 4: 681–690.

Liloyan, Tigran. 1993 (June 18). "Armenian President Calls on Opposition to Support CSCE Plan." ITAR-TASS.

Linden, Ronald H. 2000. "Putting on Their Sunday Best: Romania, Hungary, and the Puzzle of Peace." *International Studies Quarterly* 44, no. 1: 121–146.

——. 2002. *Norms and Nannies: The Impact of International Organizations on the Central and East European States.* Lanham, MD: Rowman & Littlefield.

Lynch, Allen, 2002. "The Evolution of Russian Foreign Policy in the 1990s." *Journal of Communist Studies and Transition Politics* 18, no. 1 (March): 161–182.

Magas, Branka. 20006. "The War in Croatia." *War and Change in the Balkans: Nationalism, Conflict and Cooperation*, ed. Brad K. Blitz, 118–123. Cambridge: Cambridge University Press.

Mahoney, James, and Gary Goertz. 2004. "The Possibility Principle: Choosing Negative Cases in Comparative Research." *American Political Science Review* 98, no. 4: 653–669.

Malešević, Siniša. 2002. *Ideology, Legitimacy and the New State: Yugoslavia, Serbia and Croatia*. London: Frank Cass.

Malik, Iffat. 2001. *Kashmir: Ethnic Conflict International Dispute*. Karachi: Oxford University Press.

Mann, Michael. 2005. *The Dark Side Of Democracy: Explaining Ethnic Cleansing*. New York: Cambridge University Press.

Mansergh, Nicholas. 1991. *The Unresolved Question: The Anglo-Irish Settlement and Its Undoing, 1912–72*. New Haven: Yale University Press.

Mansfield, Edward D., and Jack Snyder. 1995. "Democratization and the Danger of War." *International Security* 20, no. 1: 5–38.

——. 2005. *Electing to Fight: Why Emerging Democracies Go to War*. Cambridge, MA: MIT Press.

Mayhew, David R. 1974. *Congress: The Electoral Connection*. New Haven: Yale University Press.

McAllister, Ronald. 2000. "Religious Identity and the Future of Northern Ireland." *Policy Studies Journal* 28, no. 4: 843–857.

McIntosh, Mary E. 1995. "Minority Rights and Majority Rule: Ethnic Tolerance in Romania and Bulgaria." *Social Forces* 73, no. 3 (March): 939–968.

McLaren, L. M. 2003. "Anti-immigrant Prejudice in Europe: Contact, Threat Perception, and Preferences for the Exclusion of Migrants." *Social Forces* 81, no. 3: 909–936.

McLaughlin, Daniel. 2004 (December 6). "Hungary Divided on Extending Citizenship." *Irish Times*.

McMahon, Patrice. 1998. "The Quest for Unity: Divided Nation and Irredentist Ambitions." Ph.D. dissertation, Columbia University.

Medianu, Narcisa. 2002. "Analyzing the Political Exchanges between Minority and Majority Leaders in Romania." *Global Review of Ethnopolitics* 1, no. 4: 28–41.

Melander, Erik. 2001. "The Nagorno-Karabakh Conflict Revisited: Was the War Inevitable?" *Journal of Cold War Studies* 3, no. 2 (Spring): 48–75.

Mendelson, Sarah. 2002. "Russians Imperiled: Has Anybody Noticed?" *International Security* 26, no. 4: 39–69.

Mercer, Jonathan. 1995. "Anarchy and Identity." *International Organization* 49, no. 2: 229–252.

Metz, Helen Chapin, ed. 1996. *Turkey: A Country Study*. Washington, DC: Federal Research Division, Library of Congress.

Midlarsky, Manus I. 2005. *The Killing Trap: Genocide in the Twentieth Century*. New York: Cambridge University Press.

Mihailescu, Mihaela. 2005. "Dampening the Powder Keg: Understanding Interethnic Cooperation in Post-Communist Romania (1990–96)." *Nationalism and Ethnic Politics* 11, no. 1: 25–59.

Milic, Vladimir. 1992. "Socijalni lik politickog javnog mnjenja" (The Social Face of Political Public Opinion). In *Adanje Javnog Mnjenna I Politickih Stranaka* (Emergence of Public Opinion and Political Parties), ed. Miroslav Pecujlic, Vladimir Milic and Srbobran Brankovic, 110–135. Belgrade: Institute for Political Studies.

Miljkovic, Maja, and Marko Atilla Hoare. 2005. "Crime and the Economy Under Milosevic and His Successors." In *Serbia Since 1989: Politics and Society Under Milosevic and After*, ed. Sabrina P. Ramet and Vjeran Pavlakovic, 192–226. Seattle: University of Washington Press.

Milkenberg, Michael. 2002. "The Radical Right in Postsocialist Central and Eastern Europe: Comparative Observations and Interpretations." *East European Politics and Society* 16, no. 2: 335–362.

Miller, Nicholas J. 1994. "Serbia Chooses Aggression." *Orbis* 38, no. 1: 59–66.

——. 1997. "A Failed Transition: The Case of Serbia." In *Politics, Power and the Struggle for Democracy in South-East Europe*, ed. Karen Dawisha and Bruce Parrott, 146–188. Cambridge: Cambridge University Press.

Miller, Ross A. 1995. "Domestic Structures and the Diversionary Use of Force." *American Journal of Political Science* 39, no. 3: 760–785.

Milner, Helen V. 1988. *Resisting Protectionism: Global Industries and the Politics of International Trade*. Princeton, NJ: Princeton University Press.

Mitchell, Neil. 2004. *Agents of Atrocity: Leaders, Followers, and the Violation of Human Rights in Civil War*. New York: Palgrave Macmillan.

Moore, Patrick. 1993. "War Returns to Croatia." *RFE/RL Research Report* 2, no. 6: 40–43.

Morgan, Patrick. 2003. *Deterrence Now*. Cambridge: Cambridge University Press.

Morgan, T. Clifton, and Kenneth N. Bickers. 1992. "Domestic Discontent and the External Use of Force." *Journal of Conflict Resolution* 36, no. 1: 25–52.

Mueller, John. 2000. "The Banality of Ethnic War." *International Security* 25, no. 1 (Summer): 42–70.

Naegele, Jolyon. 2005. "A People Scattered." *New Presence: The Prague Journal of Central European Affairs* 7, no. 1 (Autumn): 32–33.

Naimark, Norman M. 2001. *Fires of Hatred: Ethnic Cleansing in Twentieth-Century Europe*. Cambridge, MA: Harvard University Press.

Nas, Beata Kovacs. 1996. "Transnational Kindred and Ethnic Conflict: The Effects of Basic Bilateral Treaties on Domestic Minority Policy." Ph.D. dissertation, University of Maryland.

Nastase, Mihnea Ion. 2002. "Communist Legacies and the Quest for European Union Membership." *Problems of Post-Communism* 49, no. 5 (September–October): 55–64.

Nelson, Daniel N. 1998. "Hungary and Its Neighbors: Security and Ethnic Minorities." *Nationalities Papers* 26, no. 2: 312–330.

——. 1992. *Romania After Tyranny*. Boulder, CO: Westview Press.

O'Neil, Patrick. 1998. *Revolution from Within: The Hungarian Socialist Worker's Party and the Collapse of Communism*. Northampton, MA: Edward Elgar.

Olson, Mancur. 1965. *The Logic of Collective Action*. Cambridge, MA: Harvard University Press.

Oltay, Edith. 1992a. "A Profile of Istvan Csurka," *RFE/RL Research Report* 1, no. 40: 26–29.

——. 1992b. "Hungarian Democratic Forum Rent by Dispute over Extremism." *RFE/RL Research Report* 1, no. 47: 22–25.

Open Society Institute. 2002. *Monitoring the EU Accession Process: Corruption and Anti-Corruption Policy*. Budapest: Open Society Institute.

Oprescu, Dan. 2002. "National Minorities in Rumania: Public Policies Between 1990–2002." Unpublished manuscript.

Owens, David. 1995. *Balkan Odyssey*. New York: Harcourt Brace.

Panossian, Razmik. 2002. "The Past as Nation: Three Dimensions of Armenian Identity," *Geopolitics* 7, no. 2: 121–146.

Patman, Robert. 1990. *The Soviet Union in the Horn of Africa: The Diplomacy of Intervention and Disengagement*. Cambridge: Cambridge University Press.

Paul, T. V. 2005. *The India-Pakistan Conflict an Enduring Rivalry*. New York: Cambridge University Press.

Pavlakovic, Vjera. 2005. "Serbia Transformed? Political Dynamics in the Milosevic Era and After." In *Serbia Since 1989: Politics and Society Under Milosevic and After*, ed. Sabrina P Ramet and Vjeran Pavlakovic, 13–54. Seattle: University of Washington Press.

Pecujlic, Miroslav. 1992. "University zacoaronom krugu politike [In the Spelled Circle of Politics]." In *Radanje Javnog Mnjenna I Politickih Stranaka- Analiza empirijskih istrazivanja u Srbiji 1990–1991* (Emergence of Public Opinion and Political Parties: An Analysis of Empirical Surveys in Serbia, 1990–1991), 75–79. Belgrade: Institute for Political Studies.

Petersen, Karen K. 2004. "A Research Note: Reexamining Transnational Ethnic Alliances and Foreign Policy Behavior." *International Interactions* 30, no. 1 (January–March): 25–42.

Petersen, Roger. 2002. *Understanding Ethnic Violence: Fear, Hatred, Resentment in Twentieth Century Eastern Europe*. Cambridge: Cambridge University Press.

Petersoo, Pille. 2007. "Reconsidering Otherness: Constructing Estonian Identity." *Nations and Nationalism* 13, no. 1: 117–133.

Petrescu, Dragos. 2004. "Historial Myths, Legitimating Discourses, and Identity Politics in Ceausescu's Romania (Part 2)." *RFE/RL East European Perspectives* 6, no. 8: 1–6.

Pettifer, James. 2001. *The New Macedonian Question*. New York: Palgrave.

Pettigrew, T. 1998. "Reactions Toward the New Minorities of Western Europe." *Annual Review of Sociology* 24: 77–103.

Pevehouse, Jon C. 2002. "Democracy from the Outside-In? International Organizations and Democratization." *International Organization* 56, no. 3: 515–550.

Phillips, R. Stuart. 1997. "Aleksandr Lebed: Soldier, Statesman, President?" *World Affairs* 159, no. 3 (Winter): 109–112.

Popov, Vladimir. 2000. "Political Economy of Growth in Russia." Working paper, Center for Strategic and International Studies.

Poppe, Edwin, and Louk Hagendoorn. 2001. "Types of Identification Among Russians in the 'Near Abroad.'" *Europe-Asia Studies* 53, no. 1: 57–71.

Posen, Barry. 1993. "The Security Dilemma and Ethnic Conflict." *Survival* 35, no. 1: 27–47.

Posner, Daniel N. 2004. "The Political Salience of Cultural Difference: Why Chewas and Tumbukas Are Allies in Zambia and Adversaries in Malawi." *American Political Science Review* 98, no. 4: 529–546.

———. 2005. *Institutions and Ethnic Politics in Africa*. New York: Cambridge University Press.

Prelec, Marko. 1997. "Franjo Tudjman's Croatia and the Balkans." In *Crises in the Balkans: Views from the Participants*, ed. Constantine P. Danopoulos and Kostas G. Messas, 75–111. Boulder, CO: Westview Press.

Prizel, Ilya. 1998. *National Identity and Foreign Policy: Nationalism and Leadership in Poland, Russia and Ukraine*. Cambridge: Cambridge University Press.

Proskournina, Olga. 2002 (April 4). "Putin's Guru Slams Russian Economy in 1990s." gazeta.ru.

Putnam, Robert. 1988. "Diplomacy and Domestic Politics: The Logic of Two-Level Games." *International Organization* 42, no. 3: 427–460.

Ranelagh, John O'Beirne. 1983. *A Short History of Ireland*. Cambridge: Cambridge University Press.

Regan, Patrick. M. 1996. "Conditions of Successful Third-Party Intervention in Intrastate Conflicts." *Journal of Conflict Resolution* 40, no. 2: 336–359.

———. 1998. "Choosing to Intervene: Outside Intervention in Internal Conflicts." *Journal of Politics* 60, no. 3: 754–779.

———. 2000. *Civil Wars and Foreign Powers: Outside Intervention in Intrastate Conflict*. Ann Arbor: University of Michigan Press.

RFE/RL. 2000. "Budapest Wants Ethnic Hungarians in Romania to Stay Put," RFE/RL report, February 24.

Rieff, David. 1997. "Case Study in Ethnic Strife." *Foreign Affairs* 76, no. 2 (March–April): 118–133.

Ringold, Dena, Mitchell A. Orenstein, and Erika Wilkens. 2003. *Roma in an Expanding Europe: Breaking the Poverty Cycle*. Washington, DC: World Bank.

Roeder, Phillip G. 1991. "Soviet Federalism and Ethnic Mobilization." *World Politics* 43, no. 2: 196–232.

———. 1993. *Red Sunset: The Failure of Soviet Politics*. Princeton, NJ: Princeton University Press.

Rohozinska, Joanna. 1999. "Romania's Ills: Strays and Stereotypes." *Central Europe Review* 1, no. 11. www.ce-review.org/99/11/rohozinska11.html. Accessed August 26, 2007.

Ron, James. 2003. *Frontiers and Ghettos: State Violence on Serbia and Israel*. Berkeley: University of California Press.

Roper, Steven D. 2000. *Romania: The Unfinished Revolution*. New York: Routledge.

Rothschild, Joseph. 1981. *Ethnopolitics: A Conceptual Framework*. New York: Columbia University Press.

Rudolph, Christopher. 2003. "Security and Political Economy of International Migration." *American Political Science Review* 97, no. 4: 603–620.

Rummel, Rudolph J. 2000. *Death by Government: Genocide and Mass Murder Since 1900*. New Brunswick, NJ: Transaction Publishers.

Russett, Bruce. 1993. *Grasping the Democratic Peace: Principles for a Post–Cold War World*. Princeton, NJ: Princeton University Press.

Rutland, Peter. 1994. "Democracy and Nationalism in Armenia." *Europe-Asia Studies* 46, no. 5: 839–861.

Saideman, Stephen M. 1997. "Explaining the International Relations of Secessionist Conflicts: Vulnerability vs. Ethnic Ties." *International Organization* 51, no. 4: 721–753.

——. 1998. "Inconsistent Irredentism? Political Competition, Ethnic Ties, and the Foreign Policies of Somalia and Serbia." *Security Studies* 7, no. 3: 51–93.

——. 2001. *The Ties That Divide: Ethnic Politics, Foreign Policy, and International Conflict*. New York: Columbia University Press.

——. 2005. "At the Heart of the Conflict: Irredentism and Kashmir." *The India-Pakistan Conflict: An Enduring Rivalry*, ed. T. V. Paul, 202–224. Cambridge: Cambridge University Press.

Saideman, Stephen M., and R. William Ayres. 2000. "Determining the Sources of Irredentism: Logit. Analyses of Minorities at Risk Data." *Journal of Politics* 62, no. 4: 1126–1144.

——. 2007. "Pie Crust Promises and the Sources of Foreign Policy: The Limited Impact of Accession Processes and the Priority of Domestic Constituencies." *Foreign Policy Analysis* 3, no. 3: 189–210.

Saideman, Stephen M., David Lanoue, Michael Campenni, and Samuel Stanton. 2002. "Democratization, Political Institutions, and Ethnic Conflict: A Pooled, Cross-Sectional Time Series Analysis from 1985–1998." *Comparative Political Studies* 35, no. 1: 103–129.

Saideman, Stephen M., David J. Lanoue, Amy Cox, and Suranjan Weeraratne. 2006. "Challenges of Democracy and the Origins of Power-Sharing: Competition, Exclusion and the Impact of Institutions." Paper prepared for presentation at the Workshop on Power-sharing and Democratic Governance in Divided Societies, Center for the Study of Civil War, Peace Research Institute, Oslo, Norway.

Salmon, Trevor C. 1992. "Testing Times for European Political Cooperation: The Gulf and Yugoslavia, 1990–1992." *International Affairs* 68, no. 2: 233–253.

Sartori, Giovanni. 1970. "Concept Misformation in Comparative Research." *American Political Science Review* 6, no. 4: 1033–1053.

Schimmelfennig, Frank. 2003. *The EU, NATO and the Integration of Europe: Rules and Rhetoric*. Cambridge: Cambridge University Press.

Schimmelfennig, Frank, and Ulrich Sedelmeier, eds. 2005. *The Europeanization of Central and Eastern Europe*. Ithaca, NY: Cornell University Press.

Schöpflin, George. 2000. *Nations, Identity, Power*. New York: New York University Press.

Schweid, Barry. 1995 (May 10). "Russia to Formalize Ties to NATO, Shelve Centrifuge Sale to Iran." Associated Press.

Selassie, Bereket H. 1980. *Conflict and Intervention in the Horn of Africa*. New York: Monthly Review.

Service, Robert. 2003. *Russia: Experiment with a People*. Cambridge, MA: Harvard University Press.

Seward, Deborah. 1992 (April 25). "Russians in Crimea Seek Independence from Ukraine." Associated Press.

Shafir, Michael. 1996. "A Possible Light at the End of the Tunnel." *Transitions* 2, no. 19: 29–32.

——. 1999a. "Radical Politics in Post Communist East Central Europe, Part VIII: Radical Continuity in Romania—The Party of Romanian National Unity." *RFE/RL East European Perspectives* 2, no. 19: 1–8.

——. 1999b. "Radical Politics in Post Communist East Central Europe, Part VIII: Radical Continuity in Romania—The Party of Romanian National Unity (B)." *RFE/RL East European Perspectives* 2, no. 20: 1–8.

——. 2000. "The Political Party as National Holding Company: The Hungarian Democratic Federation of Romania." In *The Politics of National Minority Participation in Post-Communist Europe: State-Building, Democracy and Ethnic Mobilization*, ed. Jonathan Stein, 101–28. Armonk, NY: M. E. Sharpe.

——. 2001. "The Greater Romania Party and the 2000 Elections in Romania: A Retrospective Analysis." *RFE/RL East European Perspectives* 3, no. 14: 1-7.

——. 2004. "The Politics of Public Space and the Legacy of the Holocaust in Postcommunist Hungary." *RFE/RL East European Perspectives* 6, no. 12. http://www.rferl.org/reports/eepreport/2004/06/13-230604.asp. Accessed October 23, 2007.

Shah, Mehtab A. 1997. *The Foreign Policy of Pakistan: Ethnic Impacts on Diplomacy, 1971–1994*. London: Taurus.

Shain, Yossi. 2007. *Kinship and Diasporas in International Affairs*. Ann Arbor: University of Michigan Press.

Shargorodsky, Sergei. 1993 (November 11). "EC Officials to Negotiate Partnership Deal." Associated Press.

Shleifer, Andrei, and Daniel Treisman. 2004. "A Normal Country." *Foreign Affairs* 83, no. 2: 20–38.

Shulman, Stephen. 2002. "Challenging the Civic/Ethnic and West/East Dichotomies in the Study of Nationalism." *Comparative Political Studies* 35, no. 5: 554–585.

Siddiqi, Toufiq A. 2004. "India and Pakistan: Pipe Dream or Pipeline of Peace?" *Georgetown Journal of International Affairs* 5, no. 1. http://journal.georgetown.edu/Issues/ws04/ws04_forum_siddiqi.html. Accessed October 23, 2007.

Silber, Laura, and Allan Little. 1996. *Yugoslavia: Death of a Nation*. New York: Penguin.

Simes, Dimitri. 1991. "Russia Reborn." *Foreign Policy* 85 (Winter): 41–63.

Sinn, Hans-Werner. 2000. "EU Enlargement, Migration, and Lessons from German Unification." *German Economic Review* 1, no. 3 (August): 299–314.

Smith, Alastair. 1996. "Diversionary Foreign Policy in Democratic Systems." *International Studies Quarterly* 40, no. 1: 133–154.

Smith, Anthony D. 1991. *National Identity*. Reno: University of Nevada Press.

——. 1995. "Gastronomy or Geology? The Role of Nationalism in the Reconstruction of Nations." *Nations and Nationalism* 1, no. 1: 3–23.

Smith, Gordon. 2007. *Canada in Afghanistan: Is It Working?* Calgary: Canadian Defence and Foreign Affairs Institute.

Smith, Graham. 1999. "Transnational Politics and the Politics of the Russian Diaspora." *Ethnic and Racial Studies* 22, no. 3 (May): 500–523.

Smith, Graham, and Andrew Wilson. 1997. "Rethinking Russia's Post-Soviet Diaspora: The Potential for Political Mobilization in Eastern Ukraine and North-east Estonia." *Europe-Asia Studies* 49, no. 5: 845–864.

Snyder, Jack. 1991. *Myths of Empire: Domestic Politics and International Ambition*. Ithaca, NY: Cornell University Press.

——. 1999. *When Voting Leads To Violence: Democratization and Nationalist Conflict*. New York: Norton.

Socor, Vladimir. 1990. "Forces of Old Resurface in Romania: The Ethnic Clashes in Tirgu-Mures." *Report on Eastern Europe* 15: 36–53.

Solsten, Eric, ed. *Cyprus: A Country Study*. 1993. Washington, DC: Federal Research Division, Library of Congress.

——. *Greece: A Country Study*. 1995. Washington, DC: Federal Research Division, Library of Congress.

Stan, Lavinia. 2003. "Democratic Delusions: Ten Myths Accepted by Romanian Democratic Opposition." *Problems of Post-Communism* 50, no. 6 (November–December): 51–60.

Stewart, Michael. 2004. "The Hungarian Status Law: A New European Form of Transnational Politics?" In *The Hungarian Status Law Syndrome: A Nation Building and/or Minority Protection*, ed. Zoltán Kántor et al., 120–151. Sapporo: Slavic Research Center, Hokkaido University.

Stroschein, Sherrill. 1996. "The Components of Coexistence: Hungarian Minorities and Interethnic Relations in Romania, Slovakia, and Ukraine." www.ciaonet.org/conf/ieco3/ieco3_09–96.html. Accessed September 3, 2007.

Suhrke, Astri. 1975. "Irredentism Contained: The Thai-Muslim Case." *Comparative Politics* 7, no. 2 (January): 187–203.

Szántay, Antal, and Márta Velladics. 1995. "Strangers Though Shouldst Kindheartedly Support and Respect." In *New Xenophobia in Europe*, ed. Bernd Baumgartl and Adrian Favell, 180–191. London: Kluwer Law International.

Szayna, Thomas S. 1993. "Ultranationalism in Central Europe." *Journal of Democracy* (Fall): 527–550.

Szporluk, Roman. 1992. "The National Question." In *After the Soviet Union: From Empire to Nations*, ed. Timothy Colton and Robert Legvold, 84–112. New York: Norton.

Tanner, Marcus. 2001. *Croatia: A Nation Forged in War*. New Haven: Yale University Press.

Taylor, Peter. 1999. *Loyalists: War and Peace in Northern Ireland*. New York: TV Books.

Telhami, Shibley, and Michael N. Barnett, eds. 2002. *Identity and Foreign Policy in the Middle East*. Ithaca, NY: Cornell University Press.

Thompson, Mark. 1994. *Forging War: The Media in Serbia, Croatia and Bosnia-Herzegovina*. Avon, UK: Article 19 International Centre Against Censorship.

Tismaneanu, Vladimir. 1995. "Democracy, Romanian Style." *Dissent* 42, no. 3 (Summer): 318–320.

———. 1998. *Fantasies of Salvation: Democracy, Nationalism and Myth in Post-Communist Europe*. Princeton, NJ: Princeton University Press.

———. 2002. "Discomforts of Victory: Democracy, Liberal Values and Nationalism in Post-communist Europe." *West European Politics* 25, no. 2 (April): 81–101.

Todosijevic, Bojan. 2001. "Dimensions of Nationalism: Structure of Nationalist Attitudes in Hungary and Yugoslavia." *Central European Political Science Review* 2, no. 6: 170–186.

Toft, Monica Duffy. 2002. "Indivisible Territory, Geographic Concentration, and Ethnic War." *Security Studies* 12, no. 2: 82–119.

———. 2003. *The Geography of Ethnic Violence: Identity, Interests, and the Indivisibility of Territory*. Princeton, NJ: Princeton University Press.

Tóka, Gábor. 2004. "Hungary." In *The Handbook of Political Change in Eastern Europe*, ed. Sten Berglund, Joakin Ekman, and Frank H. Aarebrot, 289–335. Cheltenham, UK: Edward Elgar.

Tolz, Vera. 1998. "Forging the Nation: National Identity and Nation Building in Post-Communist Russia." *Europe-Asia Studies* 50, no. 6: 993–1022.

Touval, Saadia. 1963. *Somali Nationalism: International Politics and the Drive for Unity in the Horn of Africa*. Cambridge, MA: Harvard University Press.

———. 1972. *The Boundary Politics of Independent Africa*. Cambridge, MA: Harvard University.

Treisman, Daniel. 1996. "Why Yeltsin Won." *Foreign Affairs* 75, no. 5 (September–October): 64–77.

Tucker, Joshua. 2002. "The First Decade of Post-Communist Elections and Voting: What Have We Studied, and How Have We Studied It?" *Annual Review of Political Science* 5: 271–304.

Tucker, Joshua, Alexander Pacek, and Adam Berinsky. 2002. "Transitional Winners and Losers: Attitudes Toward EU Membership in Post-Communist Countries." *American Journal of Political Science* 46, no. 3: 557–571.

Udovički, Jasminka, and Ejub čtitkovac. 1997. "Bosnia and Hercegovina: The Second War." In *Burn This House: The Making and Unmaking of Yugoslavia*, ed. Jasminka Udovički and James Ridgeway, 174–214. Durham, NC: Duke University Press.

Udovički, Jasminka, and Ivan Torov. 1997. "The Interlude: 1980–1990." In *Burn This House: The Making and Unmaking of Yugoslavia*, ed. Jasminka Udovički and James Ridgeway, 80–107. Durham, NC: Duke University Press.

U.S. Department of Energy. 2004. "OPEC Revenues Fact Sheet." www.eia.doe.gov/emeu/cabs/opecrev.html. Accessed September 3, 2007.

Uzelak, Gordana. 1997. "Franjo Tudjman's Nationalist Ideology." *East European Quarterly* 31, no. 4: 449–472.

Vachudova, Milada Anna. 2005. *Europe Undivided: Democracy, Leverage & Integration After Communism*. Oxford: Oxford University Press.

Vaknin, Sam. 2003. *After the Rain: How the West Lost the East*. Skopje, Macedonia: Narcissus.

Valentino, Benjamin A. 2004. *Final Solutions: Mass Killing and Genocide in the Twentieth Century*. Ithaca, NY: Cornell University Press, 2004.

Valki, László. 1999. "Hungary's Road to NATO." *The Hungarian Quarterly* 40, no. 3 (Summer): 1–18.

Van Houen, Pieter. 1998. "The Role of a Minority's Reference State in Ethnic Relations." *Archives Européenes de Sociologie* 39, no. 1: 110–148.

Venice Commission. 2004. "Opinion on the Draft Law Concerning the Support to Romanians Living Abroad of the Republic of Moldova." Opinion no. 299/2004. Venice: European Commission for Democracy Through Law.

Vermeersch, Peter. 2003. "EU Enlargement and Minority Rights Policies in Central Europe: Explaining Policy Shifts in the Czech Republic, Hungary and Poland." Draft paper for presentation at the Association for the Study of Nationalities, Columbia University.

Vickers, Miranda. 2004. "Pan Albanianism: Myth or Threat to Balkan Security?" *Transitions Online* (April): 1–3.

Volkan, Vamik. 1987. "Psychological Concepts Useful in the Building of Political Foundations Between Nations: Track II Diplomacy." *Journal of the American Psychoanalytic Association* 35, no. 4: 903–935.

———. 1999. *Bloodlines: From Ethnic Pride to Ethnic Terrorism*. Boulder, CO: Westview Press.

Waltz, Kenneth. 1979. *Theory of International Politics*. Reading, MA: Addison-Wesley.

Waterbury, Myra A. 2006. "Internal Exclusion, External Inclusion: Diaspora Politics and Party-Building Strategies in Post-Communist Hungary." *East European Politics and Society* 20, no. 3: 483–515.

Weiner, Myron. 1971. "The Macedonian Syndrome." *World Politics* 23, no. 1: 665–683.

Wilkinson, Steven. 2002. "Conditionality, Consociationalism, and Ethnic Conflict Moderation." Draft conference paper, University of Western Ontario. www.ssc.uwo.ca/polysci/necrg/powersharingdemocracy/papers/StevenWilkinsonConditionality.pdf.

Wimmer, Andreas. 2002. *Nationalist Exclusion and Ethnic Conflict: Shadows of Modernity*. Cambridge: Cambridge University Press.

Wirsing, Robert G. 1994. *India, Pakistan and the Kashmir Dispute*. New York: Palgrave Macmillan.

Woodward, Susan L. 1995a. *Balkan Tragedy: Chaos and Dissolution After the Cold War* Washington, DC: Brookings Institution.

———. 1995b. *Socialist Unemployment: The Political Economy of Yugoslavia, 1945–1990*. Princeton, NJ: Princeton University Press.

———. 1999. "How Not to End a Civil War: Bosnia-Herzegovina." In *Civil Wars, Insecurity, and Intervention*, ed. Barbara F. Walter and Jack L. Snyder, 73–115. New York: Columbia University Press.

Woodwell, Douglas. 2004. "Unwelcome Neighbors: Shared Ethnicity and International Conflict During the Cold War." *International Security Quarterly* 48, no. 1 (March): 197–223.

———. 2007. *Nationalism in International Relations: Norms, Foreign Policy, and Enmity*. New York: Palgrave Macmillan.

Wydra, Doris. 2004. "The Crimea Conundrum: The Tug of War Between Russia and Ukraine on the Questions of Autonomy and Self-Determination." *International Journal of Minority and Group Rights* 10: 111–130.

Yiangou, George S. 2002. "The Accession of Cyprus to the EU: Challenges and Opportunities for the New European Regional Order." *Journal of Ethnopolitics and Minority Issues in Europe* 2. www.ecmi.de/jemie/download/Focus2-2002_Yiangou. pdf. Accessed October 23, 2007.

Zacher, Mark W. 2001. "The Territorial Integrity Norm: International Boundaries and the Use of Force." *International Organization* 55, no. 2 (Spring): 215–250.

Zakosek, Nenad, and Goran Cular. 2004. "Croatia." In *Handbook of Political Change in Eastern Europe*, ed. Sten Berglund, Joakim Ekman, and Frank Aarebrot, 451–492. Cheltenham, UK: Edward Elgar.

Zellner, Wolfgang. 2001. "The High Commissioner on National Minorities: His Work, Effectiveness, and Recommendations to Strengthen the HCNM as an Institution." In *Europe's New Security Challenges*, ed. Heinz Gärtner, Adrian Hyde-Price, and Erich Reiter, 265–295. Boulder, CO: Lynne Rienner.

Zevelev, Igor. 2001. *Russia and Its New Diaspora*. Washington, DC: U.S. Institute of Peace Press.

Page locators in italics refer to figures and tables